EGYPT

BY K · LANGE & M · HIRMER

PHAIDON

EGYPT

ARCHITECTURE · SCULPTURE · PAINTING
IN THREE THOUSAND YEARS
BY K·LANGE AND M·HIRMER

PHAIDON PUBLISHERS INC

DISTRIBUTED BY NEW YORK GRAPHIC SOCIETY

GREENWICH · CONNECTICUT

TRANSLATED BY R. H. BOOTHROYD
FROM THE ORIGINAL GERMAN EDITION
PUBLISHED BY HIRMER VERLAG · MUNICH

ALL RIGHTS RESERVED BY PHAIDON PRESS LTD
5 CROMWELL PLACE · LONDON SW7
1956
THIRD EDITION · REVISED · 1961

TEXT PRINTED BY GEO. GIBBONS LTD · LEICESTER
PLATES PRINTED BY KASTNER & CALLWEY · MUNICH
BOUND BY A. W. BAIN AND CO · LTD · LONDON

CONTENTS

FOREWORD

THE WONDERFUL WORLD on the banks of the Nile, with its temples, its tombs and its sculptures, had an irresistible fascination for the Greeks and Romans in the days of antiquity. Ever since it has again been accessible to the peoples of the West, it has continued to exercise a magical attraction, and, as the years go by, more and more attention is paid to its contribution to civilization—that way of life which can still serve as an example. Whereas in earlier years it was Egyptian sculpture that made the greatest appeal and provided material for discussion, today interest is directed more and more towards the life of ancient Egypt in its entirety. With a sense of awe we perceive that what for us is still a problem, had already been solved in a grandiose manner in those remote times.

My first book on Egyptian art, which in a few months ran to a second edition, was published in 1939, and since then I have endeavoured to complete my knowledge of the Nile Valley and its ancient monuments by means of a fifth visit and continual study. As a result, my own standpoint has extended beyond the artistic achievement in itself, to embrace the Egyptian way of life as a whole; the longer and more thoroughly one studies this way of life, the more admirable it seems in its consequentiality based on conviction and unshakeable belief.

The present volume is a work of collaboration. The choice of the illustrations and the great majority of the photographs are due to my publisher and friend, Prof. Dr. Max Hirmer, and his are also the architectural notes in the description of the plates. The architecture of ancient Egypt, which in general has been neglected in previous works on the history of Egyptian art, thus receives adequate treatment.

I would like to join with Prof. Dr. Hirmer in thanking all those institutions and individuals who have helped in the production of this volume; on my journeys to Egypt I have invariably found a great willingness to help, especially on the part of the Egyptian Administration of Ancient Monuments and the Director of the Cairo Museum.

KURT LANGE

THE AIM OF THE ILLUSTRATIONS to the present volume is to give a general idea of ancient Egyptian art: an idea of the landscape in which the buildings erected in the course of three thousand years were, and still are, situated, and an idea of the buildings themselves and their component parts. The reader can thus deduce the details from the living whole and will not, as is the case with so many previous books on Egyptian art, have to guess from details what the whole may be or have been. The same is true of sculpture and painting, in which branches of art the work does not live as a result of its details, but the details receive life from their relationship to the whole. And lastly, sculpture and painting fulfil their real purpose only if they are one with the building to which they belong.

Even if the aim has been only partially achieved, this will represent a step forward in the presentation of ancient Egyptian art to a wider circle of readers—a step forward in that they will be led by the whole to the detail, the proper way to approach the great art of all periods.

To my friend and fellow-author Kurt Lange, who has visited and experienced Egypt five times, I express my thanks for all that he has imparted to me in the course of conversation over the course of many years, for his work in connection with the present volume, and last but not least, for his understanding acceptance of all my wishes with regard to the notes on the plates. In this way it has been possible to combine the author's own notes with the brief descriptions in that part of them dedicated in particular to architecture, for which I accept responsibility.

My sincerest thanks are due to the members of the Service des Antiquités de l'Egypte, for their cordial collaboration during the two visits I made in order to take photographs, and also to the Director-General of the Egyptian Office of Antiquities, Prof. Dr. Mustapha Amer; the Inspector-General of Antiquities in Upper Egypt, Labib Habachi; the Inspector of the Theban Necropolis, Ibrahim M. Kamel; the Custodian of Antiquities at Saqqâra, Zakarija Ghoneim; the Saqqâra archaeologist, Dr. Jean-Philippe Lauer; and lastly, the Director of the Museum in Cairo, Dr. Abbas Bayoumi. With their help and permission I was able to photograph and reproduce for wider publication certain works which previously had been reserved for special scientific research-workers: the two recently reconstructed sanctuaries from the time of Sesostris I and Amenophis I, the newly discovered tomb of Kheruef at Thebes, one of the Zoser reliefs from the king's southern tomb at Saqqâra and many outstanding works in the Cairo Museum, of which hitherto no photographs, or only inadequate ones, had been published.

I also have to thank the Director of the Egyptological Seminary of Munich University, Prof. Dr. Hanns Stock, for all the assistance I was given in his institute and in its library.

My thanks are likewise due to the Directors of the Metropolitan Museum in New York, of the National Gallery of Art in Washington and of the Museum of Fine Arts in Boston (Mass.), who generously placed photographs of the principal works in their museums at my disposal. For the same reason I have to thank the Ashmolean Museum, Oxford, and Monsieur Jacques Vandier, Conservateur en Chef, Musée du Louvre, who kindly obtained photographs of the works in his museum reproduced in the present volume, and lastly the Hessische Treuhandverwaltung des Preussischen Museumsgutes, who, through Prof. Dr. Ernst Holzinger, allowed me to take the first modern colour photograph of the Nefertiti.

Finally I must express my gratitude to Miss Julia Asen, my enthusiastic and tireless collaborator, thanks to whose technical ability many difficult photographs, especially those in colour, were successfully taken.

MAX HIRMER

INTRODUCTION

LIFE begins with fear of the unknown and, if it has been thoughtfully lived, ends with acknowledgement and self-restraint. That is true both of individuals and of the great civilizations produced by mankind. Many peoples seem to be called, but only a few are chosen to influence by the example of their achievements whole continents and periods.

The number of highly civilized peoples which, after an early rejection of barbaric elements, have contrived to develop a systematic style coinciding with the richest and purest possibilities of human endeavour, is smaller than is generally supposed. As a rule they are river-valley civilizations, created by the periodical floods of rivers on the banks of which men settled and cultivated the fields. The most praiseworthy among them seem to us to be those who, owing nothing to preceding civilizations, achieved self-realization thanks to the wealth of their own talents and, without perceptible assistance, achieved the zenith of culture, thereby laying the foundations of further progress. Such seem to us the Sumerian, Chinese and Egyptian civilizations: original sources of human development which started from the primitive organization of early mankind and after an intense fulfilment of the possibilities open to them achieved a spiritual universality the influence of which continues to this day.

Simplified by the distance from which we view it, the great drama of Egyptian civilization, more than any other, gives us an idea of the life of a creative people, with all the ups and downs inherent to the course of its destiny.

It may be due to the consequentiality and concentration of Egyptian style that the attitude of posterity towards ancient Egypt has wavered between under- and over-valuation. That is true even today and it is noteworthy that even scholars cannot always free themselves from such suggestions.

I

The susceptible mind may go so far as to see in Egypt's achievement—to use Heinrich Schäfer's words—'the ultimate aim, already once achieved, but then unhappily lost again'. To many others the prevailing impression is that of an inability, doubly evident in many of its achievements and frankly incomprehensible, to free itself from the fetters of archaism and to achieve free, progressive forms in all fields. One man sees on the banks of the Nile every phase of human development already experienced and thus anticipated as a grandiose and instructive example. Another, instead of this, sees a complacent persistence of inadequate elements in the attitude to religion, the practice of art, the progress of thought and the exercise of power—and even in the unquestionably great realization of the State he will see nothing but unalloyed despotism and the dictatorship of priests. He will agree with the saying that the Egyptians did not know how to make use of their greatest spiritual treasures. How penetratingly did Hegel in his philosophy of history explain the essence and will of Egypt—and how strangely biased and in the main supercilious is the usually cautious Jacob Burckhardt in his attitude to the Egyptian world.

This fantastically concentrated, peculiar and intransmissible civilization postulates an *aut aut* in the attitude of others towards it—either 'for me' or 'against me'. It is rarely that one comes across a sober valuation of its quality—without fantastic subtilization or extravagant enthusiasm, but also without predominance of inner conflicts of feeling. This is probably because, according to our way of thinking, the Egyptians lack the ability to meet half-way, approachability, a readiness to listen. The severity of their attitude is not inviting. They admit no compromises. One has to adapt oneself to their sphere as well or as badly as one can, one must try to feel like an Egyptian, if one wishes to avoid distorted judgements. One must know how to grope one's way backward from the spatial conceptions of the Greeks to the magical and tranquil disposition on the surface and try to recover the obvious, ideal reality of the image with which these men, still childish despite all the variety, mastered the incomprehensible and the feasible. He who is not prepared to do this, will never understand the substance of Egypt. He will be attracted by the aesthetic charm of many works, but it must be quite clear to him that in this way the core will never be revealed to his understanding. Everything Egyptian, wherever it may be, has its own atmosphere around it. Few manifestations have contrived to assert themselves for so long.

Since French fortification-works on the coast of the Nile Delta in 1799 brought to light, by pure chance, the 'Rosetta Stone', thereby discovering an important key to the deciphering of everyday Egyptian writing, further exploration has laid before our eyes an almost overwhelming abundance of the most varied materials. This material proves that no other people in the world had such a faculty, such a fixation for the production of images. Even in olden days numerous Egyptian monuments were taken away to Rome, to Byzantium and other places, while in every civilized country most of the museums and many private collections have acquired treasures of pharaonic art, yet the number of works, large and small, still in their country of origin is incalculable. Scholars are busy sifting and evaluating the discoveries of archaeologists and philologists and drawing conclusions of deep import therefrom, while stylistic criticism is also gradually coming to maturity. Opinions are becoming more and more sharply defined. More clearly than ever before, the investigations of the past years are throwing light on the specific structure of Egyptian things.

Has the extension of knowledge confirmed the evaluation or merely altered it?

Do we see the pharaonic period with its increasingly evident transformations in another light than that in which it appeared to the pioneer Egyptologists fifty or a hundred years ago? And if that is the case, is the explanation perhaps that we are projecting our own essence and will into the unfathomable mystery of ancient Egypt? Can we of today ever penetrate to the core of the nature of an age-old creative community with a way of thinking foreign to us, based on another form of human life and drawing inspiration from a different milieu? In our efforts to know, to explain and to feel ourselves corroborated, are we not attempting to grasp a mirage?

Every seeker after knowledge is bound to ask himself such questions before he turns to the sources.

These sources are not always easy to apprehend. What do we learn when we examine them?

It is inspiring and instructive to study, with the aid of the various objects found in prehistoric Egyptian tombs, the way in which the essential Egyptian element developed its language of imagery, at first hesitantly, and then by gradual stages ever more clearly towards a definite aim.

It is common knowledge that the original naïve form-renderings of all peoples resembled one another so closely that in the absence of any indication of their origin even an expert cannot assign them with certainty to definite regions. Like ancient Greece, Egypt is no exception in this respect. Curiously enough the most artistically gifted peoples show in their early years the fewest traces of their ultimate development. The little human figures from the pre-dynastic period found in the Nile Valley reveal a marked variety: on the one hand we find a primitive carelessness, on the other hand a rigid adherence to a formal world of their own, by means either of naturalistic representation, or of a geometrical compression. But only in exceptional cases are we reminded of anything typically Egyptian. The most arbitrary expression of whims and chance is naturally found in the oldest plastic experiments in Nile mud and clay. The motive is grasped in a drastic manner and often very effectively, but in the construction there is no trace of law and order. If the material chosen is stone, it seems as if the very qualities of the material had guided the hand in a given direction: both human figures and animals are rendered with more decision. Neolithic figures of game animals in flint and flat palettes of hard greyish-green slate carved in the form of animals have a special place of their own. In them the outlines begin to speak a firmer language.

These so-called cosmetics palettes give a wonderfully complete picture of the beginning and development of methodical principles in early Egyptian plastic art. The owners of these palettes, most of which have a hole bored through them to take a string, used them for pulverizing malachite and other materials in order to make eye-paint. Towards the end of the early period their inner sides were filled with semi-plastic ornament. Their size and the extent of the decoration on the finest specimens show clearly that they were not intended for ordinary, everyday use. A small pan in the middle of the figure-covered surface is the only reminder of their original purpose, and such spaces rarely show any trace of having been used. Probably they were sacred offerings made by chieftains to local divinities, and they may have played a role in religious ceremonies. Ultimately they developed until they achieved a kind of official character as tablets commemorating victories.

In them we can see all the stages on the way leading from barbarism to civilization: the rejection of the uncouth, the conquest of the fear of empty spaces in the pictorial plane, the development from a multitude of figures spread incoherently over the surface to a logical division into zones, the first appearance of a co-ordinating idea, the invention of religious or political symbols which from then on became current, the stressing of some event worthy of commemoration. We can follow the remarkably rapid development of writing from the specifically Egyptian models, perhaps inspired by passing contacts with the Sumerian precedent, but essentially independent. From the deliberately ugly scene on the so-called battlefield palette, showing among other things a maned lion—probably symbolizing the victor himself—and numerous birds of prey about to fall upon the nude bodies of fallen enemies, is derived the representation of actual historical episodes on the votive tablets of Kings Scorpion and Narmer. Incarnations of royal power hack down the brick walls of conquered cities, of which the names are given. The slaying, already considered as a symbol, of a vanquished foe held by the hair, the inspection after their execution of the fettered bodies of enemy commanders, whose heads had been laid between their feet, have become state ceremonies, which the lord of the two crowns, barefooted, solemnly performs. Standards are borne before him in the triumphal procession, symbols of the divine powers which confirm his power and vouchsafe him protection, symbols which may at the same time have been provincial emblems connected with the political organization of the country. Thus a household article becomes a historical monument.

The path of this development runs from awkward experiments to a more and more rigorous and solid conception of form. A rigid selection limits the number of types, even down to those of household vessels. Gone is the preference for all kinds of hard stones of varied colour; taste is now restricted to a few sorts of fine stones. The relief becomes shallower, but on the other hand gains in decision. That which in figures of men and animals had hitherto produced a rather feeble effect, becomes more tense. In the course of a few generations, the struggle to achieve an ideal pictorial realization, evolved from the observation of Nature, but at the same time side by side with Nature, is brought to a victorious conclusion, that ideal which in the consistency of its development according to laws of its own is one of Egypt's greatest achievements. By a process of gradual clarification and co-ordination of its characteristics, there was established a style more decisive and enduring than any the world has known. And this remarkable feat was achieved during the first two dynasties—approximately between 3000 and 2800 B.C.

We are too ready to consider the development of a style as a natural and in-evitable process—one might almost say an arbitrary emanation of the spirit of a people predisposed thereto. In reality it is anything but that; it is a wilful act and an outcome of tension, it is an achievement of the conscience, of an exhausting intensity which cannot be maintained for long. And last but not least it is a deter-mination to renounce. How short-lived, how uncertain is every creation of a stan-dard, involved in a desperate struggle against the ever-present tendency towards sluggish approximation! What a high degree of youthful determination must have been required to build that autonomous world of artistic expression which was to be the basic framework for every expression of Egypt's national spirit for three and a half thousand years!

This development of its own 'essential reality' in drawing and relief has its parallel in architecture.

Here the path of development runs from the use as building material of lumps of mud to the square, sun-dried bricks of Nile mud and finally to the great blocks of stone and thus to the lasting achievement of the artistically conceived monu-mental stone building. It had as its premise the ground-plan, and that in itself was a

6

spiritual achievement in method of the highest order. The name and work of that man who, by order of his king, used the newly discovered materials to erect the first extensive and at the same time artistic complex of stone buildings known to us, have been venerated by all succeeding generations and even the Greeks saw in him a god.

Today, on the sandy plateau of the Memphis desert cemetery near the village of Saqqâra, we can still see the gleaming white remains of those buildings which Imhotep erected as an eternal residence for his great king, Zoser. Step pyramid and sacred temple, royal pavilion, government buildings, chapels of national divinities and storehouses—the whole lying in a great rectangle surrounded by a high wall with its bays and projections that, dominated by a 200-feet high step pyramid, the design of which was altered four times, in the centre of the complex, must have made a deep impression on the men of those days.

The methodical exploration of this area has brought with it one of the greatest surprises in the history of art during our own century: here we find, at the very beginning of the development of architecture, the fluted column, not, it is true, standing free—like the contemporary fasciculated column and the base of the papyrus column—but with one part incorporated with the adjoining wall. It has no actual pedestal and resembles a plant with a grooved stalk and little leaves hanging down to form a capital at the top. The stone-cutter's work is as perfect as that of the mason who fashioned the blocks and drums out of fine-grained limestone. These fragments have an air of youth and purity. Although in the main it was a question of transferring to stone the forms hitherto used for objects made of other materials—wood in the form of whole trunks, beams and jambs, reeds and wicker-work plastered with clay—the stress is already laid on the language peculiar to stone and the original beauty of the architectural components has a stylistic emphasis which at once lifts it out of the world of imitation. Some elements without which architecture would now be unthinkable had in those days taken definite form as part of a powerful religious idea: column and pier, base and capital, astragal and flute, steps, wall niche and projection. At the same time there makes

7

its first appearance that ornamental façade decoration like a continuous frieze, which henceforward becomes a permanent feature of Egyptian art.

In a chamber built on to the north side of the step pyramid has been found the oldest life-size statue of a king that has come down to us, the seated effigy of Zoser, looking out through two openings in the wall from eyes long robbed of their sparkling inlays, gazing at the complex of buildings erected for his burial. The effigy has its place there as a guarantee of the continued existence of the individual—a permanent body which, substituting the deceased but yet filled with the actual powers of his being, offers the necessary corporal abode for his surviving personality (his 'Ka'), should it choose to visit its earthly sphere and accept offerings. It would appear that this idea of death was the origin of the portrait statue, for which the Egyptians had a special feeling. Yet certain statuettes of the first two dynasties found in Upper Egyptian temples give reason to think that there may have been another origin.

From this time on we find named portrait statues both in royal funerary temples and in the upper portions of the tombs of well-to-do private individuals, the statues being placed in an inaccessible room and usually looking out through a slit in the walls on the offerings laid before them, breathing the scent of incense and listening to the ritual prayers for the well-being of the inmate of the tomb. Both the man and his wife are commemorated by statues, sometimes with their children in a family group. To them are added at a later period figures of servants, smaller and less formal effigies of maidservants grinding corn, slaves preparing beer or sealing jars, or serving their master. At the end of the third dynasty and during the fourth, all sculptured figures of members of the royal household, including the so-called special heads, have such a marked individual character that they remain in our memory. This in itself is, to a certain extent, an answer to the question, still the subject of lively discussion, whether we have here to do with essentially typical imaginary personages or with portraits reproduced faithfully from the originals. Despite all the liberal simplification, at this stage of development the outstanding feature is the personal character of the faces, and sometimes even of the frames of the bodies. Since the discovery of the astonishing bust of Prince Ankhhaf, there can be no possible doubt that, at least in certain cases, there was a definite striving after lifelikeness. In this connection it is worth remembering that in the pyramid of King Teti near Saqqâra, in rubble two feet above the original floor-level, there was found the undoubtedly old Egyptian mould of a death-mask taken from the face of a young woman. One needs to be very insensitive to art or hidebound by theory if one cannot perceive that the constant occurrence of personal names on the pedestals or backs of statues might very well be a counterpart to an attempt to portray individual features or the whole personal appearance, always within the limits imposed on all early portraiture. How else could we explain the striking variety of the numerous and famous Old Kingdom portrait statues, which is such that we can give them their names and retain them in our memories? Whether we consider them approachable or not, the fact remains that quite apart from their artistic value we can form a kind of personal friendship with a Rahotep and a Nofret, a Hemiun, Ti, or Ranufer, or with the so-called 'village magistrate', Ka-aper. With all their sublimity, they live in a kind of private sphere and excite our curiosity as to their manner of life, their habits and occupations. With the portrait statues from the neighbouring countries of Hither Asia this is only very rarely the case.

A similar function to that of the statue, storing up its strength in its chamber in the upper part of the tomb, is fulfilled by the reliefs covering the walls of the sacrificial chapel and other apartments in the mausoleum, like a carpet of inexhaustible themes. They and the sculptures in the round presuppose one another—there is a relationship of meaning which in a museum can seldom, and even then only partially, be perceived. We tend to regard this magical picture book with its numerous hieroglyphs as a charming, amusing and instructive panorama of life in an old patriarchal country—and who will grudge this sensation to spectators unhampered by specialist knowledge? But in reality every one of the scenes in these cycles crowded with figures, which Ludwig Curtius has rightly called one of the greatest objective representations of human existence, has a close connection with

9

the offerings to the dead which were made in these rooms. The material needs of the departed are thus assured in a magical way. Should it ever happen that no offerings are made, then the deceased, with his knowledge of magic, can conjure up and make use of everything he needs. He has everything with him, for every possible eventuality; not only food, drink, clothing and toilet requisites, but everything necessary for the joys of the chase and for social relaxation. It enhances the significance of these carefully planned and yet unrestrained pictures that room is found in them for amusing and lovable, though useless, things. In spite of its amplitude, the theme—recurring time after time with slight modifications—preserves a strict order, even in the distribution of the single zones and masses. Like the custom, dating from the first dynasties, of using every kind of expedient in order to preserve the corpse, this provision for bodily needs is an expression of that determined affirmation, carried almost to the point of absurdity, of personal existence, which places the religion of Egypt in diametrical contrast with the negation of self in the teachings of Buddha.

In the meantime written characters had taken on their definitive form, which in vividness and clarity remained unsurpassed. One must compare them with the earliest examples on the jar sealings, the cylinder seals, ivory tablets and gravestones of the first dynasty, in order to realize what an achievement this was. The uncertain outlines and faulty alignment have now been replaced by a noble rigidity, combining the highest degrees of expression with a sober economy in the employment of means. The little pictures which were the basis of Sumerian-Accadian writing and of the cuneiform characters of Hither Asia seem clumsy indeed when compared with the severe calligraphy of these eloquent hieroglyphs.

To the word-sign which alone or in combination with others stands for a consonant, a syllable or the meaning of a word, and which preserved all its beauty on monuments throughout millennia, whereas in everyday use it tended more and more towards the cursive form, there is now added the significant symbol. This too achieved perfection of form and retained its magical power until the beginnings of Christianity. Indeed, even modern eyes cannot resist the charm of its suggestive significance. Egyptian sculpture has aptly been described as a three-dimensional hieroglyph. Starting with the conventional application of the image on the side of the square block it achieves spatial depth, though it never reaches the high quality of Greek statues. No one can understand the nature of Egyptian sculpture who has not realized this fact—the fact that every work of Egyptian sculpture is fundamentally a written representation, pointing to a higher spiritual relationship, however plastic and corporeal it may seem. It is practically never an aim in itself. And that is why a purely aesthetic valuation will never do full justice to it.

Nowadays no discerning critic will talk of the immutability of the form and manner of Egyptian art. The theory of an archaic rigidity excluding all change has been as thoroughly demolished as the theories of a dictatorship of priests opposed to all progress and the Egyptian incapacity to achieve clarity of thought and rid themselves of 'the ballast of obsolete stages of civilization'. Our knowledge and our ability to understand have become deeper in the course of the last decades. We know now that the impressive continuity of Egyptian civilization, which survived every crisis, was based on that very attachment to what had been sanctioned by usage and proved to be valid, that conservatism condemned by earlier critics as a whim of the Egyptians. At the same time we also know that the constant transformations characteristic of all life and thus also of the life of nations, those transformations which constitute the history of mankind, sometimes took place in Egypt with surprising rapidity and that these often stormy events, so pregnant with consequences, were clearly reflected in the world of Egyptian art. That is particularly true of the early and late Old Kingdom and also of the Middle Kingdom, the importance of which in the history of the human mind cannot be exaggerated. Even under the New Empire, when Egypt was a world power, there were continual changes: one need only think of the changes in the social structure, phase by phase, under the eighteenth dynasty and of the difference between the Egyptians of the nineteenth and twentieth dynasties and those of the eighteenth.

The first mighty achievement due to the combined efforts of the nation was the establishment of the Old Kingdom (ca. 2778-2662 B.C.) around Memphis, with

11

its strict social order and astonishing planned economy, which made immense undertakings possible and yet did not sever the individual from his rooted attachment to the soil.

Under Snofru, on whose outstanding figure recent excavations near Dahshur have thrown further light, and the subsequent rulers of the fourth dynasty, of whose lives and doings we unfortunately know little, the genuine, standard type of pyramid was developed. As there are no indications of the presence in Egypt at that time of large numbers of prisoners of war or of the existence of a kind of slavery (the sources, on the contrary, reveal the prevalence of a patriarchal regime), we can only suppose that a youthful and pious people, by building the pyramids, with its hard and enthusiastic work extolled itself as well as its god-kings. Even we of today, accustomed as we are to the wonderful achievements of science, cannot withhold our admiration when we see them: royal tombs of unequalled dimensions, the definitive form of which must be related to that of the sacred Benben stone in the neighbouring city of the sun, Heliopolis, and thus to the sun-god himself, as the sunships discovered in the rocky ground near the pyramids also prove. The idea of the monumental sun throne coincides with that of the dominating royal tomb. The immortalized king enters once again into the mystical relationship with his father, the sun god, every time the sun shines on the smooth gleaming sides of the gigantic triangles and rests upon them during its daily course through the heavens, as it did the first time it shone on the mysterious stone monument at Heliopolis.

The royal pyramid dominates the desert plateau and in the same way the might of the god king dominates the community of the dwellers on the banks of the Nile. The king assigns to each of his subjects a suitable task and in return guarantees his existence. His family, courtiers and functionaries are grouped around him, just as their graves are grouped around his huge monument: a reproduction in stone of the state organization for the visitor of today. So limitless and all-pervading did the might of the incarnate 'Great God' appear to the Egyptians of those days, that no priests ministered to his person during his lifetime and no divine images were needed in the chambers of his tomb. The heedless touching of his emblems might be as lethal as a flash of lightning, if the king did not absolve the unwary with his blessing. When he appeared, there resounded, just as it did when the divine images appeared at festivals, the warning cry: 'Earth, beware! The god is coming!' That, notwithstanding this, the king was not abhorred as an incalculably tyrannical despot, as ignorant generations two thousand years later told the traveller thirsting for knowledge, is proved by the meaning of the proper names of the pyramid period, which attribute to the head of the state all the benevolent virtues of the god—'Cheops has shown mercy', 'Userkaf is friendly', 'Pepi it is who brings peace', 'Merirê lives for us', 'Good is the love of a king'. Another proof of the popular regard for the person of the ruler is provided by the Sphinx at Giza: that huge couchant lion with its hooded king's head, gazing toward the sunrise—for all its mutilation and decay the greatest work of sculpture produced by mankind.

As the dynasties and rulers changed, this early form of human social organization and the divine monarchy on whose omnipotence it rested passed through many crises and many periods of tension, until after lasting for fifteen hundred years its mechanism broke down and it outlived itself under the all-too-long rule of a weak monarch.

It would seem that by the end of the fifth or the beginning of the sixth dynasty the rise of individualism had led to a conventionalism which was too perceptibly oppressive.

Before that time there had been no lack of sharply defined royal personalities: figures like Zoser and Snofru have all the characteristics of a sharply marked individuality. It would be making the problem too easy if we were to assume that the form of community life prevailing at that time was a kind of collective existence resembling that of insects and governed by impulses. On the contrary an autonomous individualism with definite social aims was beginning to come to the fore among categories which hitherto had been inarticulate. Royal pyramids became smaller and less massive, while the tombs of influential courtiers and landowners became more and more considerable in their dimensions and the number of chambers they contained. Whereas at the beginning sculpture in the service of royalty had achieved a lofty aloofness, it later began to lose ground to the art of the private portrait. There are many other signs that the local princes and vassals were becoming more and more conscious of their importance and more and more headstrong in opposition to the claims of the crown. Moreover new hostile forces were pressing their way up from below. The provinces, awakening to historical consciousness, began to assert their claims. Finally the order which had lasted so long was shattered by a social catastrophe in which whole classes of the nation threw off the burden of obligations obviously felt to be intolerable, and resorted to violence in order to realize their claims to prosperity and possessions, thereby bringing about a revolution which left country and customs defenceless and brought the under-dog to the top. The fury of the mob spared neither royal monuments nor the archives of government buildings, and even the hallowed tombs were not respected. From the cemeteries of the great, blocks of stone were removed and used for the tombs of little men.

As a result a whole world was rent asunder.

It can be taken for certain that no influences from outside brought about this supreme crisis. Before it broke, the Nile Kingdom, so far as we know, had not undertaken any important or lengthy military operations, nor had it been attacked by external enemies. Nor can it have been a question of over-exploitation of the national potential by indulging in vast building plans: the period of huge pyramids was a thing of the past. Moreover it is becoming more and more evident 'that this achievement did not imply the enslavement of the nation, but that an equally grandiose system of state-organized planning with a religious base was behind it. There must obviously have been some kind of official obligation to work, which made it possible to mobilize unemployed workers for building projects especially during the flood season, that is to say at a time of year when the transport of building materials, which in Egypt was always effected by water, was easiest. The provision of work at this season, however, meant economic security for innumerable members of the population, since the work was paid for (accounts relating to work have been preserved).' (E. Otto).

It must therefore have been the steadily growing disproportion between the inviolable possessions of the economically independent pyramid towns, religious temples and private funerary institutions on the one hand, and the similarly increasing burdens imposed upon the rest of the population and on the country districts directly administered by the state on the other hand, which finally resulted in poverty, famine and serious social dissension. The pretensions of the gods and the departed, which religion recognized as natural and reasonable, became in practice too overwhelming in their totality and jeopardized the existence of large categories of the living. Conversely, every disturbance of the social order imperilled the flow of supplies to the chief centres which by now had become populous cities. One may therefore say that the course of events in the Egyptian system was inevitably predestined and fulfilled itself according to a kind of fatal necessity.

A detailed account of the disturbed conditions at that time has come down to us in the 'Admonitions of Ipu-wer', which one cannot read without emotion and to which Egyptologists in our own time rightly attach a special importance. For a whole century or more the way of life and the practice of art declined, not only in the provinces, but also in the neighbourhood of the old capital, until it reverted to a helplessly primitive stage, and the unfettered impulses reigned triumphant, whereas at the courts of individual local rulers the remnants of the old tradition which remained after the radical upheaval were combined to form a new mode of existence.

The whole process is of great interest to students of the history of the mind. To see in it only an Egyptian revolution would be to underrate its significance. It was a revolution in the story of human development.

Men learned that what had seemed to be inviolably permanent, could be destroyed. They saw that statues of kings could with impunity be reduced to splinters, tombs desecrated, the most sacred monuments of the past destroyed.

Men who previously had felt themselves more or less secure in their bonds, lost their innocence and their convictions—those convictions which were based on unthinking faith in the validity of tradition. Once the material impulse was stilled, there arose doubts and heart-searchings. Kings and gods could be destroyed. What had long seemed irremovable, reasonable and seemly, might become the reverse. . .

People now began to become gradually conscious of the loss of a moral perception which they had previously possessed without knowing it. From now on throughout the ages there resounds more or less clearly, but without ever ceasing completely, the lament that all guarantees against mortality and oblivion are of questionable value. Amidst the joys of feasting and merriment it may suddenly strike a sinister chord; the secret consciousness of the vanity of all efforts to achieve immortality in this world henceforth becomes part of the Egyptian attitude of mind. The soul of ancient Egypt never recovered completely from the shock of this decisive change. There is an echo of it in those minstrels' songs inscribed upon Theban tombs of the New Empire:

'*I have heard all that happened to my forefathers—*

. . . .

Their houses have fallen to ruins.
Their market-places are no more.
They are like to a thing that has never been
since the days of the god.

. . . . .

Think not of that day of the "Come!",
until thou goest towards the West as a votary:
lo! what the priests in panther's skins strew on the ground,
what they place on the table of sacrifice, to what purpose is it?
Celebrate a beautiful day seemingly!
Multiply the good by thy wisdom!
Behold! Fate does not multiply its days,
Time comes at its hour, no more is given. . .

No man who has gone away, has ever returned.'

16

The form which this consciousness took in the Late Period is vividly described by the Greek historian Herodotus: 'At feasts in the houses of the rich, when they have sat down, a man carries round in a coffin a wooden image of a dead man, which is very naturally painted and fashioned and is usually one or two ells long. He shows it to each guest and says: Look upon this, and then drink and make merry, for when thou art dead, thus wilt thou be! Thus do they do at their feasting.'

With the loss of the age-old belief that divinity and monarchy, sacred images and statues of rulers were inviolable things, began the conception of the responsibility of the individual. Such was the situation at the beginning of the Middle Kingdom. The objectivity of its funerary offerings and the painful doubt of its laments breathe a profound scepticism. Personal loneliness—a new discovery—is silently expressed in the gravity of its portrait sculpture. It is significant that a long time has still to elapse before this newly acquired experience achieves a mature form in the features of royal statues. The strength of conviction in Old Kingdom portraits was based on a sublime ingenuousness, but the features henceforth are stamped with an inner, highly personal consciousness.

Energetic local kings endeavoured, by extending and consolidating their power, to put a stop to the spread of disorder in the country. The political instinct, gradually regaining strength, tended towards centralization. In opposition to it, the noble families, powerful in their own possessions, defended their privileges, many of which dated from long ago and had been exercised to the benefit of the population, not only in times of distress.

The monarchy ruled the country from Thebes. This hitherto insignificant provincial town became the home and residence of the new dynasty and consequently the capital. The strict and wise regime of the princes of Herakleopolis succumbed to its warlike fury after a hard struggle. Mentuhotep Nebhepetrê, whose strong-limbed seated effigies in the funerary temple of his family in western Thebes express his ruthless energy, like Menes before him held both countries in a firm grip. One hundred and fifty years later, the great Sesostris Khakaurê completely overcame the provincial princes and made them vassals of the crown. During his reign, the princes abandoned their custom of building imposing and at the same time habitable tombs in the cliffs of the desert plateau along the Nile.

The newly founded state had once again powerful and courageous monarchs. It reunited the areas into which Egypt inevitably splits after every political crisis; purposefully and coherently it organized all the forces of the Nile valley for all national emergencies, and in particular for defence against foreign invaders. Something resembling a caste of professional soldiers, a royal army relying on the help of the provincial militias, began to form itself. Material civilization flourished, nobler and richer than ever before.

But this kingdom, which held undisputed sway over the country and the people, differed from the Old Kingdom.

It was now a monarchy based on its own strength—it knew that it was vulnerable and transient. It drew its strength not from the harmony, but from the tensions within the state, the unity of which was henceforth symbolized by effigies of the national gods at the sides of the thrones of statues of kings. Its rulers had to be constantly on the watch to suppress opponents. We know that Ammenemes I, the founder of the glorious twelfth dynasty, was the victim of a court conspiracy. In a treatise on kingship, his son and successor, Sesostris I, attributes to him the following melancholy comment on those times: 'Trust not even thy brother, have no friends, no confidants; all that is of no avail. When thou sleepest, guard thy own heart, for on the day of misfortune no man has true followers...'

It was not by chance that nearly all the kings of this dynasty appointed their sons and heirs co-regents. The pledge of their security was the example they set: the strict fulfilment of their duties and the sense of responsibility which they showed to their subjects. That the energetic Sesostris III and his son Ammenemes III did not take life easily is proved by their striking portraits, even if, in the treatment of form and the worn, disillusioned expression, the spirit of the times found stronger expressions than in the actual features of the rulers. In these effigies the careful anatomical structure of the faces endows the two kings with a striking personality, combined with a capacity for awakening human sympathy which we rarely find in Egyptian art.

The Middle Kingdom (ca. 2060-1680 B.C.)—that second golden age with its many profound and mighty creations—eventually dissolved in a way which has not yet been historically explained. The decline lasted for more than half a century during which no attack from outside the borders weakened its foundations.

Why did its strength decline? Did the very loftiness of its ideas, its separateness and acquiescence, bring it to ruin? Did its gifted royal family in the end wear itself out? The conformity to rule of its instincts and works gained for its creations— and not least for its writings, the form and content of which still appeal to us—the reputation among succeeding generations of a classical validity. The portraiture of the early Late Period followed reverently in its footsteps, drinking in the mighty impulses of the models, which for all their formal severity are frequently impregnated with a kind of hopeless melancholy.

At the end—and in the circumstances it could hardly have been otherwise—all kinds of adventurers fought their way up to power—freebooters and generals and a few real, born rulers, though of all these happenings nothing has come down to us except long lists of names, huge mutilated statues and a dim inkling of changing and in the main barbaric conditions.

Then, after sporadic incursions of individual tribes into the Delta area, there came from Asia a flood of foreign invaders. First, under the pressure of an extensive migration of peoples in the North, heterogeneous hordes lusting for plunder, who left no original monuments, no visible tokens of their ways and ideas. Their kings, some of whom bore Semitic names, controlled the valley of the Nile from their fortress of Avaris in the eastern Delta, imposing the yoke of foreign domination on the Egyptians for at least a century. This period, still obscure from the historical point of view, represented a decisive turning-point in the course of Egyptian civilization. It would seem that, as early as the end of the Old Kingdom, there was an influx of foreigners into Egypt, but they have left us no tangible traces. On the other hand, the domination of the so-called Hyksos effected considerable transformations in the character and customs of the Egyptians, though the material traces left by these fierce intruders were scanty. What is important is that their appearance widened the Egyptian outlook; only from that time onwards was there an Egyptian foreign policy in the strict sense of the word. It seems almost symbolic of this involuntary broadening of outlook, that they brought to the conquered people horses and chariots, thus providing them with unexpected possibilities for what later became a successful method of fighting.

With the expulsion of the Asiatic oppressors and the ensuing pursuit, which brought a clan of minor Theban rulers, known as the seventeenth dynasty, into Palestine, the New Kingdom (ca. 1580-1085 B.C.) began to take shape—that era of world power which was to offer Egyptian talent and skill its greatest opportunity.

Attention was now directed towards the outside world and it soon became evident that the power of Egypt had not been broken, but, after a temporary setback, had become greater than ever before.

It is true that no new fundamental cultural values were produced and no royal statue, no sphinx of the New Empire can vie in inner content and external form with those of the great eras of the past. Activity takes the place of creativeness. But this activity is of such intensity and extent, that in this case quantity becomes in itself quality.

The utmost was accomplished in every field, especially in the subjection and administration of the Palestinian and Syrian principalities and in the final colonization of Nubia, which under the Hyksos appears to have made itself independent under its own chieftains. Egypt became an empire—and this in reality was foreign to its nature and was maintained by succeeding generations for several centuries only at the cost of tremendous effort; its Theban city god became the imperial god whose glory outshone that of other gods and brought the sun god Rê under his sceptre. This essentially peace-loving nation of peasants, among whom the conscientious functionary was respected and the scribe revered as a sage, was seized with military ambition and the officer home on leave proudly flaunted in family gatherings the 'gold of honour' conferred upon him by the king. Thebes, the capital of Upper Egypt, whence had come on two occasions the idea of founding a unified state, now became a metropolis:

'. . . . . . . *where the houses are rich in treasures,*
she has a hundred gates and from each issue forth to battle
two hundred doughty warriors with their steeds and weapons.'
(*Iliad* IX, 381-4)

The wide circle of its fruitful countryside now became filled with huge temples and palaces, with increasingly splendid residential and industrial areas, stretching right to the edge of the desert. In the limestone foothills of the western mountains, the walls of the habitable chambers in the tombs were adorned with those cycles of pictures which vividly portray the life of the time, and even the details of costumes and usages: the performance of official duties and the exercise of professions, the supervision of the harvest and the joys of the chase, all kinds of characteristic figures from near and far, the monotonous passage of the weeks and gay festivals, and at the end of life's journey the solemn voyage on the Nile, the funeral procession 'to the West' and the rites solemnized by the priests of the dead before the mummy embalmed with myrrh at the gateway to the tomb.

The warlike, industrious and vigorous centuries of the Tuthmosis and Amenophis have been called the golden age of the Pharaohs, and certainly in Tuthmosis III they had a statesman of universal talents in the style of Julius Caesar —a military commander, an organizer and a ruler of the first rank—and in the splendour-loving Amenophis III a princely promoter of welfare of no mean proportions. But why is it that for all our admiration for their extent and magnificence and inventiveness we remain dissatisfied as we wander from building to building, from statue to statue, if we have previously steeped ourselves in the creations of the pyramid area? Why does the visitor feel a kind of homesickness for the golden desert silence of the pyramid zones and the Old Kingdom funerary mounds near Saqqâra? In the olden days a naïve confidence in this world and in the world to come, an affable self-assurance and human charm left their imprint on the rich abundance of works, but all this is now replaced by a reserved business civilization. Then, as now, the magical cult of the dead in their 'eternal dwellings' was depicted, but now there is no communication, in so far as private feelings and thoughts are concerned. At the same time convention has retreated inward. Courteous, one might almost say lovable, are the notably feminine stone features of the statues, even if they represent influential men—officers and functionaries of the Pharaoh's immediate entourage—but they remain inscrutable. There is in them a gradual penetration of that Levantine-Oriental element which we hardly ever encounter in the older portraits of men. The architectural components are imposing and, in their way, noble, but their formal language is already too much imbued with superiority to make communication possible and it may be that on beholding their haughty features we feel a secret longing for the modest, appealing nobility of the past. In the one case dignity and restraint border on over-refinement, in the other on arrogance, and the monumental element has a touch of insolence. Among the innumerable masterpieces of craftsmanship, what was formerly a restrained obviousness and an aloof distinction, now becomes merely charming and at times amusing. However great the effect of the material charm and artistic ability of the treasures from King Tutankhamun's tomb, nevertheless not one of his numerous gems can vie in intimate charm with the graceful jewels which the princesses of the twelfth dynasty took with them to their last dwelling-place.

The elements in the colossal statues and large edifices which served to heighten the national consciousness were used more and more for the glorification of power. The reaction under the self-willed and biased religious fanatic Akhnaton did not check this process for long. His authoritarian artistic experiment coupled with his programme of religious reform reveals, in addition to virtues which the chisels of sensitive masters converted into works of sublime charm, many signs of decadence. And this is true of other fields influenced by the example of the court. In the spiritual history of the East in olden days there are not many figures of the same importance, concerning whom so much can be said in one breath to their credit and discredit. What happened was that arbitrariness and individualism threatened

22

at that time to imperil the structure of Egypt which was in any case being gradually transformed by influences from outside, and the reaction against this obvious degeneration signified—if one can call it so—a third salvation of the country. In this connection it must not be forgotten that in the Amarna years the germs of vital and religious feeling reached a stage of development which subsequently ripened to a significant maturity, the results of which cannot be disregarded in the history of Egyptian spiritual development. It was at that time that a new ideal replaced that of the preservation of what was hallowed by custom, of the accumulation of wealth and the enjoyment of life. And can one ignore the fact that many of the sculptural works at Amarna have exercised a deep and lasting influence on the artistic ideas of our own time?

Akhnaton's religious campaign did not win the people over to his side. The claims of the royal ego were too absolute, in most cases not equal to the requirements of his office and at bottom thoroughly unpopular. The artistic style inspired by Akhnaton, however, achieved during the reigns of Tutankhamun and Haremhab a wonderful fusion with the old convention of Thebes and Memphis and its influence on sculpture in the round and on relief can be traced for a long time.

There followed the noble classicism, presented, it is true, with a certain academic coolness, of Sethos I, who in his military campaigns made a vigorous attempt to save the prestige which Egypt had almost entirely lost, especially in the north, owing to Amarna misrule. He evidently had a flair for finding unusually gifted masters to supervise artistic production in his workshops: his many-chambered tomb, driven deep into the heart of the western mountain at Thebes, surpasses in its layout and adornment all the other royal graves in the Valley of Tombs, and the beauty of the figured mural decorations in the temple which he caused to be erected at Abydos, leaves an indelible impression on the minds of all who behold it.

Under the long reign of his famous son, Ramesses II, Egypt entered upon that problematic period which is the inevitable lot of every advanced civilization: that busy period in which a brisk vivacity takes the place of tranquil, creative emotion, but in which, on the other hand, understanding of the world and a non-dogmatic

23

piety become more evident. A kind of evening glow suffuses the historically not very important, but in their way venerable exponents of such late periods: a Ramesses, an Assurbanipal, a Nebuchadnezzar, or even a Hadrian.

The love of the colossal and the imposing now surpasses itself. It is as if the whole Nile Valley had become a gigantic stonemason's yard whose task it was to give monumental expression to the complacency of the rulers.

The massiveness of buildings and sculptures is such that one is tempted to call it a form of exhibitionism carried to a degree of titanical absurdity. Individual works of high quality are still produced. But viewed as a whole, all this magnification of the Good God, of his fellow gods and of the achievements of the time is spoilt by its exaggeration of effects, its disproportionateness, its unwieldiness and restlessness. What is certain is that at that time more stone was hewn than under any of the pyramid kings, and the visitor today has difficulty in discovering the traces of more refined stages of civilization amidst the all-pervading works of the great Ramesses. In view of the historical situation it is not surprising that during the sixty-six years of this Pharaoh's reign, there was a marked penetration of foreign elements into the manner of life and customs of the Egyptians, even in their everyday speech and dance steps. Disintegrating forces entered everywhere into the essence of Egyptian life. Scepticism and satire were rampant and openly derided the most sacred things.

When Egypt was drawn into the field of outside political forces, many changes occurred. The son of Re became a royal man of the world, foreign princesses populated his harem, while a continual stream of foreigners poured into the Nile valley, as immigrants, as gifts of allied rulers or as captives taken in battle. For years the court of the Pharaohs had conducted active diplomatic negotiations with the kings and city governors of the western Asiatic countries—negotiations in which the queen participated. For imperative reasons of world policy the seat of government was moved to the area of the Delta, though Thebes retained its old glory and in their extent the new buildings put those of earlier periods in the shade. One must have seen with one's own eyes the mighty witnesses in the area of Luxor to the assertiveness of the time, if one is to form a true idea of what those generations attempted and of what by dint of titanic labour they achieved. The gigantic dimensions of buildings and sculptures surpass all expectation, however great: on every papyrus capital in the middle aisle of the great hall of pillars at Karnak it has been calculated that a hundred men could stand, and the walls surrounding the complex of the Amun sanctuary could easily contain ten European cathedrals.

Ramesses III, with whom Egypt's twentieth dynasty begins, strove valiantly to rival his predecessor and namesake in the exercise of power and in building, but despite the eloquence of the reliefs of the period, with their instructive representations of foreign peoples and historical events, hardness and coarseness steadily invade the pictorial decoration of temple walls. The sense of proportion becomes uncertain, the execution noticeably uneven. The expression is that of a certain exhaustion of the national strength, which is not surprising after such fantastic efforts. From the beginning of the eighteenth dynasty the Pharaohs had to be ever on the watch to defend their northern frontiers and to this end they recruited mercenaries wherever they could find them. For years the mode of life and artistic expression clung to the examples of the days of the great Ramesses Miamun: even his features were perpetuated in the portraits of private individuals and—like Julius Caesar, who later bequeathed his name as the greatest of all titles to the great ones of our world—for many generations to come it was unthinkable that anyone could assume the office of Pharaoh without at the same time being a Ramesses.

A change in this respect came about, after many internal upheavals, only as a result of the foreign dominations which followed one upon the other during the first millennium B.C.—Libyans and Ethiopians, Assyrians and Persians, Greeks and Romans. What in the intervening period seems like new blood in the manner and expression of life is perhaps but a return to the achievements of the creative days of long ago. Naturally the conditions of existence and outlook underwent constant change and at the same time taste was evidently influenced by foreign ways. There was also no lack of genuine efforts to achieve a new artistic expression. Until a few years ago the criticism and evaluation of the phenomena of the Egyptian Late Period were treated far too light-heartedly; after all it was a period of intense historical and cultural development which lasted a full thousand years! Even if Egyptian civilization in its old age was incapable of providing the necessary energy for the exploitation of such attempts, that does not mean that it assumed an attitude of courtly senility and unapproachability, as is commonly believed even today. It is true that as regards the human portrait it adhered to a conventional type, which could not stand up to closer investigation, but this type, emptied though it was of all form, had yet enough consistency to inspire the evolution of the Greek sculptured figures of youths, destined to achieve an unparalleled artistic development. In any case it would be wrong to generalize from this case. With the close-fitting draperies, giving the impression of nudity, of the sculptured bodies of the Ethiopian and following periods, a feeling for the human body appears which exploits wantonness as a means of producing effect. More than ever before the treatment of the nude tends towards a plastic sensuality— long before the irresistible, mature Greek model became known to the Egyptians. And when this model finally revealed the full force of its charm, Egypt did not reject it. Meanwhile, especially in portraiture, plastic, individually striking solutions of single problems had been found, which prove that the age-old feeling for reserved, highly expressive form had not been extinguished. Side by side with the smooth stone features of the kings of the Late Period, smiling coldly and aloofly despite, in most cases, the bravure of the technique, we find masterpieces like the grandiose Mentuemhet in Cairo and the incomparably moulded 'Green Head' in the museum in Berlin, which in their way can hold their own beside the best creations of the older period. In particular, the late Memphite portraits have a kind of urbanity which makes many famous works of European art seem provincial by comparison. It is clear that this tradition had considerable influence on Roman portraiture of the late Republican era.

The fact that, not only under the able and talented twenty-sixth dynasty, but also under the last Egyptian rulers of the thirtieth, a by no means despicable late flowering of the arts took place, is partly due to Egypt's firm adherence to the symbol and type as laid down by hieroglyphic tradition—that adherence to a fixed system which to the end was one of the mainstays of the state, of religious practice and of society. Figured hieroglyphics from the Ptolemaic period, cleverly fashioned in coloured porcelain and inlaid in the wood of coffins, can vie in every respect, in severity and beauty of style and craftsmanship, with those of earlier times. Figures of animals—especially couchant lions—with a striking power of expression, produced by a later generation which had long lost all national feeling and had to be satisfied if it pleased foreign tastes, reveal a deliberate and daring return to New Empire models. There is something miraculous in the constancy of Egyptian sculptural vision through the millennia. To that must be added a gift for handling the materials and a degree of skill which made it possible for Egypt to produce convincing works even in its decline.

Are we not justified in assuming that this astonishing productive capacity was the natural result of a well-balanced national life?

The fantastic course of this national life, with its constant changes combined with conservatism, its outstanding achievements and renunciations, lends itself all the more easily to comparison with other civilizations and to the formulation of fruitful theories on the history of mankind, because its modes of expression can easily be grasped and in many respects are akin to our own. For all the strangeness of individual works, the European of today not only finds it easy to become conversant with the world of Egyptian art, but he even gets to like it, once he has decided to make a thorough study of it. Egyptian art is far more easy to approach than that of the Middle or Far East, or India, or even the ancient art of America, despite all the insight into the latter which we have recently acquired. Indeed, the spell which ancient Egyptian art casts upon many of us is accompanied by the danger that aesthetic delight and thoughtless assimilation of the strange elements to our own way of thinking may make us forget its peculiarity—a peculiarity which exhaustive studies are stressing more and more.

27

How are we to explain this ease with which we 'feel ourselves at home' in the Egyptian world, so different from our own in its mode of expression?

Is it the exotic charm, the fairy-tale element in all these people, animals, plants and articles of everyday use, so strange and yet so familiar in appearance, that attracts us? Is it because the Egyptians carried to its logical conclusion and then applied in practice that universal, original mode of representation which is that of children and of all adults uninfluenced by teaching or by models? The high quality of Egyptian architecture and sculpture is due mainly both to the admirable draughtsmanship and to a *mastery* convincing despite all the peculiarities, to a not easily definable classical element in substance and effect which I would tentatively describe as a 'protoclassical', to avoid bringing confusion into the normal terminology. No Sumerian-Babylonian work of sculpture in the round can vie in equilibrium of proportions and mastery of form with the Egyptian masterpieces, however expressive individual religious works of that astonishing race may be. Despite the innate dignity and authority of early Mesopotamian sculptures, they still—like the grandiose human figures of mature Assyrian art—retain an alien ethnographical element which keeps the spectator at a distance, and which Egyptian sculptors of all periods replaced with a universal, human effect. The ideal of the nude, as developed in the Nile Valley from the earliest times, is found nowhere else in the Eastern world, but on the other hand provided the immediate inspiration for the incomparable Greek conception. This nation of sculptors, with their happy knack of seeing things as Adam saw them, had a mysterious understanding of the original scale of measurements dating from the Creation, on which, in reality, the whole persuasiveness and beauty of form is based. Goethe was right when he ranked the Egyptian works of sculpture 'of ancient basalt, black and severe' with those of the Greeks 'of marble, white and charming'. Works like the enthroned King Chephren receiving the blessing of the falcon-god, the noble statue of Ti, or the maned sphinx of Ammenemes III have never been surpassed in the power of their inner and external classicism. The admiration they arouse confirms their quality. If the term 'classic' were to be reserved for 'Antiquity' in the narrower sense of the term, what words could express this convincing, universal quality, perfect in itself?

Is it also possible to speak of a proto-Christian element in the ancient Egyptian moral code?

From the fall of the Old Kingdom Osiris played an increasingly important role in religious thought. This mythical king of olden times and god of agriculture, who was treacherously murdered by his brother Set and rose again from the dead, became in Upper Egypt the Lord of the Underworld and the judge of the dead. It is true that the confession which the deceased had to make to him concerning their behaviour in this world was purely negative, consisting as it did of a recital of numerous punishable offences which they had *not* committed, wherein the influence of magic is evident. It is likewise true that the active spiritual attitude of Europeans in this respect begins only with the positive and categorical 'Thou shalt not' of the Commandments of Moses. Nevertheless, we find here for the first time —more than a thousand years before similar ideas became prevalent in neighbouring countries—a religious conviction that our fate in the world to come depends on our moral behaviour in this life, which we shall have to justify before the throne of God. On entry into the kingdom of the dead, apart from the simultaneous oral declarations, the heart of the deceased had to be weighed before the eyes of the divine judge—and no other people except the Egyptians has expressed such an idea so clearly in words and in pictures. By contrast the old Mesopotamian conception of the world to come seems hopelessly gloomy, and that of the Greeks would have been colourless and inadequate, if the mysteries had not provided a certain compensation.

Whether we can speak of a genuine monotheistic tendency in early Egyptian religion, is debatable. There is, however, no doubt whatever that in the earliest phases of Egyptian religion known to us there emerges a God Almighty, whose presence fills the whole region of the skies and whose eyes shine like the sun and the moon; this god of heaven is called 'the Great', 'the Lord of All', and 'He who is'; and notwithstanding the multiplication of gods which soon took place, the surviving texts, whether inscriptions on tombs or treatises on worldly wisdom, refer to him simply as 'the god'. And those who have made a deeper study of the history of religion are acquainted with the solar monotheism of King Akhnaton, that doctrinal belief in one all-embracing, creative and protective divinity, worshipped in the image of the gleaming disc of the sun, which provides even the smallest of its creatures with all they need. That, however, is the sum of its activity, and there is no mention in this doctrine, in so far as we know it, of sin or repentance, or of right and wrong. Nevertheless it would appear that portions of the Amarna hymn to the sun have been incorporated in the 104th Psalm and it is certain that many axioms of Egyptian worldly wisdom found their way into the Jewish scriptures in the eighth or seventh century B.C. The primitive representation of the maternal Isis nursing her mystically conceived son in her lap, after passing through intermediate stages in Greek art, became the Byzantine Madonna. And for the first Christians in the Nile valley it was easy to embellish their new faith with long-revered symbols and to identify the Cross of Jesus Christ with the hieroglyphic looped cross, or 'ankh', which for them signified 'life'.

If we can only free ourselves from the current prejudices, we perceive, when we study the sources, that from the earliest times a sense of fittingness and integrity was an Egyptian characteristic. Everywhere there emerges a tolerant way of thinking, averse to the violent or the drastic, which has a congenial 'bourgeois' touch, with a delicate respect for social propriety and the need for restraint. It is all these qualities that distinguish the inhabitants of the Nile valley, with their by no means robust physique, their rustic love of peace and their indefatigable zeal for writing, from many of the conquering peoples who later played a role in the history of the eastern Mediterranean countries.

Typical is the honourable place assigned to women in ancient Eygpt. Their position was considerably better than that of the Greek women of antiquity. Old Kingdom portrait groups show them as the equals of their husbands—pillars of the state like the men. The title by which they were known, 'nebt-per'—'mistress of the house'—is in itself significant. In Egyptian law a matriarchal trend can be

30

clearly discerned. In the question of legitimate succession to the throne, the queen was as important as the descent of the king. Absolute legitimacy could thus only be achieved by marriages between royal brothers and sisters, which were probably far more frequent than would appear from the historical records that have come down to us. Even as early as the pyramid era, in a trial for high treason in the harem, we see the accused queen being interrogated by a tribunal specially created by the king for this purpose, a tribunal of which the chief judge—probably because he was too close to the Pharaoh and might therefore be suspected of undue influence—did not form part. The great American orientalist J. H. Breasted rightly remarks in this connection that it was a striking proof of the king's lofty sense of justice and of the surprising legal-mindedness of the time that a person suspected of a conspiracy in the king's harem could not be sentenced to death without a lot of fuss. Breasted goes on to say that an immediate death-sentence, without any attempt to prove the legal guilt of the accused, would have seemed quite justifiable barely a century ago in the same country.

Soon after the year 2500 B.C., the vizier Ptahhotep included the following among his rules of life: 'When thou hast achieved something and founded a household, love thy wife in thy house, as is seemly. Care for her bodily needs, clothe her back; ointments for the care of her body are a balsam for her limbs. Gladden her heart, so long as thou livest: she is a field, the tilling of which brings reward to him who possesses her.' One of the axioms of the sage Ani runs: 'Rebuke not a woman in her house, if thou knowest that she is capable. Say not to her: Where is that? Bring it to me! if she has put it in its right place. Let thy eye look, whilst thy tongue remains silent, so that thou canst appreciate her good deeds.' The following maxim is a reminder of the duty to love one's mother—a moral obligation which was profoundly felt: 'Double the bread which thou givest to thy mother; support her, as she bore you. She had much labour with thee; when thou wast born after thy months, she suffered still further, for her breast was in thy mouth for three years. She did not shrink from nursing thee; she sent thee to school, when thou hadst learned to write, and every day she was there with bread and drink from her house. When thou art a young man and takest unto thyself a wife and art thyself the head of a household, remember how thy mother bore thee and reared thee in all ways. May she never have to blame thee or to raise her hands to God—and may He never have to hear her lament!'

A sense of justice and sympathy with the oppressed are continually affirmed in the autobiographical writings that have been preserved. Naturally, at no time and in no country was life really so patriarchally humane as the descriptions would have us believe. Even under the Pharaohs only a few can have followed literally the ethical precepts of the royal doctrine. But the predisposition towards them is in itself of value as representing a moral aim, for they gave us a notion of the ethical ideal to which the author and the times subscribed.

The pseudo 'Instruction of King Ammenemes to his son' represents the subsequently murdered founder of the twelfth dynasty as saying: 'I gave to him who asked and nourished the orphans; I admitted the destitute to my presence, as I did those who had authority,' thus giving us an example of the Egyptian ideal of a ruler in those days. In the inscription on his tomb, the provincial chieftain Henku begs the inhabitants of his former territory to bring the offerings to the dead, reminding them of his care for them: 'O all ye people of the region of Snake Mountain and ye great chieftains of other regions, who pass by this tomb: I am Henku, who speaks well: offer water and bring bread, cakes and beer to Henku, who was honoured by his lord. For I was an honoured man, beloved of your fathers, praised by your mothers, who buried your old men, who loosed the fetters of the humble . . . Never did I enslave the daughter of any among you, so that she turned her hands against me . . . I gave food to all the hungry of the region of the Snake Mountain and clothing to the naked who were there. I filled the land on the river banks with cattle and the pastures with sheep, pigs and goats. I sated the wolves of the mountains and the vultures of the sky with the excrement of the cattle, for I desired that every man in the region should remain unmolested.' As early as the fifth dynasty affirmations of the following tenor are found on tombs: 'I gave barley from my estate in Upper Egypt to the poor of this land! And if I found in this land one who had a debt of corn to another man, I paid it to their master from my estate. I provided every man in this land who had no son with textiles from my possessions. I protected the weak against those who were stronger. I judged the litigants in a lawsuit so that they were (both) content. I was the darling of his father, praised by his mother, loved by his brothers . . .'

Noteworthy are the instructions as to his duties, derived from two texts inscribed in four New Kingdom tombs, but certainly dating from the late Middle Kingdom, which it was customary for the king to give to a newly appointed vizier. They begin with a solemn warning: 'Watch carefully over the hall of thy office and over everything that happens there, for on it depends the order of the whole country. Not sweet, nay, somewhat bitter is the office of a vizier, it signifies being as the ore which encloses the gold of the house of his lord. It signifies that he shall not bow to princes and officials and shall not procure for himself followers among all kinds of people.' Later, among other things, we find: 'It is an abomination in the sight of God if one shows partiality. Should a suppliant come from any part of the country, thou shalt see that everything is done according to its order and thou shalt help every man to obtain justice. A prince stands before the eyes of the public. Water and wind tell of everything he does; no thing that he does remains unknown. The best safeguard for a prince is to act according to the law . . . The suppliant who is summoned shall not say: I was not helped to obtain justice. Look upon the man thou knowest as on the man thou dost not know, on the man who stands close to the king as on the man who stands far from him. A prince who acts thus shall remain in this place. Dismiss no suppliant without having listened to his words . . . Be angry with no man without reason; be angry on account of those things for which it is right to be angry. To inspire too great fear is foolish, for men will not then say: That is a righteous man. Of all men the vizier is he who should practise righteousness. Therefore do not fail to be righteous and remember that the king loves the meek more than the bold. Mayst thou act according to these instructions, which are given to thee for thy welfare, for thus does man become happy.'

Among the teachings of learned and experienced men handed down from mouth to mouth through the centuries, but also given to young men in schools to copy, we find maxims like the following: 'If thou wilt that thy state be good, if thou wilt preserve thyself from all evil, then beware of covetousness. A man proves himself if his whole criterion is that which is right, if he follows the path laid down for him. By so doing he will acquire riches, but the covetous man will remain without a tomb. The brave man who does not yield to his whims, will be master of himself and a master of things. The man of weak heart, who follows his impulses, will incur hatred instead of love. If thou tillest the field and it brings forth and God gives thee a rich harvest, do not boast of it to thy neighbours. To exercise the discipline of silence is a great thing. If thou art a man in a leading position, listen patiently to the words of a suppliant. Do not dismiss him before he has emptied his soul of that which he has to say. It is not necessary to grant all that he asks, but good listening alone soothes the heart.' (Maxims of Ptahhotep, ca. 2450 B.C.) 'Do right, so long as thou dwellest on this earth; soothe him who weeps, offend no widow, deprive no man of the possessions of his father, harm not the counsellors in their work. Take heed not to inflict unjust punishment. Be not angry; it is good to be friendly. Make thy popularity a permanent monument to thyself. The good behaviour of the righteous is more acceptable (to the gods) than the ox sacrificed by the evil-doer' (Teachings of King Achthoes II, written for his son Merikarê, about 2100 B.C.). 'Let there be no dissension between thy heart and thy tongue. In this wise will thy plans succeed and thou wilt achieve importance in the eyes of the multitude. And thus wilt thou remain unscathed in the hand of God: God hates the hypocrites and his greatest abomination is the man full of contradictions. If thou findest that a poor man has arrears of debts, divide them into three parts and remit two of them—thou wilt find that such are the ways of life. To be praised as a friend of mankind is worth more than riches in the storehouse' (Teachings of Amenemope, ca. 1100 B.C.).

Such is the message that ancient Egypt has handed down to us through the ages, the message of a simple, but venerable humanity, expressed in the form of carefully formulated maxims. And the author of the Teachings of King Achthoes was already well aware that 'after his death, the man alone remains and his deeds are heaped up beside him'.

In view of all this energetic and disciplined effort on behalf of morality, can we claim that Egypt was the cradle of our Western civilization?

Egypt always looked towards the Mediterranean and not towards Africa. The fundamental contributions of Memphis, the ancient home of the creative and artistic divinity Ptah, and of Heliopolis to Mediterranean civilization can be perceived only in outline.

The question arises whether we are right when we maintain, as is still too often the case, in our schools that the discovery of that spirit which still sustains us was due exclusively to the Greeks and consequently tend to neglect the role played by ancient Egypt.

Was Egypt the mother of our civilization and do we persist in disowning her?

The whole problem of our appreciation and interpretation of ancient Egypt in reality consists in the fact that we rely on modern methods of thinking in our attempts to decipher her peculiar intuitive world.

This inevitable position leads us to take an over-complicated view of things which to the natural intuition of the men of those days were irrefutable. The most learned scholars of today rack their brains in their efforts to explain the ideas of primitive men whose processes of thought were based on the observation of nature and on the most elementary facts of life. This lack of the sense of proportion often borders on the grotesque. For example, the elucidation of the symbolic meaning of the so-called pyramid texts demands an almost impossible degree of perspicacity on a spiritual level which simply did not exist for the men who wrote them. On the other hand, things to which the ancient Egyptians devoted much thought are for us today, owing to their very nature and our processes of thought, practically void of interest, and one, among many, of the problems we have to solve is what precisely attracts us so strongly in Egyptian works of art. Is it the striking ingenuousness with which they expressed something never quite forgotten, something universal, with an unfailing clarity and mastery of form? One has an uneasy suspicion that the qualities which we most appreciate in these works, were by no means the most important for the ancient Egyptians.

We must, therefore, endeavour to get to the bottom of the feelings and thoughts of the former inhabitants of the Nile valley by means based on very different premises. This involves an enormous effort which few laymen would care to undertake; apart from a thorough knowledge of the countless writings on the subject, it would involve delving into the objective analytical processes of modern thought, in the hope of perceiving at least the outlines of what originally seemed quite clear without any amplification—and it is doubtful whether we could often achieve even that.

Therein lies the whole charm, and also the whole tragedy, of our relationship to the Egyptians of olden times.

Nowadays, when their way of thinking or expressing themselves is to us not immediately comprehensible, we take good care not to accuse the Egyptians of being muddle-headed or incapable of setting out their observations in a methodical manner, an accusation which even experts were thoughtlessly inclined to make not so very long ago. Such opinions, based on a positivism proud of its progress, have now merely historical interest. Among the initiated, there can be few doubts remaining that the way of thought of the ancient Egyptians was extremely clear and consequential—the proofs can be found in every one of their theological systems, in every masterpiece of their disciplined art, those masterpieces which were not just vague outpourings of sentiment but demanded a rigid concentration on form, and lastly in those manuals of a scientific nature such as the celebrated Edwin Smith surgical papyrus. This mode of thought, however, achieved fulfilment by means different from those of post-hellenic European thought based on Greek models, means which cannot be comprehended by timid souls who rely on logic alone. According to the Egyptian conception, the heart was not only the seat of the feelings, but also—very characteristically—the seat of intelligence. The Egyptian did not think with the aid of ideas, but with the aid of figures and pictorial associations. In contrast, as Max Picard has rightly remarked, never have pictorial representations had so little influence on the spirit and the soul, on society, economics and politics, as in our own time.

In contrast to our own deliberate, reflective method of thinking, one might, in the case of the Egyptians, speak of vegetative, intuitive thinking, which had a logic of its own and the results achieved by which do not necessarily differ from those reached by other processes. Nevertheless, since we can only reconstruct its ideas on the basis of the expressions of them which have come down to us, there always remains the danger that we may insert European conceptions into the Egyptian sphere, and assign old Egyptian modes of expression to modern categories of thought. Here we have to be careful. If we wish to get as near as possible to what is specifically Egyptian, we must first of all learn how to consider it as something completely alien. This paradox is true, to a certain extent, of Greek art and thought as well.

For Egypt belongs to us, not as a component part of our being, but as an example. She did not inaugurate the epoch of Mediterranean humanity which produced European thought; she developed, realized and perfected herself on a stone-age basis common to all mankind, and in an extremely curious way.

One is tempted to say that certain definitely stone-age characteristics of the structure of the Egyptian mind remained her own until the end. Typical of Egypt's intermediate position in the history of the spirit was her attitude towards the animal world, which the Hellenes viewed with astonished respect and the Romans could not understand ('I worship only gods, not oxen', was Emperor Octavian's reply when he was invited during his visit to Egypt to pay homage to the sacred bull of Apis). The tail of an animal which primitive hunters attached to the back of their girdles, like the poisonous snake standing erect on their forehead, formed part of the ornaments worn by Egyptian rulers for three thousand years, for Alexander and the Roman Emperors, when they became rulers of Egypt, were still given these attributes of the Pharaonic office. Divinities with the form or the heads of animals, divinities put together out of parts of the bodies of several animals and thus producing an effect which for us is abstruse, were not only tolerated down to the very end by the soul of the Egyptian people, but were actually *believed in* with confidence and respect. Where in the course of European development after the appearance of the Greeks would a royal title like 'Strong Bull' have been thinkable? It is surprising enough that long after the diffusion and adoption of the sophistic doctrines they were ready to accept in their own world the ram's horn of Amun on a statue of Alexander.

Typical is Egypt's method, based purely on experience, of studying nature, typical is her 'additive' method of constructing images, typical her instinctive adherence to the surface, her reluctance to expose herself to the dangers of space and perspective, and lastly—and above all—her retention of magic, which time and again raises its head through every phase of the development of the inner life. It is highly significant that Herodotus, the Greek historian of the classical period, should not only be full of astonishment and admiration for everything he saw, but in the introduction to his account of Egypt should lay emphasis on the fact that the inhabitants of the Nile valley do everything differently from the Greeks.

It would appear to be no mere chance that the later Egypt, with the paroxysm of her animal cult, the sterility of her ritual, the whimsicality of her numerous styles, should appear to be not nearer to us, but more alien than the earlier epochs. Here is no genuine continuum, no living and fruitful effort pointing the way to the future, an effort which would have something in common with early European trends, but the calcification, the ageing and finally the death through old age of a state of human affairs, which passed away because its time had come.

The fact that many Egyptian formal elements became permanent features in Western European civilization does not impair the truth of this statement. The Egyptian style—which in itself must be considered one of the most notable systems evolved by mankind—when later generations tried to imitate it proved to be quite untranslatable. In its artistic borrowings from this self-contained art posterity has never gone beyond an amusing miscomprehension.

Nevertheless, as an example of a proud, self-sufficient civilization obedient only to its own inner laws, Egypt has exercised a notable influence on those nations which subsequently dwelt on the shores of the Mediterranean. Its dignity spoke for itself. From it they received powerful formulative impulses and by it they were inspired to achieve a greater, more joyous fulfilment of their own tasks. In innumerable inventions, in the form of almost all the utensils produced by craftsmen, and, last but not least, in the field of architecture, we owe a deep debt of gratitude to Egyptian skill. From Moses to Solon, Thales, Plato and Plotinus, the experience and knowledge of Egypt have had their effect on the productive spirits of the Mediterranean world. And not as models demanding to be imitated, but as an irresistible lure to the fulfilment of one's self. Here all eyes could see what can be made out of human existence.

The peculiar characteristics of Egypt, which transformed a nameless barbarism into a historical social order, and gave to the state organization, to its laws and its religion a form and an inspiration still valid in our eyes, did not *found* European civilization but they *helped it to rise*. That feeling of timid respect which posterity feels for the example set by Egypt might well change to one of gratitude. Not because Egypt has given anything to us—her alien successors. But because she was self-sufficient and remained steadfastly true to that which she had once recognized as valid. And by so doing she has laid us under an obligation.

THINITE PERIOD

(Ca. 3000-2778)

1   Lion. About 3000 B.C. Berlin

2 Cosmetics palette with desert animals and fabulous beings. Oxford

3 Above: Cosmetics palette with giraffes and palms. Paris
Below: Part of a victory tablet. Cairo, Museum

4   Victory tablet of King Nar-mer. Cairo, Museum

5   King Nar-mer. Cairo, Museum

6   Tombstone of King „Snake"

OLD KINGDOM

THIRD DYNASTY (2778-2723)

7   Step-pyramid of King Zoser and tomb area, Saqqâra
View from the Unas Pyramid towards the north-east

8   Zoser tomb area: Papyrus half-columns of the north house

9 Zoser tomb area: Perimeter wall, with portal

10   Zoser tomb area: Portico of the hall of pillars

11   Zoser tomb area: Hall of pillars

12   Zoser tomb area: At the southern tomb

13   Zoser tomb area: Temple

14 King Zoser, detail from plate 15

15 King Zoser, mural relief in the southern tomb

16   King Zoser. Cairo, Museum

17   King Zoser. Cairo, Museum

18   Wood reliefs from the tomb of Hesirē'. Cairo, Museum

19   Hesirēʿ at the offering-table. Cairo, Museum

FOURTH DYNASTY (2723-2563)

20   The Dahshur pyramids

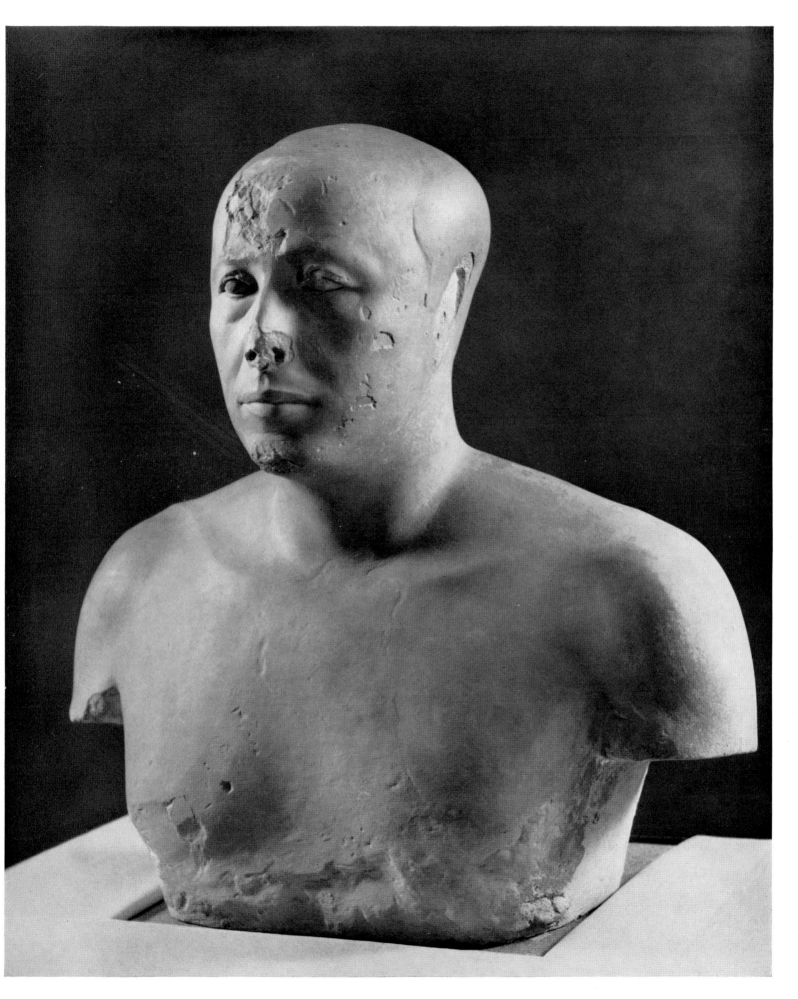

21   Prince Ankhhaf. Boston

22   Prince Rahotep and his wife Nofret. Cairo, Museum

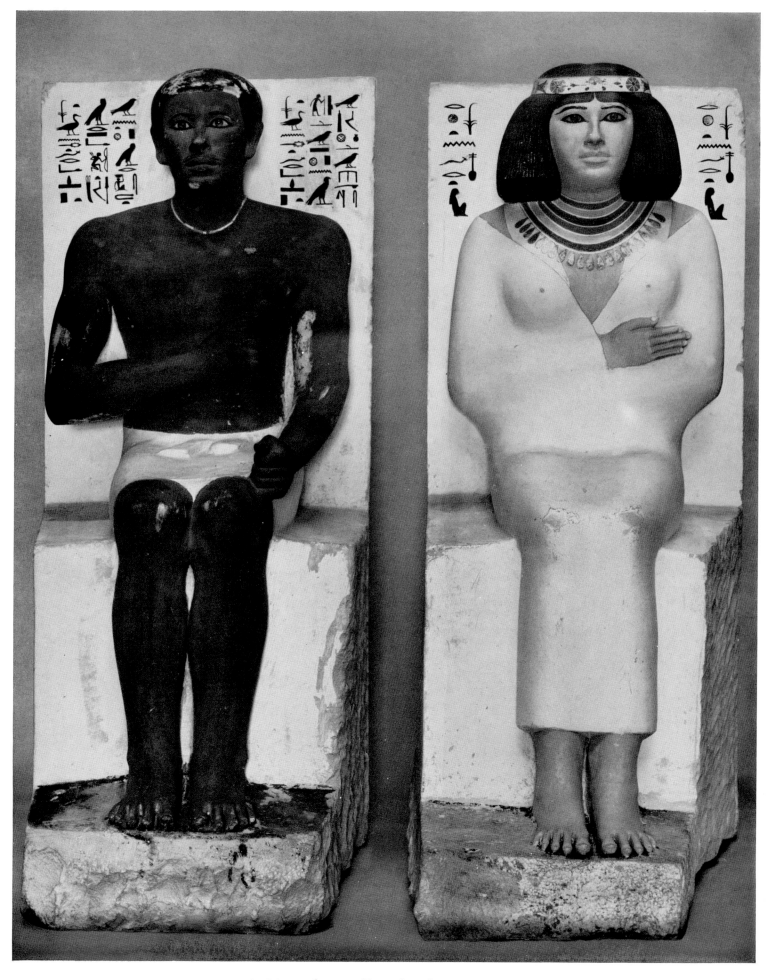

23 Prince Rahotep and his wife Nofret. Cairo, Museum

24 Nofret. Cairo, Museum

25   Prince Rahotep and his wife Nofret. Cairo, Museum

26   The pyramid and tomb zone at Giza, as far as the Sphinx, seen from the south-west

27   The Giza pyramids from the south

28　The Sphinx and the Valley Temple of King Chephren

29　The great Sphinx

30   Southern portion of the Giza pyramid zone

31 Pyramid of Cheops, Sphinx and Valley Temple of Chephren

32   Mastaba cemetery near the pyramid of Chephren

33   Funerary temple of Mycerinus, in background the pyramid of Chephren

34   Valley Temple of King Chephren: the wide chamber and hall of pillars

35   Valley Temple of King Chephren: middle aisle of the hall of pillars

36 King Chephren. Cairo, Museum

37　King Chephren. Cairo, Museum

38 King Chephren. Cairo, Museum

39   King Chephren. Cairo, Museum

40   Portrait head from the royal cemetery at Giza. Cairo, Museum

41   Portrait head from the royal cemetery at Giza. Profile of head shown in plate 40

42   Portrait head from the royal cemetery at Giza. Cairo, Museum

43 King Mycerinus. Cairo, Museum

44   King Mycerinus and Queen Khamerernebti. Boston

45   King Mycerinus and Queen Khamerernebti. Boston

46 King Mycerinus between Hathor and the local deity of Diospolis Parva. Cairo, Museum

47 King Mycerinus between Hathor and the local deity of Kynopolis. Cairo, Museum

48 Granite pillar with palm capital from the funerary temple of King Sahurē at Abusir.
Cairo, Museum

49   Sarcophagus of Rawer. Cairo, Museum

50 King Userkaf. Cairo. Museum

51   King Userkaf. Cairo, Museum

52 Rawer. Alabaster relief. Cairo, Museum

53   Rawer. Cairo, Museum

54   Ka-aper. Cairo, Museum

55   Ka-aper. Cairo, Museum

56   Girl grinding corn. Cairo, Museum

57 Girl grinding corn. Cairo, Museum

58   Scribe portrait of an unknown man. Cairo, Museum

59   Scribe portrait of an unknown man. Cairo, Museum

60　An official writing.　Paris

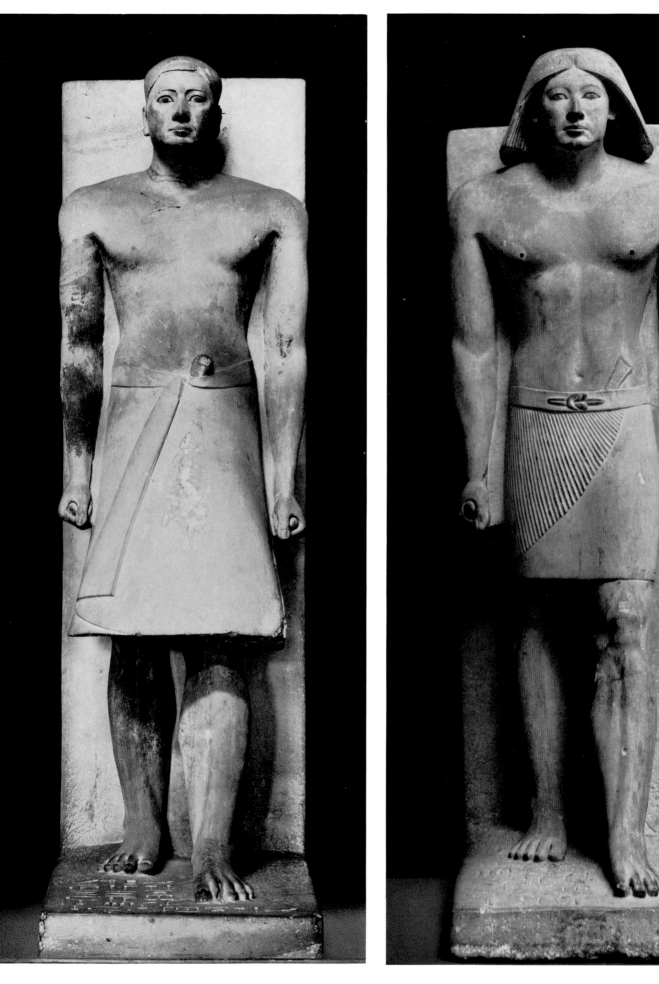

61   Ranufer. Cairo, Museum

62 Ranufer. Cairo, Museum

63   Ranufer. Cairo, Museum

64   Ranufer. Cairo, Museum

65   Ranufer. Cairo, Museum

66 Ti. Cairo, Museum

67   Ti. Cairo, Museum

68   Ti hunting hippopotami. In the tomb of Ti, at Saqqâra

69 Ti and his wife Neferhotpes. In the tomb of Ti, at Saqqâra

70   Return of the herd and donkeys. In the tomb of Ti, at Saqqâra

71   Detail from Plate 70. In the tomb of Ti, at Saqqâra

72   Ptahhotep at offering-table. From his tomb at Saqqâra

73   False door from the tomb of Ateti. Cairo, Museum

74 Herwadjetkhet, wife of Mereruka. In his tomb at Saqqâra

75   Mereruka. In his tomb at Saqqâra

76   A drive in the papyrus thicket. In Mereruka's tomb at Saqqâra

77   Harpooning of a hippopotamus. In Mereruka's tomb at Saqqâra

78   King Pepi I. Cairo, Museum

79 Urchûu. Cairo, Museum

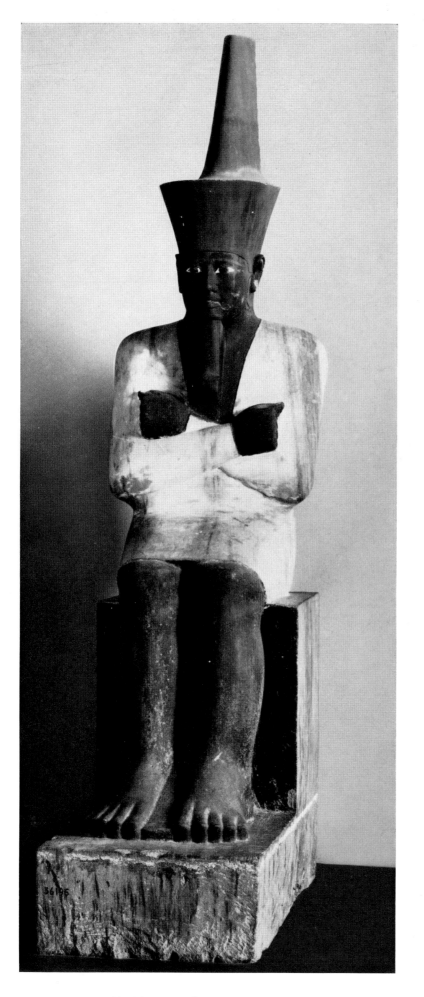

MIDDLE KINGDOM

ELEVENTH DYNASTY
(2133-1992)

80· King Mentuhotep. Cairo, Museum

81 King Mentuhotep. Cairo, Museum

82   King Mentuhotep striking an enemy. Cairo, Museum

83   Above: Detail from the sarcophagus of Queen Kawit. Cairo, Museum
Below: Sarcophagus of Queen 'Ashait. Cairo, Museum

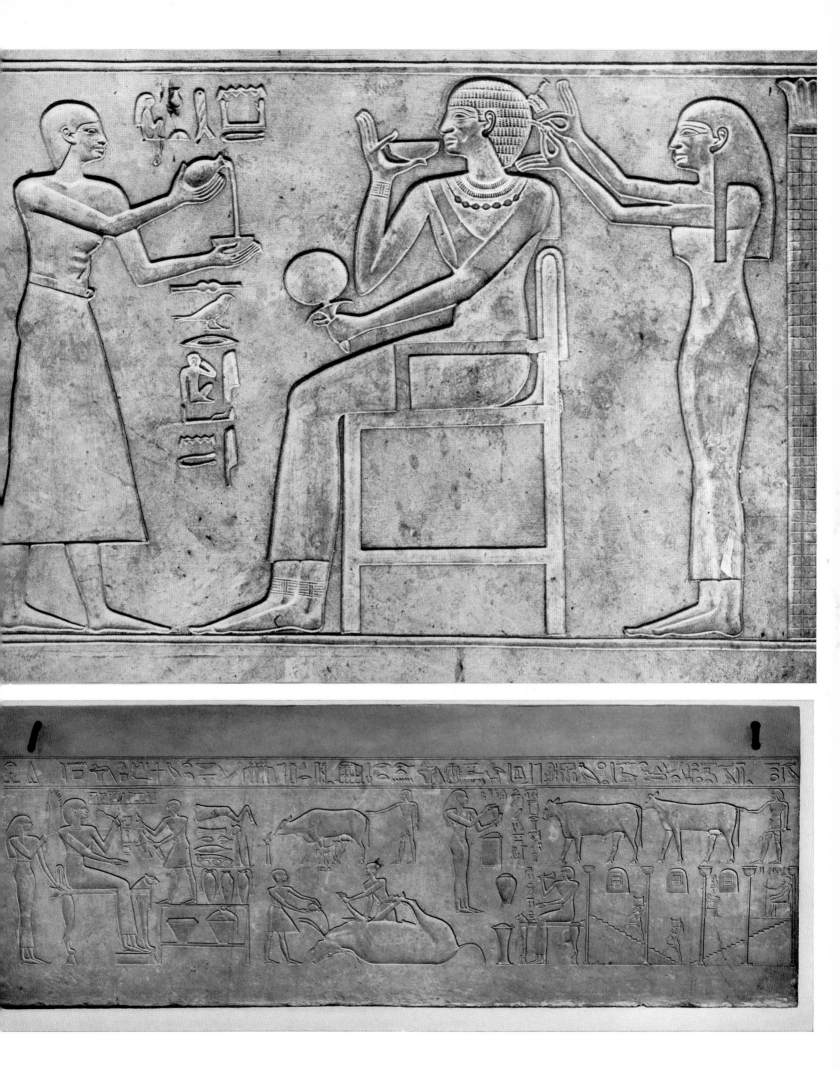

84   Unknown woman. Cairo, Museum

85   King Sesostris I. Cairo, Museum

86 Horus and Set on the throne of Sesostris I. Cairo, Museum

87 The regional gods of Upper and Lower Egypt on the throne of Sesostris I. Cairo, Museum

88 Princess Senui. Boston

89   Princess Senui. Boston

90   Chapel of Sesostris I in Karnak

91   Chapel of Sesostris I in Karnak

92   Detail of the chapel of Sesostris I in Karnak

93 Pillar from a building of Sesostris I, two sides. Cairo, Museum

94　King Sesostris I and the god Atum. Pillar relief. Cairo, Museum

95 King Sesostris I and the god Ptah. Pillar relief. Cairo, Museum

96   Upper portion of the pillar from a building of Sesostris I from Karnak. Cairo, Museum

97   Upper portion of the pillar from a building of Sesostris I from Karnak. Cairo, Museum

98   King Sesostris I and the god Ptah. Pillar relief. Cairo, Museum

99   Rock tomb of Prince Sirenpowet, son of Sat-Kheni. At Assuan

100 Prince Sirenpowet, son of Satet-hotep, at table. In his tomb at Assuan (cfr. Plate 101)

101   In the rock tomb of Prince Sirenpowet, son of Satet-hotep. At Assuan

102   Door-lintel: King Sesostris III at the feast of Jubilee. Cairo, Museum

103   Door-lintel: King Sesostris III at the feast of Jubilee. Cairo, Museum

104   King Sesostris III in the Hebsed pavilion (cfr. Plate 102–103). Cairo, Museum

105 King Sesostris III. Washington

106   Sphinx of King Sesostris III. New York

107   Sesostris III. Cairo, Museum

108   King Ammenemēs III. Cairo, Museum

109   King Ammenemēs III. Cairo, Museum

110 Maned sphinx of Ammenemēs III. Cairo, Museum

111   Maned sphinx of Ammenemēs III. Cairo, Museum

112   Ka statue of King Hor. Cairo, Museum

113   Ka statue of King Hor in his shrine. Cairo, Museum

NEW EMPIRE
EIGHTEENTH DYNASTY (1580-1314)

114   Alabaster Sphinx in the Memphis Temple Zone

115   Karnak. Shrine for the Bark of Amun, erected by Amenophis I

116 Karnak. Amenophis I and Amun, from the shrine of Amenophis I

117 Amenophis I. Part of the mural relief in Plate 116

118 Karnak. Temple of Amun: Pylon and obelisk of Tuthmosis I and obelisk of Queen Hatshepsut

119   Temple of Queen Hatshepsut at Thebes (Der-el-bahri)

120　Temple of Queen Hatshepsut at Thebes (Der-el-bahri)
Tuthmosis III and the god Amun, from the Hall of Birth

121　Temple of Queen Hatshepsut at Thebes (Der-el-bahri)
Porch of the Anubis chapel and Hall of Birth

122   Temple of Queen Hatshepsut at Thebes (Der-el-bahri)
Royal vulture in the porch of the Anubis chapel

123   Temple of Queen Hatshepsut at Thebes (Der-el-bahri)
Ahmes, the mother of Queen Hatshepsut, from the Hall of Birth

124   Temple of Queen Hatshepsut at Thebes (Der-el-bahri). Upper court

125 Temple of Queen Hatshepsut at Thebes (Der-el-bahri)
Chapel of Hathor: Hatshepsut drinking from the udder of the Hathor cow

126   Sarcophagus of Queen Hatshepsut. Cairo, Museum

127   Queen Hatshepsut. New York

128　Karnak, Temple of the national god Amun:
The god Amen-Rê and the Queen, from an obelisk of Queen Hatshepsut

129   Karnak, Temple of Amun.
Southern court and Hall of Annals of King Tuthmosis III

130   Queen Hatshepsut. Detail of the relief on the obelisk in Plate 128

131 King Tuthmosis III offering sacrifices. Cairo, Museum

132   King Tuthmosis III. Cairo, Museum

133   King Tuthmosis III. Cairo, Museum

134   King Tuthmosis III. Cairo, Museum

135   King Tuthmosis III. Cairo, Museum

136   Karnak, Temple of Amun.
Seventh pylon: King Tuthmosis III smiting the Asiatics

137   Karnak, Temple of Amun.
Ceremonial temple of King Tuthmosis III, west front

138   Karnak, Temple of Amun.
Ceremonial temple of King Tuthmosis III, the three naves seen from the south-west

139   Karnak, Temple of Amun.
Ceremonial temple of King Tuthmosis III, the three naves seen from the north

140   Festival scenes from the tomb of the Vizier Rekhmirê

141   From the tomb of Userhêt, secretary to King Amenophis II, in Thebes: Userhêt hunting

142   The sacred cow of Hathor, with King Amenophis II drinking from her udder. Cairo, Museum

143   The sacred cow of Hathor.   Cairo, Museum

144   Queen Merit-Amun, wife of King Amenophis II. Outer coffin

145   King Amenophis II offering sacrifices. Cairo, Museum

146   Hunting in a papyrus thicket, from the tomb of Menna at Thebes

147 Festival scenes from the tomb of Nakht, priest of Amun at Thebes

148   Queen Tio, from the portrait group in Plate 149. Cairo, Museum

149   King Tuthmosis IV and his mother Tio. Cairo, Museum

150 Preparations for a festival, from the tomb of Djeser-ka-rê-seneb at Thebes

151   The daughters of the deceased, from the tomb of Djeser-ka-rê-seneb at Thebes

152   King Amenophis III and Queen Tiy at the feast of Sed, from the tomb of Kheruef at Thebes

153   Cha-em-hêt praying, from the tomb of Kha-em-hêt at Thebes

154 Procession of princesses carrying sacred vessels.
Left half of the relief in the tomb of Kheruef at Thebes

155   Procession of princesses carrying sacred vessels.
Right half of the relief in the tomb of Kheruef at Thebes

156   Amenhotep, son of Hapu, chief architect of King Amenophis III in Thebes. Cairo, Museum

157   Amenhotep, son of Hapu, in his last years. Cairo, Museum

158   Luxor, Temple of Amon-Mut-Khôns. Peristyle of King Amenophis III, seen from the west.
On the left, the great court and pylon of King Ramesses II

159   Luxor, Temple of Amon-Mut-Khôns.
Porch of the temple house of King Amenophis III, seen from the west

160   Luxor, Temple of Amon-Mut-Khôns.
The great court of King Amenophis III and porch of the temple house, seen from the north

161   Luxor, Temple of Amon-Mut-Khôns.
The great court and peristyle of King Amenophis III, seen from the east

162　The "Memnon Colossi". In the background the Theban Necropolis on the western mountain

163   The "Memnon Colossi", the only remains of the funerary temple of King Amenophis III at Thebes

From the tomb of the Vizier Ramose at Thebes.
164 Above: The hall of pillars. — Below: Frieze with funeral procession on the south wall of the hall of pillars
165 Scenes from the funeral procession

166   Entrance wall of the hall of pillars in the tomb of Ramose at Thebes:
      The ceremonial purification of Ramose

167   Entrance wall of the hall of pillars in the tomb of Ramose at Thebes:
Ramose, detail of the relief in Plate 166

168   Entrance wall of the hall of pillars in the tomb of Ramose at Thebes:
A festive gathering, left part of the relief

169   Entrance wall of the hall of pillars in the tomb of Ramose at Thebes:
A festive gathering, middle part of the relief

170   Hall of pillars in the tomb of Ramose at Thebes.
Detail of the festival relief: the parents of Ramose

171 Hall of pillars in the tomb of Ramose at Thebes.
Detail of the festival relief: the brother of Ramose and his wife

172   Hall of pillars in the tomb of Ramose at Thebes.
Detail of the festival relief: the sister-in-law of Ramose

173 Hall of pillars in the tomb of Ramose at Thebes.
Detail of the festival relief: the brother of Ramose

174 Hall of pillars in the tomb of Ramose at Thebes.
Entrance wall: Almsgiver with papyrus

175   From the tomb of the sculptors Nebamun and Ipuki at Thebes.
Above: Funeral ceremony at the entrance to the tomb. — Below: Mourners at the funerary shrine

176 King Amenophis IV, later Akhnaton.
From a pillar statue in the temple of Aton near the temple of Amun at Karnak. Cairo, Museum

177   King Amenophis IV, later Akhnaton.
From a pillar statue in the temple of Aton near the temple of Amun at Karnak. Cairo, Museum

178   Queen Nefertiti. Cairo, Museum

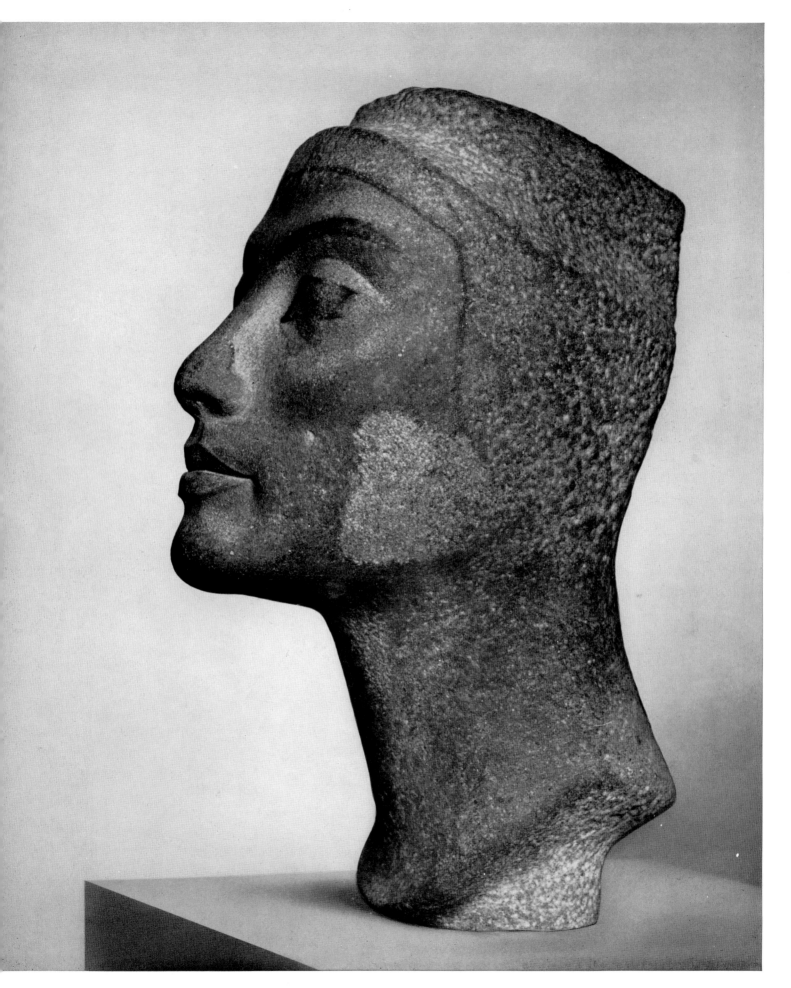

179   Queen Nefertiti. Cairo, Museum

180 King Akhnaton. Paris

181   Queen Nefertiti. Berlin

182   King Tutankhamun. Cairo, Museum

183   Gold mask of King Tutankhamun. Cairo, Museum

184   Gold coffin of King Tutankhamun. Cairo, Museum

185   Gold coffin of King Tutankhamun. Cairo, Museum

186   Footplate of the middle coffin of King Tutankhamun. Cairo, Museum

187   Gold coffer from the tomb of King Tutankhamun. Cairo, Museum

188   Detail of the gold coffer from the tomb of King Tutankhamun:
King Tutankhamun, at his feet Queen Ankhesenamun. Cairo, Museum

189 Detail of the gold coffer from the tomb of King Tutankhamun:
Queen Ankhesenamun placing a gold collar round the King's neck. Cairo, Museum

190   Throne of King Tutankhamun. Cairo, Museum

191   Back of the throne of King Tutankhamun. Cairo, Museum

192   Back of the cedarwood chair of King Tutankhamun. Cairo, Museum

193   Lid of an ivory chest from the tomb of King Tutankhamun:
The King with his wife Ankhesenamun. Cairo, Museum

194 Lid of a receptacle for intestines from the tomb of King Semenkhkarê. Cairo, Museum

195   Lid of a receptacle for intestines from the tomb of King Tutankhamun. Cairo, Museum

196 Priest offering sacrifices, and musicians. From the tomb of Paatenemheb near Saqqâra. Leiden

197 Blind harp-player. From the tomb of Paatenemheb near Saqqâra. Leiden

198 Haremhab as highest state official. New York

199   Haremhab as highest state official. New York

200–201 From the tomb of general (later king) Haremhab near Saqqâra. Procession of prisoners. Leiden

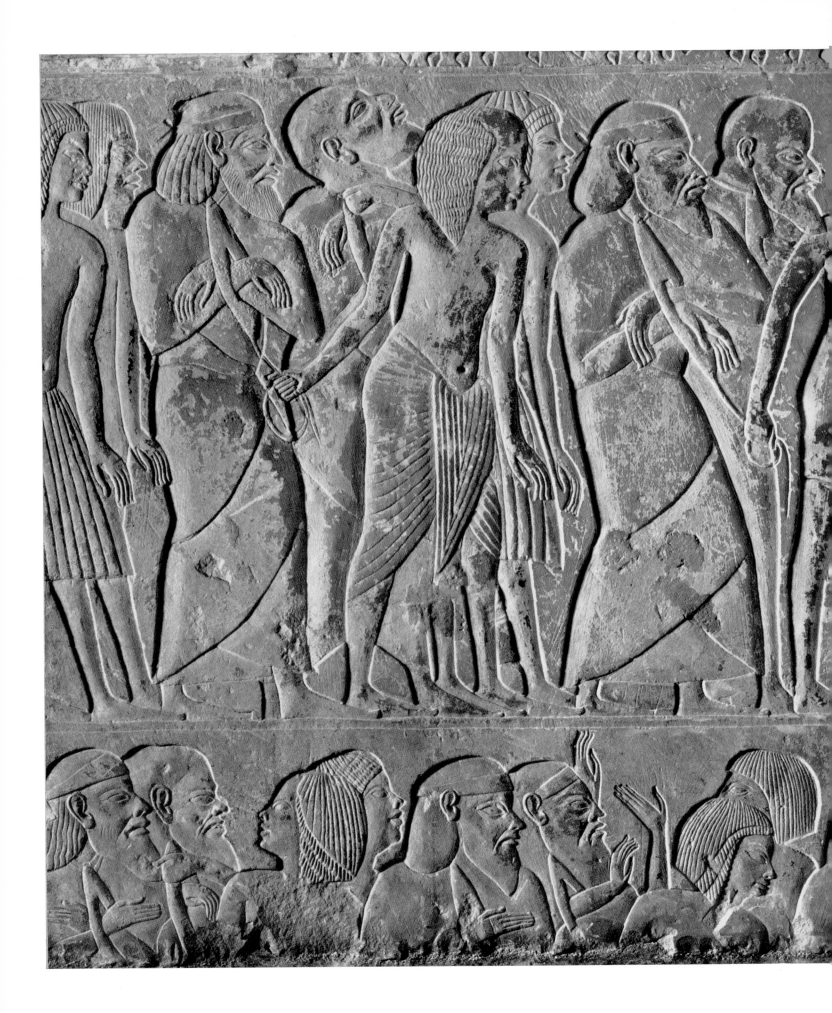

202 From the tomb of general (later king) Haremhab near Saqqâra. Procession of prisoners. Cf. pl. 200. Leiden

203   From the tomb of general (later king) Haremhab near Saqqâra. Haremhab. Cf. pl. 201. Leiden

204   The moon god Khôns, son of Amun and Mut. Cairo, Museum

205 The goddess Mut, wife of Amun. Cairo, Museum

206   The court official Maia and his wife Merit. Leiden

207   The court official Maia. Leiden

208   From the statue of Merit, wife of Maia. Leiden

209   Merit. Cf. pl. 208. Leiden

210   The valley of the queens' tombs on the southern edge of the Theban necropolis

211   The valley of the kings' tombs in the Western Theban mountains

NINETEENTH DYNASTY (1314-1200)

212 From the tomb of King Sethos I in the valley of the kings' tombs:
The King offering sacrifices

213   From the tomb of King Sethos I in the valley of the kings' tombs:
The goddess Isis

214   From the tomb of King Sethos I in the valley of the kings' tombs:
The King before Maat, goddess of truth and righteousness. Preliminary drawing for a relief

215   From the tomb of the high priest Userhêt at Thebes:
The mother and the wife of the deceased

216   Temple of King Sethos I at Abydos.
Hall of pillars in the second court

217   Temple of King Sethos I at Abydos.
The second hall of pillars, seen from the north

218   Temple of King Sethos I at Abydos.
The hall of Nefer-tem and Ptah-Soker: view of the north-west wall

219   Temple of King Sethos I at Abydos.
A king and a prince capturing a bull

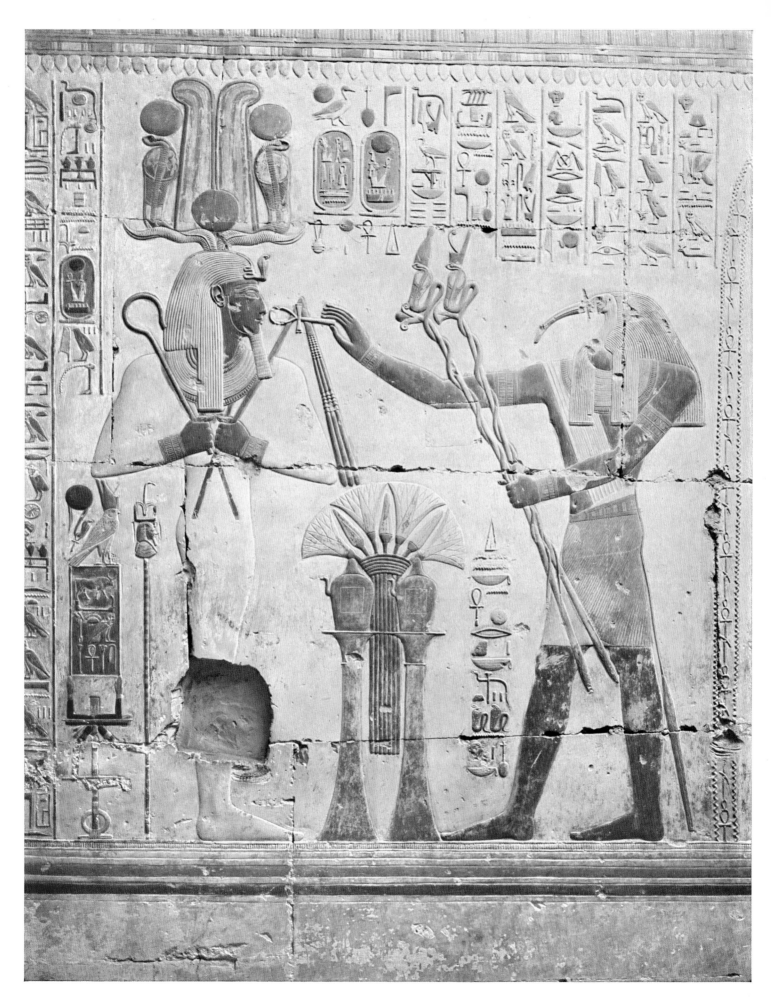

220 Temple of King Sethos I at Abydos.
The Osiris chapel. Sethos-Osiris and the god Thoth

221 Temple of King Sethos I at Abydos.
The Isis chapel: King Sethos I with offerings, before the goddess Isis

222 Temple of King Sethos I at Abydos.
Hall of Nefer-tem and Ptah-Soker: King Sethos I before the death god Soker

223   Temple of King Sethos I at Abydos.
Sanctuary of Rê-Harakhte: King Sethos I before the universal god Atum

224   Temple of King Sethos I at Abydos.
Chapel of Osiris: the goddess Isis

225 Temple of King Sethos I at Abydos.
Chapel of Isis: King Sethos I offering sacrifices (cfr. Plate 221)

226 Karnak, Temple of Amun.
The great hall of pillars of Kings Sethos I and Ramesses II, seen from the Sacred Lake. In the background the first pylon

227   Karnak, Temple of Amun.
The great hall of pillars of Kings Sethos I and Ramesses II. In the foreground the obelisk of King Tuthmosis I

228   Karnak, Temple of Amun.
The great hall of pillars of Kings Sethos I and Ramesses II, seen from below

229   Karnak, Temple of Amun.
The great hall of pillars of Kings Sethos I and Ramesses II, seen from the north

230   King Ramesses II. From Karnak. Turin

231   King Ramesses II. Cf. pl. 230. Turin

232 Funerary temple of King Ramesses II and landscape near Thebes and Luxor

233   Thebes. Funerary temple of King Ramesses II, seen from the north.
In the foreground the ruins of the store-rooms

234   Funerary temple of King Ramesses II.
The second court seen from the south-west

235   Funerary temple of King Ramesses II.
The north-west side of the second court; behind it, the great hall of pillars

236   Thebes. Funerary temple of King Ramesses II, seen from the west,
with view of the three main naves and the two south-western lateral aisles of the hall of pillars

237 Funerary temple of King Ramesses II.
View of the central and north-eastern main naves

238   The Necropolis of Thebes, seen from the funerary temple of King Ramesses II.
On the right, Middle Kingdom rock tombs

239 Luxor, Temple of Amun-Mut-Khôns. South-western portion of the great court of King Ramesses II;
behind it, the peristyle of King Amenophis III

240   Luxor, Temple of Amun-Mut-Khôns. Statue of King Ramesses II from the first court;
beside it the little figure of his wife, Queen Nefertari

241   Luxor, Temple of Amun-Mut-Khôns. First court.
Queen Nefertari beside one of the large statues of King Ramesses II

242   Mit-rahina. Colossal statue of King Ramesses II

243   Abu Simbel. One of the four colossal statues of King Ramesses II in front of the entrance to the temple

244 Abu Simbel. Front of the rock-temple erected by King Ramesses II with the four colossal seated statues of the king

245   Abu Simbel. Central aisle of the great hall of pillars with the statues of King Ramesses II

246   Entrance room to the tomb of Queen Nefertari at Thebes

247   In the tomb of Queen Nefertari at Thebes: Queen Nefertari guided by Isis

TWENTIETH DYNASTY (1200-1085)

248   Thebes (Medinet Habu). Funerary temple of King Ramesses III, seen from the south

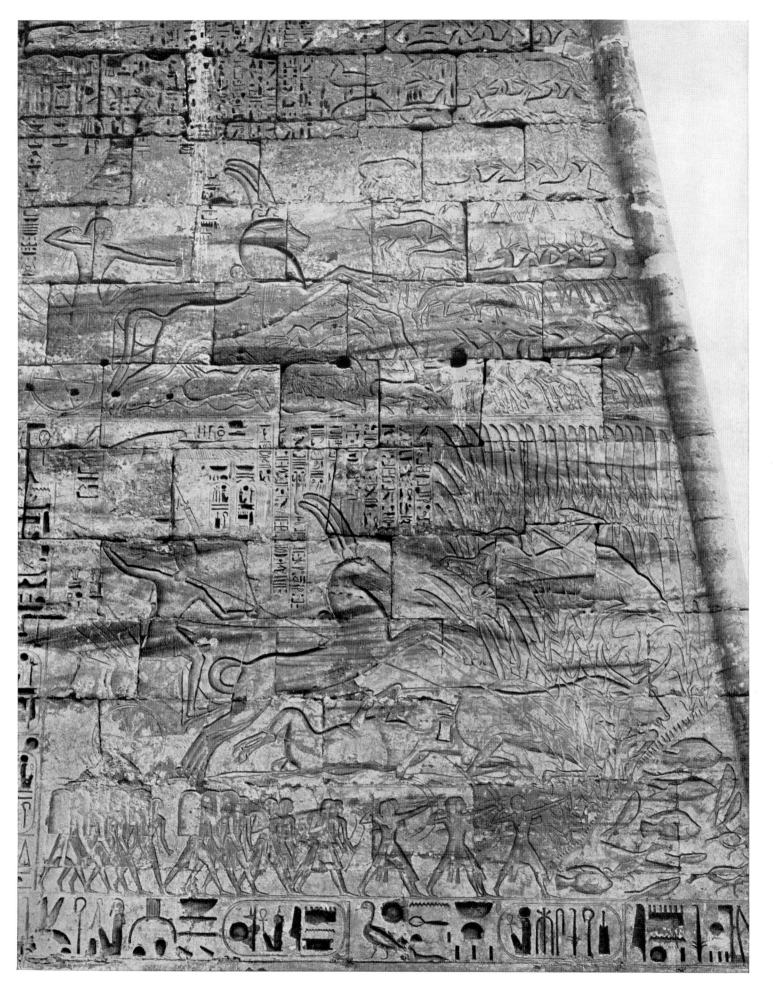

249   Thebes (Medinet Habu). The King hunting, from the first pylon of the funerary temple of King Ramesses III

LATE PERIOD
TWENTY-FIFTH AND TWENTY-SIXTH DYNASTIES (715-663-525)
Ethiopian and Saïtic Period

250   Upper portion of the tomb of the viceroy Mentuemhêt at Thebes.
In the background the western mountains with El Qorn

251 The viceroy Mentuemhêt. Cairo, Museum

252   The priest Pediamenopet. Berlin

253   Head of a priest. Paris

TWENTY-SEVENTH TO THIRTIETH DYNASTIES (525-341)
Persian domination

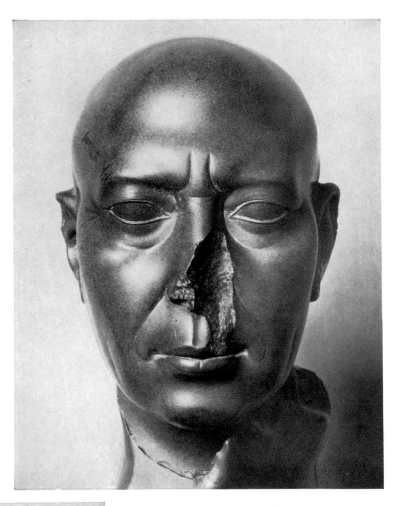

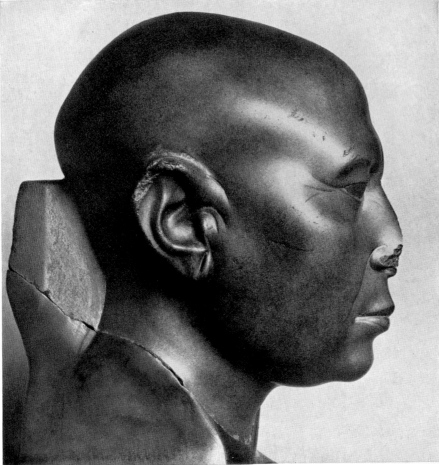

254 Head of a priest, the so-called Green Head. Berlin

255   Edfu, Temple of Horus.
General view from the west. In the foreground, the huge store-rooms

256   Edfu, Temple of Horus.
View of the south side of the large court and the pylon

257   Edfu, Temple of Horus.
The porch of the temple seen from across the court

258   Edfu, Temple of Horus.
Diagonal view of the temple porch

259 Edfu, Temple of Horus.
The hall of pillars and the holy of holies with the two antechambers. In the holy of holies, the granite chapel of Nektanebos II

260 Kom Ombo. Twin sanctuary of Suchos and Haroêris

NOTES ON THE PLATES

FOREWORD

The historical monuments of Egypt, admired by travellers of ancient times as wonders of the world, can be divided into a number of principal groups which provide an impressive panorama of the golden age of the civilization of ancient Egypt. On the normal route between Alexandria or Port Said and Cairo and on through Central and Upper Egypt, the visitor to the Nile Valley comes upon the ancient monuments in an order corresponding more or less to the historical process of development from the foundation of the kingdom to the time of the successive foreign dominations.

The extensive desert cemetery of the old northern capital, Memphis, about twenty miles south-west of Cairo near the present-day village of Saqqâra, and the impressive pyramid zone near the modern village of Giza, about five miles from Cairo, introduce us to the buildings and sculptures of the archaic period (ca. 3000–2778) and of the Old Kingdom. In Central Egypt, we find the rock tombs, adorned with sculptures, of the regional princes of the Middle Kingdom (ca. 2050–1680), the free-standing structures of which have unfortunately been as good as completely lost to posterity. In the neighbourhood of Luxor and in Nubia, when we see the huge temple ruins and statues of kings and penetrate into the royal tombs at Thebes, driven deep into the heart of the Western Mountain, we are able to form an idea of the grandeur and talents of the New Kingdom, that period during which Egypt became a world power (ca. 1580–1085). On the site of the old provincial capital of Dendera near Kena, and between Luxor and Assuân with its temple-island of Philae, we encounter finally the surprisingly well preserved sacred places of the Late Period, built under the domination of Graeco-Macedonian rulers and Roman Emperors. It is as if a kind of Ariadne's thread guided us through the monumental labyrinth of an immense historical development—monuments which have excited the admiration of all succeeding generations and which cannot fail to impress even the spoilt children of the twentieth century, accustomed to fantastic technical achievements of every kind. At almost every bend of the Nile there rise before our eyes towering stone witnesses to a proud past dating back many thousands of years. Witnesses which challenge us to more profound historical study and, in their timeless majesty, leave a lasting imprint on the minds even of those who, before seeing them, have paid little attention to the heritage of antiquity.

In the well-known words of Herodotus, who traversed it about 445 B.C., the long valley of Egypt is a gift of the Nile. This mighty stream, in its 4000-mile course through half of Africa, gradually dug the valley out of the gravel-strewn desert plateau of north-eastern Africa, filling it year by year at the same season with rich, bluish-grey mud, fertilising the soil from which sprang abundant harvests, insofar as the irrigation systems of the peasantry were capable of absorbing it.

Life and death are close neighbours in this peculiar landscape. Almost at every point it is possible to see from one side to the other of the cultivated zone, which, with its populous cities and often considerable villages, its palm groves and fields filled with luxuriant and glistening crops, is bordered on either side by the pale slopes of the Great Desert. Sometimes approaching, sometimes receding, during the whole of the long journey through the land they accompany the banks of the river, that slow-flowing, long-revered giver of life, whose course, like that of no other stream, is woven about with the glamour of legend. The sight of it awakens thoughts and impressions of a peculiar kind. These waters coming from the tropical interior of the dark continent have glided over the backs of hippopotami and over the armour-plates of crocodiles; lions have drunk of them; up in the Sudan wiry, naked black hunters have piloted their reed canoes along the gentle stream of the young Nile. Curious outlines arise before the eyes of those endowed with a feeling for history: the god-kings of Pharaonic times are joined by the fascinating figures of an Alexander, a Caesar, an Antony, of the immortal Cleopatra whose memory lives on in the realm of dreaming fantasy, by the figures of the coolly daring conqueror Octavian, of Hadrian, and finally the silhouette of Napoleon. All of them have left indelible traces of their lives on the soil of this ancient land of wonders.

The spiritual fruit of a journey to the Mediterranean, which for the thoughtful will always represent an apprenticeship to the comprehension of Europe, is incomplete without the experience of Egypt and it is no mere chance if the world of the Nile has a quite unusual attraction for the visitor from western Europe, thirsting for impressions.

EARLY DYNASTIC PERIOD AND THE OLD KINGDOM

The remains of settlements and cemeteries of the oldest Nile Valley cultures, scattered in groups over the foreland of the desert never reached by the waters of the Nile, though they may have escaped the notice of non-Egyptologists, have now been in the main systematically studied by scientists, but the traveller on his way along the western foot of the desert between Cairo and the oasis of Fayûm will constantly come across imposing structures dating from the earliest times. Here among drifting sand lie the cemeteries of Memphis, the 'balance of the lands'. The houses built of sun-dried mud bricks of this great city, founded according to tradition about 3000 B.C. by King Menes, the consolidator of the kingdom, have long since crumbled to dust; the Arab writer Abd-ul-Latif, who lived at the end of the twelfth century A.D., described the beauties of the city as amazing and indescribable. Today the site is occupied by palm groves and the villages of Saqqâra, Mit-rahîna and Abusîr, and only occasional masses of ruins and gigantic structures bear witness to the former glories. The extensive cemetery zone was used for burials at all periods of Egyptian history and it has yielded rich booty both to thieves hungry for gold, who sometimes appeared in organized bands, and to excavating scholars. With the exception of the large subterranean burial vault of the sacred Apis bulls, all of its most impressive monuments date from the Early Dynastic Period and the Old Kingdom. Here, during the last few decades, excavation has uncovered a number of important early tombs, the numerous accessories of which have revealed names of individual kings of the first dynasty and give reason to suppose that tombs of these rulers exist. During the reign of the outstanding King Zoser, the first monarch of the third dynasty, who is named on the monuments as the Horus falcon-headed deity 'Neter-khet', an enterprising generation erected at Saqqâra, about 2760 B.C., the first artistically planned monumental stone structures known to us—the imposing step-pyramid of the king rising amidst the silence of the desert and surrounded by government and religious buildings and storehouses, all enclosed within an organically constructed wall—an 'eternal dwelling' dating from the dawn of the pyramid period. Nearby under the veil of the desert sand are traces of other tombs of later kings. Among them is the recently explored base of the pyramid of Sekhem-khet, comprising numerous chambers and a mysterious alabaster coffin which, on being opened, was found to be empty.

The first of those mighty builders, the kings of the fourth dynasty, Snofru, erected, a little further to the south near Dahshûr, two square-based pyramids about 300 feet high; recent exploration of the gate temple of one of these has yielded rich finds in statues and reliefs. It has not yet been possible to ascertain who erected the pyramid near Medûm, three steps of which still remain.

Snofru's successors turned north and created the most famous of all pyramid groups: the majestic triple structure near Giza, to which the great Sphinx, carved out of rock and completed in ancient times with layers of ashlar, also belongs. Of the temples pertaining to these pyramids, that of Cheops has unfortunately disappeared except for a few fragments; of the Chephren complex, considerable portions of the actual funerary temple and the valley temple, deeply impressive in the severity of its architectural conception, have been preserved. The religious buildings in front of the pyramid of Mycerinus, also built of massive square blocks, and the valley temple belonging thereto were never completed.

In the neighbourhood of the royal pyramids, there are many smaller ones which were erected for the burial of queens, but in some cases they seem to have been used for other purposes. Adjoining them are often found tombs of princes and princesses, of high court functionaries and of favourite officials. At Giza they were designed in such a way as to form whole burial quarters, with straight passages running between the sloping superstructure.

The Pharaohs of the fifth and sixth dynasties returned to the neighbourhood of King Zoser's step mastaba, where they built themselves much more modest tombs. The most important pyramids are those of Kings Sahurê, Neferirkarê and Ne-userrê, near the village of Abusîr. Of the sanctuaries which these rulers erected to the memory of their father the sun-god, on the edge of the desert, that of Ne-userrê near Abu Gurob, excavated by German archaeologists, with its large alabaster altar and the ruined pedestal which once bore a stumpy obelisk, is a fine example of a temple of that period. In the interior of the pyramid of Unas, now reduced to a low mound of debris, to the south-west of the tomb of Zoser at Saqqâra, the oldest Egyptian religious texts known to us can be seen.

From the statue chambers of such tombs come the famous stone or wooden likenesses of the dead monarchs which surprise us with their artistic charm and the vivacity of effect when we see them in museums. These natural and dignified figures are the forerunners of the heroic statues of nude youths which Greek sculptors produced nearly two thousand years later.

Artistic achievement in the provinces during the Old Kingdom was far inferior to that of the capital, Memphis. The reliefs in some of the rock-tombs of princes near Elephantine opposite Assuân can compare with the productions of the Memphis workshops as regards composition and craftsmanship, but these form an exception. The fundamental first creative phase of old Egyptian culture reached perfection in the area between Abu Roâsh to the west of Cairo and Medûm to the south.

Egyptian chronology is based on the reigns of their kings (Pharaohs). Following the history of Egypt written by Manetho of Sebennytus in the Nile Delta during the reign of the Macedonian ruler Ptolemy II (285–246 B.C.) we divide the pharaonic period into dynasties. From the foundation of the State to the reign of the last native king before Alexander the Great, there were thirty dynasties.

The fragment of an Old Kingdom annals stone, now preserved in Palermo, and other inscriptions give us the names of certain rulers who are not mentioned in later lists of Egyptian kings, e.g. *Seka, Chaju, Tesh.*, etc., *Scorpion, Narmer*.

The last two are represented as wearing the crowns both of Upper Egypt (the stretch of valley running south from Memphis to the Assuân cataract zone) and of Lower Egypt (the Delta); in other words they were rulers of both countries. According to Egyptian tradition, King Menes united the two countries and founded Memphis; with him begins the First Dynasty. No certain reference to Menes has yet been found on monuments of the period.

FIRST DYNASTY: *Horus Aha (Menes?), Djer Wadji (Djet), Den (Udimu), Adjib, Semerkhet, Ka.*

SECOND DYNASTY: *Hetep-sekhemui, Nebrê (Neb-nefer), Nineter, Uneg* (position in dynasty uncertain), *Senedj, Peribsen, Khasekhem, Khasekhemui.*

Collateral Lower Egyptian dynasty during the reigns of the two last-named: *Neferkarê, Neferkasokar, Hudjefa, Djadja* (identical with *Khasekhemui?), Nebka.*

The historical period of Egypt begins with the 'Union of the Two Lands', which took place about the year 3000. The first two dynasties are known as the Thinite period, for the earliest kings, according to tradition, came from Thinis in Upper Egypt and the tombs of the kings of the First Dynasty and of some of the Second Dynasty (Peribsen, Khasekhemui) have been found at Abydos near Thinis. These kings were Upper Egyptians who made themselves masters of the whole of Egypt. Although the differences between the two regions continued after the union and renewed struggles flared up until the end of the Thinite period, the Upper Egyptian kingdom remained victorious throughout. On the other hand—and that is the essential and decisive element of this union—no attempt was made to subjugate, let alone exterminate, the defeated Lower Egyptian population. This attitude is symbolized by the fact that the king wears sometimes the crown of Upper Egypt, sometimes that of Lower Egypt, and further that he is not only the 'victorious Horus falcon' of Upper Egypt, but calls himself also the 'Two Lords'. From the beginning a high political wisdom aimed at a levelling and fusion of the two populations and of their cultural peculiarities. As the monarchy gains in strength, so, from the early Thinite period onwards, the Egyptian world takes shape in its religion, statecraft, society, historiography and art. The invention and development of hieroglyphic writing and the establishment of the calendar are the two fundamental intellectual innovations of that time.

It is not known whether the idea of the double kingdom also involved a double burial, one grave and one cenotaph. In any case, tombs have been found quite recently near Memphis within the precincts of the so-called Archaic cemetery (near Saqqâra) of kings of the First Dynasty who have their tomb monument at Abydos.

The palace architecture of the Thinite period can be visualized from the royal palace of Wadji (Djet) (plate 6). These structures were built of bricks made from Nile mud and were either crowned by a continuous cornice above a façade divided by pillars or they had a kind of defensive turrets projecting in front of the actual façade.

The brick tombs of the kings at Abydos, a compact group, are relatively small, some with a central room separated from the adjoining store rooms by wall pillars, others structures of many chambers with a larger burial chamber and a number of store rooms.

Much larger than the tombs at Abydos are the imposing royal tomb monuments which have been excavated in Saqqâra. Two of these have been identified by W. B. Emery, the tomb of king Wadji (Djet) and that of king Ka-a. Both of them are mastaba tombs of the characteristic slab shape which is typical for the whole period of the Old Kingdom.

The tomb of King Wadji (Djet) is a mastaba about 150 feet long and 63 feet wide with outer fronts enlivened by projections and recesses. The interior follows the peasant tradition: in the centre the tomb chamber, surrounded by numerous store rooms of varying sizes, the whole with a flat roof. Around all four sides of this mastaba slab, which was about 24 feet high, there ran a low wall, on which were arranged bulls' heads made of sun-dried clay, but with real horns, in a row. Whether these referred to the number of the animals sacrificed or were magic apotropaic symbols is not clear. The whole complex was surrounded by an enclosure wall. Outside this there were on three sides rows of tomb chambers for the servants who probably died by poison and had to follow their master into the next world.

Compared to the mastaba of King Wadji (Djet), that of king Ka-a, the last ruler of the First Dynasty, is more advanced in its arrangement, with a funerary temple adjoining the sepulchre, as later in the step-pyramid of Zoser and the pyramids of the Fourth Dynasty. The mastaba of Ka-a, like that of Wadji (Djet), has the usual slab shape and an area of 107 × 74 feet and a height of 25 feet. Of the frontage, only three sides are articulated. Walls of over 15 feet thickness enclose a central core which is made of rubble. Only below this lies the real tomb chamber, 30 feet long and accessible from the east by a descending corridor with a store room on either side. Surrounding the mastaba is again a low wall which seems to have carried bulls' heads, and beyond this there is again another wall, 9 feet thick, with an opening on the north side towards the precincts of the funerary temple. This consists of a ritual chamber in the south-west and of a number of rooms and passages. The mastaba and the funerary temple are again surrounded by an enclosure wall opening towards the east, and the entire complex is 117 feet wide and over 195 feet long. The frontages of the mastaba are surprisingly well preserved: on the projections and recesses there is the thick original stucco covering with geometrical paintings of still perfectly fresh colours, red, white, black, blue, green and yellow, imitating matting. In the actual tomb chamber there was found the collapsed sarcophagus, and in the temple, plinths and feet of two wooden statues.

1. LION. Speckled granite. Late predynastic or early dynastic period. Length 12½ inches. Berlin, State Museums, No. 22,440.
This type of lion, with menacing open mouth and tail curving over on to its back, is also found in smaller sculptures in similar material. It has no base and reveals no typically Egyptian characteristics of style. This type was later replaced by a more temperate conception.

2. COSMETICS PALETTE WITH DESERT ANIMALS AND FABULOUS CREATURES. Slate. End of the predynastic period. Height about 17 inches. Oxford, Ashmolean Museum.
From Hierakonpolis (*Kôm-el-Ahmar*). On the edges two slender, counterpoised beasts of prey with freely rendered heads. An instinctive fear of empty spaces has resulted in the filling of both sides of the palette with figures of animals. Of actually existing animals are represented the lion, leopard (?), hyena, buffalo, giraffe, steinbock, several species of antelope, hunting dogs with collars and a grallatory bird. Among the imaginary animals are some short-jawed beasts of prey with exaggeratedly long necks, a four-footed griffin with the head of a bird of prey and wings opening like combs on its back, and an erect jackal-like animal with a double waist and genitals, which appears to be playing a flute (a magician?). In the centre of one side of the palette is a pan in which malachite and other materials were mixed to make eye-paint.

3. Above: COSMETICS PALETTE WITH GIRAFFES AND PALM. Slate. End of predynastic period. Height 12¼ inches. Paris, Louvre.
On both sides enframed by four beasts of prey of similar species. In addition, on the side containing the pan, a long-necked fabulous animal, a lion and an ibis, and on the other side two giraffes and a palm. The eyes of the animals were at one time inlaid.
Below: VICTORY TABLET. Fragment. Slate. Beginning of early dynastic period. Height about 11 inches. Cairo, Museum. Tablet commemorating the victory of a king, probably King 'Scorpion'. On one side of the tablet, beneath a crosspiece, above which feet can be seen, are the names of seven conquered localities, symbolically represented by the hieroglyphs for owl, akh-bird, wrestler, beetle, Ka, casket and reed, and surrounded by walls and bastions which are being demolished by animal symbols of royalty—falcon, lion, Set animal, scorpion, etc.—On the other side of the tablet are oxen, donkeys and rams in rows (captured animals?); beneath, plants and a cipher.

4–5. VICTORY TABLET OF KING NARMER. Slate. Beginning of the early dynastic period. Height 25 inches. Cairo, Museum, No. 3055.
From Hierakonpolis (*Kôm-el-Ahmar*). As commemoration of a victory, this is related to the fragment reproduced in Plate 3. Above, on either side, are heads of the heavenly goddess Hathor with ears and horns of a cow; between

them in the centre, the name of the king. Beneath, on the side containing the pan, are three pictorial strips. Above: The king, wearing the crown of Lower Egypt, on his way to witness the execution of fettered enemies, whose heads are laid between their feet. Behind the monarch is a personal attendant with his master's salve box and sandals, in front of him an official with writing materials and four standard-bearers; the emblems on the standards raised on staffs symbolize the divine might of the king. Below: two bearded men leading two fabulous animals whose long necks twine round the pan. Such animals appear not only on similar tablets (cf. Plates 2 and 3), but also on old Babylonian cylinder-seals, and later we find them in the name of the Upper Egyptian town of Kusai. Here one may suppose that some political union is symbolized and it is not improbable that it was a manner of expressing the union of Upper and Lower Egypt, since on both sides of the tablet Narmer is wearing the crowns of both countries. Beneath, the king in the shape of a wild ox batters down the wall of a fortified settlement, at the same time trampling on the arm of a conquered foe. *Other side of the tablet*: The king, wearing the crown of Upper Egypt, strikes down an enemy held by the hair, a victory motive which persists throughout all the periods of Egyptian history. Behind the king is the sandal-bearer with his box. Above the kneeling victim, whose home is given as 'the place of harpoons'(?), is a symbolical representation: the king in the shape of a falcon god is holding by the lip the head of a captive rising out of the hieroglyph meaning 'land'. The six plants (papyrus?) nearby may symbolize six thousand captives, but perhaps also Lower Egypt. Below: Two naked fallen enemies with names of districts or tribes.

5. The king wearing the crown of Lower Egypt and a coat supported by a band over his left shoulder, together with an ornamental apron divided in two; behind, on the girdle, is the traditional oxtail; in his raised right hand he holds the ceremonial flail, in his left hand the pear-shaped mace, with the Horus falcon on the lower part of the handle. In front of the monarch is his name, expressed by the hieroglyphs for sheath-fish and chisel, behind him the attendant with his sandals, which he had probably discarded on this occasion for religious reasons.

6. TOMBSTONE OF KING WENEPHES (WADJI)-DJET, 'SNAKE'. Limestone. First Dynasty. Width 25½ inches; original total height 98 inches. Paris, Louvre.
From Abydos. Each tomb had two such stones. The work shows a surprising artistic maturity together with a partially antiquated treatment of form. The Horus name of the king is rendered with a fine feeling for form and arrangement: a serpent with raised head against the background of the palace, the fluted façade of which comprises three towers and two lofty gates; above, the king-god in the shape of a falcon.

OLD KINGDOM

THIRD DYNASTY (2778-2723): *Zoser, Zoser-Atoti (=Sekhem-khet, Zeserti-ankh?) Sanakht, Khaba, Neferka, Hu(ni)*.
The centre of political life shifts to Memphis. Notable achievements in many fields. Development of building in stone: construction of King Zoser's step-pyramid and of the residence-buildings pertaining thereto; also of the similar, unfinished monumental tomb complex of King Sekhem-khet near Memphis (near the modern village of Saqqâra).

7-15. THE TOMB COMPLEX OF KING ZOSER, SAQQÂRA. The complex of edifices surrounding the step-pyramid of King Zoser (Figs. 1 and 2) comprises the king's funerary temple on the north side of the step-pyramid and the southern tomb, and consists of a temple, palaces and chapels, which were used by the king on the occasion of the Jubilee festival. A spacious hall connects the only entrance at the south end of the east wall with the great court (between the pyramid and the southern tomb), in which the king's ceremonial race in honour of Apis took place. The whole complex—the achievement of the subsequently deified Imhotep—is the first great architectural work in stone. The architectural forms are still based on the custom, usual when building with bricks of Nile mud, of employing bundles of reeds as supports for the walls, or wooden logs trimmed with the adze, and ceilings consisting of closely-packed rows of round wooden beams. The facing with glazed composition tiles of the walls in three rooms underneath the pyramid, and of three rooms in the southern tomb, is merely a highly skilful imitation in stone and glazed composition of mats made of vegetable materials. The step-pyramid itself was developed out of the mastaba, a kind of tomb originally of bench shape.

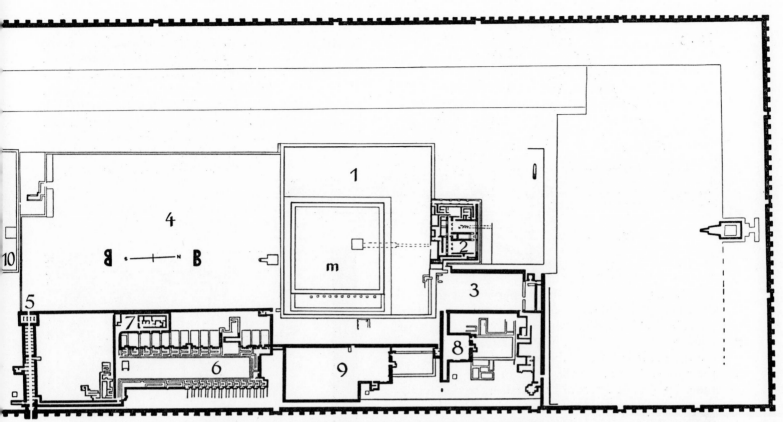

FIG. 1. Plan of the area of King Zoser's tomb, Saqqâra.

1. The step pyramid (cf. Plates 7 and 13) arising out of the original square mastaba (m); adjoining it, to the north, the funerary temple of King Zoser (2). 3. The court, with the Serdâb in its SW corner, in which the statue of the king was found (cf. Plates 16 and 17). 4. The great court with the altar (near the southern edge of the pyramid) and the two B-shaped stones, which probably served as turning-points during the king's race in the course of the Jubilee festival (cf. Plate 15). 5. The entrance hall (cf. Plate 11). At its western end the portico (cf. Plate 10); at the eastern end, the only gate in the surrounding wall (cf. Plate 9). 6. The Jubilee court, with the sham-chapels of Upper Egypt on its western side and those of Lower Egypt on the east; these accommodated the Administrators of Upper and Lower Egypt when they attended the Jubilee festival. 7. The small temple (cf. Plate 13). 8. The court in front of the northern palace; on its east side the façade shown in Plate 8. 9. The court of the southern palace. 10. The southern tomb (cf. Plate 12). Inside it, at a depth of 91 feet, rooms with walls faced with glazed composition tiles and in one of these three reliefs of the king during the ceremonial race (cf. Plate 15).—The western side of the tomb area is occupied by sham-terraces, the middle one containing galleries filled with thousands of jars and human bones. In the centre of the north side of the area was another large altar.—After *J. Ph. Lauer* 1936, drawn by *M. Hirmer.*

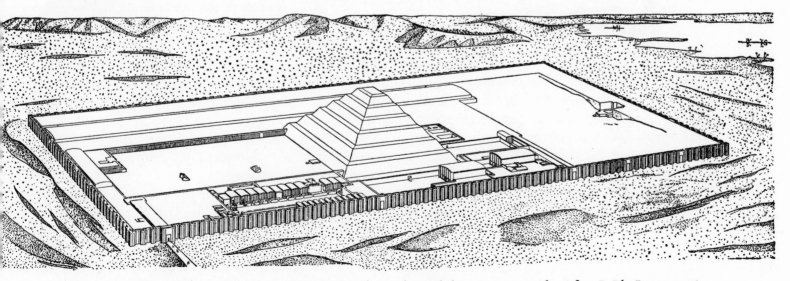

FIG. 2. Bird's-eye view of the area of King Zoser's tomb, with his step-pyramid—After *J. Ph. Lauer* 1936.

FIG. 3

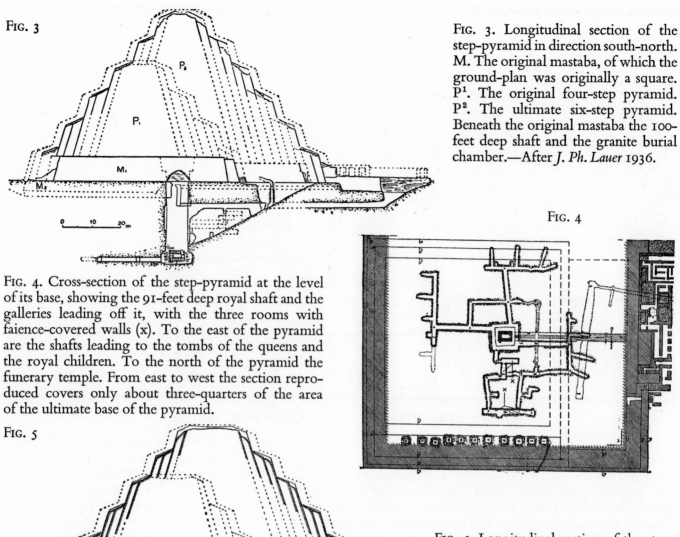

FIG. 3. Longitudinal section of the step-pyramid in direction south-north. M. The original mastaba, of which the ground-plan was originally a square. P¹. The original four-step pyramid. P². The ultimate six-step pyramid. Beneath the original mastaba the 100-feet deep shaft and the granite burial chamber.—After *J. Ph. Lauer* 1936.

FIG. 4

FIG. 4. Cross-section of the step-pyramid at the level of its base, showing the 91-feet deep royal shaft and the galleries leading off it, with the three rooms with faience-covered walls (x). To the east of the pyramid are the shafts leading to the tombs of the queens and the royal children. To the north of the pyramid the funerary temple. From east to west the section reproduced covers only about three-quarters of the area of the ultimate base of the pyramid.

FIG. 5

FIG. 5. Longitudinal section of the step-pyramid in direction east-west. Beneath the original mastaba (m), the 91-feet deep shaft leading to the granite burial chamber (GR). To the left one of the rooms with walls covered with glazed composition tiles (B). On the east side of the mastaba one of the 104-feet deep shafts leading to the tombs of the queens and the royal children.—After *J. Ph. Lauer* 1936.

This mastaba stood over the 100-feet deep shaft (Figs. 3–5) leading to the royal burial chamber. From this shaft there ran numerous corridors (Fig. 4), originally filled with household utensils and stone jars, as well as three chambers with the above-mentioned glazed composition facing on their walls and reliefs of the king, similar to those in the southern tomb (Plate 15).

The original mastaba, above which the step-pyramid was subsequently erected, measured 205 ×205 feet and was 25 feet high. It was built of fragments of stone faced with blocks of masonry, which were afterwards strengthened to a thickness of 10 feet all round the mastaba.

Along the east side were shafts 104 feet deep, each leading to a gallery 97 feet long (Figs. 4 and 5). These contained the tombs and offerings for the queens and prematurely deceased children of the royal family.

As the original dimensions of the mastaba were not sufficient to contain all these, it was extended towards the east, its original square shape being thus converted into an oblong with a longer east-west axis (Figs. 1 and 5).

The fact that the flat top of the mastaba was lower than the surrounding wall and thus invisible from outside, must have persuaded the architect Imhotep to erect a tomb rising by steps, which would be visible from a distance, 'a gigantic flight of steps reaching up towards the sky, which would enable the soul of the dead king to ascend towards the sun, his father Rê' (Lauer).

The original four-step pyramid, after its north-south axis and also its east-west axis had been lengthened, became that east-west oblong, six-step, 195-feet high pyramid which still remains as a monument to a great king and a gifted architect of the early Old Kingdom.

7. VIEW FROM THE UNAS-PYRAMID TOWARDS THE NORTH-EAST. In the foreground the southern part of the perimeter wall; in front of it, a building of mud bricks; beyond, close to the wall, the southern tomb. In the background the great court, on the northern edge of which rises the step-pyramid. To the east of the great court, remains of the temple and the Jubilee Court can be seen. In the distance, the dark strip is cultivated country; behind it, the pale cliffs of the eastern desert near Tura.

8. FAÇADE ON THE EAST SIDE OF THE COURT BEFORE THE NORTHERN PALACE.
Papyrus-shaped columns, papyrus being the plant symbol of the North. Wonderfully realistic representation.

9. SOUTHERN END OF THE EAST SIDE OF THE PERIMETER WALL WITH THE ONLY GATE.
Built by utilizing old blocks. The wall encircled the whole tomb area, with a length from north to south of about 610 yards (=1000 Egyptian cubits) and 306 yards from east to west; the original height was 65 feet. It is built after the manner of archaic mastabas, with recesses. Along its four sides are 14 bastions. The only gate, at the southern end of the eastern portion, leads into the great hall (cf. Plate 11) and thence through the portico (cf. Plate 10) to the great court. The eight rows of holes on the upper portion of the wall correspond to the extremities of the wooden beams used to strengthen walls built of mud bricks; in this stone wall, they form an effective and vivacious element. Like all the other buildings in the tomb area, the wall is built of Tura limestone from the mountain on the opposite, eastern bank of the Nile. This wall may well be considered a small-scale imitation of the 'White Wall' with which Menes, the founder of the city, encircled Memphis.

10-11. PORTICO OF THE HALL OF PILLARS AND THE HALL OF PILLARS SEEN FROM THE EASTERN ENTRANCE.
The 58-yards long hall of pillars comprises two rows each of 20 three-quarter columns, in the shape of bundles of reeds, 19½ feet high, each pillar terminating the ends of short transverse walls. The two outside walls have window-like openings in the top portion between the transverse walls. The ceiling was an imitation in stone of a wooden ceiling made of semicircular wooden beams, set close together and transversely (in the second picture, the modern ceiling is not yet in position). The portico consists of eight pillars, placed in pairs on either side of short connecting walls. The shape of the three-quarter columns in the hall is found here too: the pillars resting on cylindrical pedestals have 'reed-stems' at their tops, as if held together by a covering ceiling. At the entrance to the portico is a wall with an open gate also constructed of stone.

12. CORNER OF A WALL OF THE SOUTHERN TOMB WITH FRIEZE OF SERPENTS.
This wall, rebuilt from fragments, formed part of the superstructure of the southern tomb which was demolished during the Nineteenth Dynasty. The wall-surfaces are broken by false-door niches. The round staves are reminiscent of the wooden rollers by which the reed mats were lowered when doors were closed. The row of erect cobras crowning the wall is the primitive form of a symbolical ornament which lasted down to very late periods and probably points to Lower Egypt. There are good grounds for believing that the internal organs of the king were buried in the southern tomb. The enclosure contains a shaft 91 feet deep, which, as in the case of the pyramid, leads to a chamber faced with granite. From the bottom of the shaft a passage leads to three rooms, the walls of which, like those beneath the pyramid, are faced with turquoise-coloured glazed composition tiles. One of these rooms contains three slabs, designed to imitate doorways, with reliefs of the king (cf. Plates 14 and 15).

13. THE TEMPLE.
Rectangular shape, with rounded corners. Three of the walls terminate on the inner side in fluted three-quarter columns which, like those of the hall of pillars, were presumably crowned only with an abacus. On the eastern side of the temple we again find a half-open stone door, this time opening towards the inside.

14-15. KING ZOSER DURING THE CEREMONIAL RACE.
One of the three mural reliefs in the southern tomb. The king is shown taking part in the ritual race which formed part of the celebrations during the periodical jubilee festivals. He is lifting the ritual flail and another object

which cannot be identified with certainty. In front of the king is a long pole bearing the figure of a divinity in the shape of a jackal, before which a cobra stands erect. Above the monarch hovers the divine falcon with a symbol of life. To the right, symbols of health. In front of the king's head, his Horus name: Neter-khet.

16–17. KING ZOSER. Limestone. Traces of painting. Cairo, Museum, No. 6008.
This lifesize statue was found in the northern annex of the step-pyramid, the Serdâb (Figs. 1, 3), a limestone chamber, in the sloping front wall of which were two peepholes. It is the oldest lifesize royal statue known. The eyes, formerly inlaid, are now empty. The pointed royal head-dress, the wig of strands and the long holder for the beard are un-usual and stress the antiquity of this statue with its strik-ingly individual features. On the pedestal are the title and name of the king, always called Neter-khet on contempor-ary monuments; the name Zoser does not occur until later. Traces of colouring: white on the mantle, brown on the skin, black in the hair.

18. WOOD RELIEFS FROM THE TOMB OF HESI-RÊ at Saqqâra. Height, 45 inches. Cairo, Museum, No. 88.
Eleven wooden reliefs (in varying states of preservation), belonging to the eleven niches in the interior of the mastaba have been found; the six best-preserved of these are today in the Cairo museum. Hesirê, who as 'confidant of the king' and 'great man of the South' was one of the leading officials in Zoser's time, is shown on one of the reliefs here repro-duced, standing erect, with the emblems of his rank and writing materials, and on the other seated before an offer-ing-table. In the latter he is wearing a wig of ringlets, in the former the strand coiffure. Portraits and hieroglyphs are wonderfully fresh and delicate in their execution. Although the two relief figures already show the typical hieroglyphic character which prevailed from this time on, the features and certain details of the bodies are treated with a realism found only exceptionally in later Egyptian reliefs. On the upper lip, a short moustache.

19. HESIRÊ AT THE OFFERING-TABLE.
Detail of the relief shown on the left of Plate 18. Hesirê holds in his left hand the long staff and the club-like sceptre of his rank. From his shoulder hang the writing materials, consisting of palette, rush-box and water-container. The chair has slender ungulate legs, the seat having the shape of a papyrus stem. Above the table, consisting of support and slab, with its so-called 'breads'—the name is actually derived from this relief—are various articles of food. The practice of depicting foodstuffs in front of the deceased in his tomb goes back to the ancient Egyptian idea that, so long as the dead man has food and drink at his disposal, even if only in a picture, his 'ka', i.e. the imperishable essence of his being, can continue to exist.

FOURTH DYNASTY (2723–2563): *Snofru, Cheops (Khnum-khufu), Djedefrê, Khephren (Khafrê), Mycerinus (Menkaurê), Shepseskaf.*
Deliberate concentration and direction of popular energies under the leadership of the divine-royal monarchy. Construction of the great pyramids with their temples. Reduction of number of types and abandonment of decorative imitation in favour of simple and powerful forms. Little is known of the historical events or of the personalities of the rulers. In addition to the kings named, there were probably others of which no monuments have so far been discovered.

20. THE PYRAMID AREA OF DAHSHÛR.
View from the Unas pyramid at Saqqâra, looking south. In the middle distance, on the left, pyramids of the South Saqqâra group. In the centre of the background the so-called 'Bent Pyramid' (height 316 feet); on the right, the so-called 'Red Pyramid' (height 339 feet), the oldest royal tomb in pure pyramid form. Both of these were erected for the founder of the Fourth Dynasty, King Snofru.

21. PRINCE ANKHHAF. Limestone faced with stucco, painted. Height 23 inches. Boston, Museum of Fine Arts.
From the prince's tomb near Gizeh. As the third husband of Princess Hetepheres, the vizier Ankhhaf was the son-in-law of King Cheops. He was both vizier and superintendent of the royal buildings. This bust obviously had a religious pur-pose different from that of the damaged statues of the prince which have been found. The bust was modelled out of a layer of stucco spread in varying thicknesses over the limestone. The arms are cut off at the level of the armpits, the torso has been cut away beneath the breast. The over-painting is of a light reddish-brown. For unexplained reasons the ears have been trimmed like those of the so-called reserve heads, to which this work is closely related. The unusually realistic features, with their elaboration of individual details of form, give this bust a special place among the sculptures of the time.

23–25. PRINCE RAHOTEP AND HIS WIFE NO-FRET. Painted limestone. Height about 4 feet. Cairo, Museum, No. 223.
From the tomb of the prince—who was probably one of King Snofru's sons—at Medûm. As high-priest of Helio-polis, army commander, etc., Rahotep occupied a number of the highest offices. As a favourite of the king, his wife

Nofret was a member of the court. The animated effect produced by the colouring gives these two figures a pre-eminent place among ancient Egyptian statues. The eyes are inlaid with dull and light-coloured quartz and surrounded by a border reproducing the black-painted edges of the lids. The left sides of the high-backed cube-shaped seats were hewn off with rough blows in ancient times. The prince is wearing a simple apron, with an amulet on his

collar of tubular beads. Nofret—this favourite woman's name can mean either 'the good' or 'the beautiful'—is wrapped in a close-fitting mantle. The fillet in her hair shows a pattern of flowers. The customary difference between the colour of a man's skin and a woman's should be noticed. Whereas the woman's is in the main a sort of creamy yellow, that of the man varies in the different works from a light to a dark brown.

26–35. THE PYRAMID AREA OF GIZA. This great tomb area contains, in addition to the three most celebrated pyramids, the burial places of the most important personages of the Fourth and also of the Fifth Dynasty. Each pyramid complex consists of four buildings lying one behind the other, the whole stretching from the edge of the cultivated zone towards the west as far as the cliffs of the desert plateau. The four buildings are: the gate or valley temple; the covered causeway, with openings to admit light; the funerary temple in front of the pyramid, in which the rites in memory of the deceased ruler were celebrated; and lastly the pyramid itself as the monumental climax.

In the northern part of the area lies the oldest and at the same time the largest pyramid, that of *Cheops*, the son of Snofru and Hetepheres. At the base the sides are about 750 feet long (=440 Egyptian cubits) (north side 755 feet, south side 762 feet) and at an angle of 51° 52′ the flanks originally reached a height

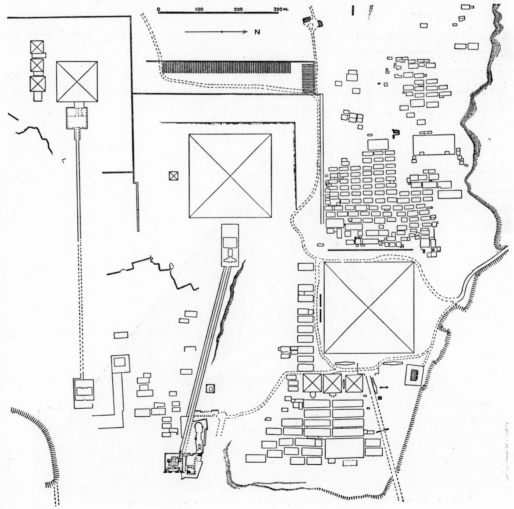

FIG. 6. The pyramid area of Giza with the three great pyramids of Cheops (right), Chephren (centre) and Mycerinus (left). (Cf. the text to Plates 26–35.) To the south of the Cheops pyramid, the two ships (shown by two lines) discovered in 1954. On the eastern side of each pyramid is its funerary temple, to which the causeway from the valley temple leads; in the case of the Chephren and Mycerinus pyramids, these temples have been preserved, but that of the Cheops pyramid has to a large extent been destroyed. Near the Chephren valley temple is the Sphinx.— After G. A. Reisner 1942.

297

of 475 feet (present height 446 feet). Adjoining it on the west is the royal cemetery, with the mastaba roads running from north to south and from east to west, laid out according to a uniform plan in the Fourth Dynasty for the members of the royal family and the high state officials, and bounded on the south by a wall. In front of the pyramid—as can still be seen in the case of the two later pyramids— lay the funerary temple, to which a causeway led from the valley temple on a branch of the Nile. Immediately adjoining the eastern side of the pyramid, two depressions for the ships. The two ships discovered in 1954 lie to the south of these. To the east, in front of the Cheops pyramid, are three smaller pyramids for close relatives, probably daughters of the king. Adjoining them is another mastaba area.

The pyramid shown in the centre of the plan, that of Chephren, the son of Cheops, originally had sides 700 feet long (present length 684 feet) and at an angle of 52° 20′ reached a height of 466 feet (present height 443 feet); at the top a considerable part of the casing remains, which originally covered the whole pyramid. The funerary temple, the approach causeway and especially the valley temple of this pyramid are very well preserved.

The southernmost and smallest of the three pyramids is that of Mycerinus. Its sides were once 285 feet long (now 258 feet) and its angle 51°. Its height was formerly 216 feet (now 201 feet). Clearly visible remains of the funerary temple, causeway and valley temple have been preserved. In front of it on the south there were also three small pyramids.

Between the causeways to the two last-named pyramids there is another large mastaba zone, with tombs mainly of prominent personages of the Fifth Dynasty.

On one side of the beginning of the causeway from the Chephren valley temple lies the Sphinx. In front of it is the Sphinx temple (not to be confused with the Chephren valley temple, which writers often wrongly describe as the Sphinx temple).

The principles of pyramid construction, differing in their details from one pyramid to another, can best be illustrated by the pyramid of Cheops, which surpassed the others both in its main conception and in the construction of the inner chambers.

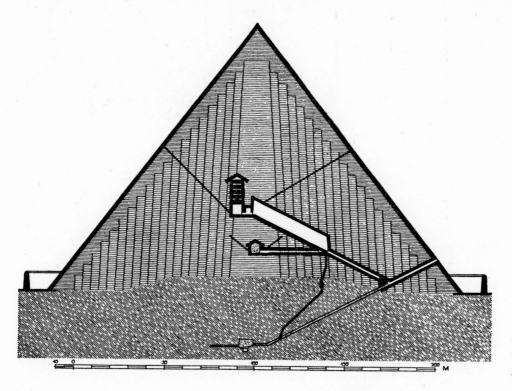

FIG. 7. Longitudinal section, direction south-north, of the Cheops pyramid.—After *L. Borchardt* 1932.

298

The framework consists of irregularly placed, rough-hewn stone blocks, with an outside casing of carefully dressed limestone, 17 feet thick. The layout of the internal construction was changed three times.
As in all other pyramids, the entrance is on the north side. In this case it is at a height of 49 feet above ground level, the passage at first sloping downwards for 62 feet and then rising. At the point where it begins to rise, the passage was blocked by a number of large granite blocks, as a protection against tomb thieves. The passage then leads into the great chamber, which rises with a gradient of 26.5°; it is 30 feet high, 153 feet long, with a maximum breadth of 7 feet 3 inches. Faced with polished Mokattam limestone, it is a masterpiece of masonry work. From it a short passage leads to an antechamber shut off by four granite blocks. At a height of 137 feet above ground level is the royal funerary chamber, with a north-south length of 17 feet and an east-west width of 34 feet. The chamber is faced with Assuân granite. At the western extremity is the king's granite sarcophagus. From the funerary chamber two air-shafts lead towards the outside; they run at different gradients and measure 6 × 8 inches; one of them is 173 feet long, the other 231 feet; they probably had a religious significance. Above the funerary chamber are four horizontal stone ceilings separated by empty spaces, and a gable roof of blocks inclining towards one another, to protect the funerary chamber from the pressure of the top of the pyramid.
The pyramids of the kings of the Fourth Dynasty lie on the eastern edge of the Western Desert, occupying an area with a north-south length of about 92 miles. Two of Snofru's pyramids are at Dahshûr (Plate 20), more than 25 miles to the south of Giza, and the third, probably finished during his reign, is at Medûm, nearly 85 miles south of Giza. The remains of the pyramid of Djedefrê, successor to Cheops, are near the modern village of Abu-Roâsh, 11 miles to the north-west of Giza. Near the modern Saqqâra, in the neighbourhood of Memphis, there is only the tomb of Shepseskaf, the last king of the Fourth Dynasty.

26. THE PYRAMID ZONE OF GIZA, SEEN FROM THE SOUTH-WEST.
In the foreground the unfinished pyramid of Mycerinus with the three subsidiary pyramids built at intervals. In the centre, the pyramid of Chephren. Behind the latter, the pyramid of Cheops. The view stretches eastwards as far as the Chephren valley temple and the Sphinx, the head of which is visible about an inch from the right edge of the picture. In the background, the dark strip is the cultivated zone in the direction of Cairo.

27. THE PYRAMID ZONE OF GIZA FROM THE SOUTH.
In the photograph the funerary temples in front of the two more recent pyramids can be clearly seen: that of Mycerinus (which in the photo appears to be in front of the pyramid of Chephren), and that of Chephren (in the photo, in front of the Cheops pyramid).

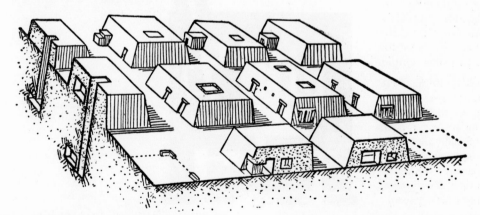

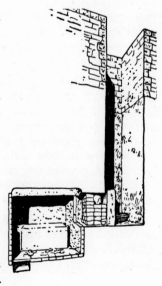

FIG. 8. Bird's-eye view of a group of Fourth-Dynasty mastaba tombs. On the left of the drawing the sides of two mastabas have been cut away to show the deep shafts leading to the funerary chambers. After *A. Badawy* 1954.

FIG. 9. Longitudinal section of a shaft and funerary chamber in a Fourth-Dynasty mastaba. The antechamber between the two shows the position of the 'substitute head'. After *A. Scharff* 1939.

28–29. THE GIZA SPHINX.

This rock statue, a colossal couchant lion with a hooded king's head was carved out of the heart of a limestone quarry whence King Cheops obtained the blocks for his pyramid and the superstructures of the tombs of his high officials. This mighty work is generally ascribed to the reign of King Chephren, but certain details, such as the type of features and the receding lateral surfaces of the head-gear, point to an older origin. Under the New Empire this sphinx was believed to be a portrait of the sun-god Rê-Harakhte of Heliopolis.—The paws and the outer sides of the trunk are built up out of ashlar blocks. In 1925–26, when the huge monument was again completely cleared, cement supports to hold up the head were placed beneath the hood on either side. On the cheek, in front of the ear, are traces of reddish-brown colouring. The damage to the head dates from the iconoclastic disturbances about 1380 and further damage was later inflicted by the Mamelukes.

Despite the gigantic dimensions (height about 65 feet, length 238 feet) it harmonizes well with the surrounding landscape. Its size can be gauged by comparing it in Plate 28 with the Chephren valley temple, in the left background at its feet.

In Plate 28: Immediately in front of the Sphinx, the remains of a temple which probably existed at the time of King Chephren; at an angle to the foreground, a monument dating from the New Empire. Behind the Sphinx, the causeway running from the Chephren valley temple to the pyramid temple. Above the head of the Sphinx can be seen an Arab cemetery.

In Plate 29: In the background behind the Sphinx, the pyramid of Cheops.

30. SOUTHERN PORTION OF THE GIZA PYRAMID ZONE, FROM THE EAST.

In front of the Sphinx, ruins of a temple probably dedicated to him; adjoining it, the Chephren valley temple. From this the ancient causeway leads up to the funerary temple of the Chephren pyramid (on the right in the photo). In the centre of the background, the pyramid of Mycerinus.

31. PYRAMID OF CHEOPS, SPHINX AND VALLEY TEMPLE OF CHEPHREN, FROM THE SOUTH.

In front of the eastern side (lying in the shadow) of the Cheops Pyramid, the three subsidiary pyramids. Note the mighty blocks of the walls of the Chephren valley temple.

32. OLD KINGDOM MASTABA CEMETERY, THE CHEPHREN PYRAMID and its funerary temple.

To the south of the causeway leading to the funerary temple of the Chephren pyramid stand the numerous rows of superstructures of private graves of officials, mostly of the Fifth Dynasty. In their statue-chambers many statues have been found, representing the occupants of the tombs and their servants. In front of the eastern side of the pyramid (lying in shadow), the funerary temple can be clearly seen.

33. FUNERARY TEMPLE OF MYCERINUS, SEEN FROM THE SOUTH-EAST CORNER OF THE MYCERINUS PYRAMID.

In the background, the Chephren pyramid.

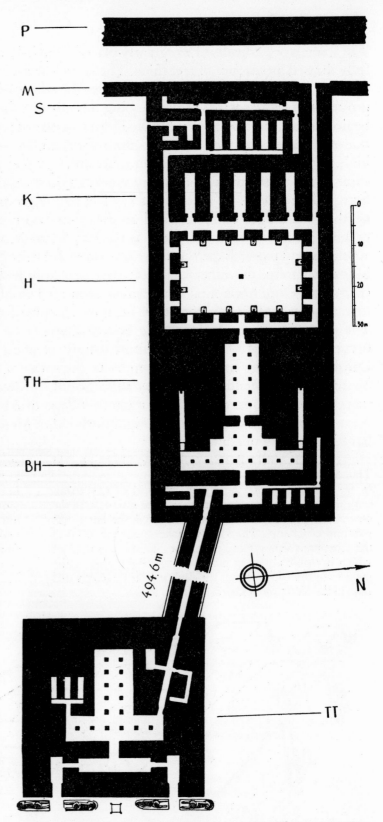

FIG. 10. Funerary temple and valley temple of King Chephren. TT: The valley temple. From it the 500-yard causeway leads north-west to the funerary temple in the centre of the eastern side of the pyramid (P). Its western flank adjoins the inner enclosing wall (M) of the pyramid. BH: A broad hall, narrowing in step-wise fashion from east to west. On either side are apartments believed to have been Serdâbs. TH: Long hall. H: The great court. Adjoining it, five chapels (K). S: The Holy of Holies.

VALLEY AND FUNERARY TEMPLES OF CHEPHREN. The valley temple, often described as a 'gateway', lay on a branch of the Nile. This magnificently simple building is in shape almost a perfect square. It is distinguished by the beauty of its proportions and the brilliance of the materials, which even today is still striking; these are characteristic features of Fourth Dynasty buildings.

In front of the two entrances in the eastern façade there probably stood two sphinxes. Both entrances lead to a transverse corridor from the middle of which we gain access to the 'broad hall'. Adjoining this are the three aisles of the 'long hall', with monolithic granite pillars 13 feet 6 inches high. Light entered this hall through oblique openings which still exist. Against the walls there once stood 23 statues of kings; holes in the plaster (Plate 34) still show the positions of their square pedestals. From the south-west corner of the 'broad hall' a corridor leads to a group of store-rooms, arranged in two rows of three each. The north-west corner is at the end of the corridor leading to the passageway.

The *funerary temple*, which adjoins the eastern flank of the pyramid, is likewise built of massive blocks of local limestone faced with granite, out of which the necessary rooms seem to have been fashioned as if they were hollowed out. In the great court, which likewise contained statues of the king, the sacrifices were made. It is the centre of the so-called 'public' part of the temple. Its columns were of Assuân granite, in front of which were seated statues of the king. Adjoining the court to the west are five chapels, in each of which the Pharaoh was worshipped under one of his five names. Each chapel contained a statue of the king and probably a bark as well. These may well have been the five barks excavated in the vicinity of the funerary temple. Behind the court was the 'intimate' part of the temple, with the alcove of the Holy of Holies, to which only the officiating priests had access. In front of the great court, near the entrance, we again find the system of the 'long hall' with the 'broad hall' lying before it, as in the valley temple, but in this case the 'broad hall' is larger. 'The funerary temple, today unfortunately almost destroyed, must have given additional force to the severe impression, aiming at might and grandeur, created by the valley temple.' (A. Scharff.)

34. VALLEY TEMPLE. Oblique view from the 'broad hall' with its single row of columns into the 'long hall' with its three pillared aisles.

35. VALLEY TEMPLE. The middle aisle of the 'long hall', seen from the 'broad hall'.

36-39. KING CHEPHREN. Diorite. Height 66 inches. Cairo, Museum, No. 138.
This seated portrait statue, together with eight other more or less complete statues of the king, was found in the 'well shaft' of the valley temple. In this particular statue, to the figure of the king is added the royal god Horus in the shape of a falcon, which, sitting on the back of the throne, lends its protecting strength to the monarch. This powerful pictorial conception is not often found in statues of Egyptian kings and nowhere has it achieved more effective form than here. The throne has lion's legs; each pair of front legs is joined to the forepart of a lion by a maned lion's head. On the sides of the throne, the symbol of the union of the two Egypts, the hieroglyph 'sema' (='join'), around which are wound the emblematic plants of Lower and Upper Egypt, the papyrus and the so-called 'lily'. On the pedestal, to right and left in front, the name. The clenched fist of the king grasps a folded cloth with hanging ends of unequal length. Between the heels is a round depression, the purport of which has not been explained. Above the centre of the forehead, lying flat against the hood,

is the erect forepart of the divine cobra which symbolized the royal power and threatened the enemies of the 'Great God' with destruction.

40-42. PORTRAIT HEADS FROM THE ROYAL CEMETERY AT GIZA. Limestone. Lifesize. Cairo, Museum, Nos. 6003 and 6005.
These separately carved heads belong to a particularly interesting group, which appears to be limited to statue-less tombs of members of Cheops' and Chephren's families at Giza, although similar heads have occasionally been found elsewhere. They come from the subterranean sarcophagus chambers, in the entrances to which—towards the shafts—they were obviously erected. The most important examples are in the museums of Boston, Cairo and Vienna. The hair is depicted like a close-fitting cap, the eyes are not inlaid, the broad and simple treatment of the features gives an effect of portraiture. The ears have been more or less hacked off. At the back of the head and neck are vertical notches; on the throat, just above the base, there are often light horizontal grooves. All this points to some local burial custom, perhaps going back to age-old conceptions, or connected with the passage in the so-called pyramid texts: 'Arise! Take thy head, pick up thy bones, gather together thy limbs!' According to H. Junker, these heads were intended to help the wandering soul on its way back to the tomb, a kind of physiognomical signpost to the buried body to which it belonged.

In connection with these portrait heads, which writers often describe as 'reserve heads', a word about *Fourth-Dynasty private tombs* in general is necessary. Their slab-like form, expressed by the name 'mastaba' (=bench), can be seen in the reconstruction in Plate 10. A simple monumentality is characteristic of these tombs, which lay alongside the roads leading at right angles to the pyramids of Cheops and Chephren. Built only of massive stone blocks, the mastabas of the Fourth Dynasty, in accordance with the wishes of the great rulers, had no ritual chambers adorned with sculptures, although such chambers are found in mastabas of important personages from the time of the third dynasty at Saqqâra and Medûm (cf. Plates 18–19 and 22–25). Only a small place for sacrifices on the southern flank of the eastern side, which gave shelter to the offerings and served as a store-room, was henceforth allowed. The Serdâb with its statue disappeared together with the ritual chamber, and there remained only the shaft faced with limestone blocks and the burial chamber with its simple limestone sarcophagus. The shaft was blocked up after the funeral. The 'reserve heads' were placed in the little antechamber between the shaft and the burial chamber.

43. KING MYCERINUS. UPPER PART OF THE SEATED STATUE IN ALABASTER. Lifesize. Cairo, Museum, No. 157.
From the king's funerary temple in front of his pyramid at Giza. The material and the conception give this seated statue a peculiar charm. As is usual in statues of this monarch, the features have all the characteristics of portraiture.

44–45. KING MYCERINUS AND QUEEN KHA-MERERNEBTI. Slate. Traces of painting. Height, 56 inches. Boston, Museum of Fine Arts.
From the king's valley temple in front of his pyramid at Giza. This unfinished, only partially polished work is the earliest known example of a type which later became very common in statues of private individuals and eventually developed into the family group. The difference between the robust, masculine features of the king with their expression of watchful expansiveness and the more placid expression of the woman's features, is striking and is a proof

of the fact that the art of this period was not dominated by any ideal pattern.

46–47. KING MYCERINUS BETWEEN TWO GODDESSES. Green slate. Height 38½ and 37 inches. Cairo, Museum, Nos. 180 and 149. From the king's valley temple at Giza.
46. On the right of the king, who is wearing the crown of Upper Egypt, is the goddess Hathor; on his left, the regional goddess of Diospolis Parva, with the regional symbol above her head.
47. On the king's right, the goddess Hathor; on his left, the regional goddess of Kynopolis, with the regional symbol above her head. Both goddesses have their right arms raised behind the king's back, grasping his upper arm. On the pedestal are the king's title and name.
In a recess in the king's valley temple, unfinished at the time of his death and completed in brick by his successor Shepseskaf, several similar triads have been found. They are now divided between the museums of Cairo and Boston.

FIFTH DYNASTY (2563–2423): *Userkaf, Sahurê, Neferirkarê, Shepseskarê, Ne-userrê, Menkauhor, Asosi, Unas (Onnos)*.
The cult of Rê, the sun religion of Heliopolis, became the state religion. Growing importance of high priests and state officials. Golden age of the art of sculpture.
The first monarchs of the brief Third Dynasty, Zoser and his successor Sekhem-khet, had their tombs erected in the immediate neighbourhood of the capital, Memphis, on the western edge of the desert near the modern Saqqâra, and also began the unfinished pyramid of Neferka only fifteen miles to the north near the modern Zâwijet-el-Arjân, while the pyramid of the last Fourth-Dynasty king is likewise close to Memphis. Similarly, it was in the neighbourhood of the capital Memphis that the kings of the Fifth and the following Dynasties built their pyramids. These monuments, however, were not built with the same care for their survival as those of Zoser, Snofru, Cheops, Chephren and Mycerinus. All that is left of them today consists of pyramid-shaped heaps of stones, without that crystalline nobility which distinguished the pyramids of the Fourth Dynasty.

Close to Zoser's step pyramid, lie the pyramids of Kings Userkaf and Unas, while a little further south rises that of Asosi. Some four miles to the north, near the modern Abusîr, we find the three pyramids of Kings Sahurê, Neferirkarê and Ne-userrê. Slightly north of this, near Abu-Gurob, is the sun sanctuary of Ne-userrê, the only one of which considerable portions have been preserved among those mighty sanctuaries with obelisks dedicated to the sun, which made their appearance during the Fifth Dynasty and the form of which has fortunately been preserved in a hieroglyph.

48. GRANITE COLUMN WITH PALM CAPITAL FROM THE HALL OF PILLARS IN THE FUNERARY TEMPLE OF KING SAHURÊ AT ABUSÎR.
Height of the capital (from the lowest ring to the upper surface of the abacus): 78 inches. Assuân granite. Cairo, Museum, No. 135.
The palm fronds rise from the supporting capital as if bound round with several coils of cord. On the lowest cord there is a manifold loop. On the shaft of the column, the name and title of the monarch.—The palm columns from Abusîr are the oldest so far discovered and at the same time the most beautiful examples of this long-lived type, which occurs two thousand years later in temples of the Ptolemaic period.

49. SARCOPHAGUS OF RAWÊR. Limestone. Cairo, Museum, No. 519.
From the tomb of Rawêr at Giza. The sarcophagus has been carefully designed to represent a palace with doors, windows and niches. It gives a good idea of the arrangement and ornamentation of a palace built of sun-dried bricks of Nile mud.

50–51. KING USERKAF. Assuân granite. Height 26 inches. Cairo, Museum, No. 6051.
From the funerary temple of this king's pyramid at Saqqâra. The body belonging to this severe, truly monumental head has not been preserved. Among the colossal statues of old Egyptian kings, this is, according to the present state of our knowledge, the oldest. The pupils of the eyes were indicated by colouring, traces of which remain.

52. ALABASTER STELE WITH PORTRAIT OF RAWÊR IN RELIEF. Cairo, Museum, No. 6267.
From Rawêr's tomb at Giza. At the top are the titles and name of the subject. Traces of colouring have been preserved. The body and draperies are indicated only by chiselled contours. The material, with its softly shimmering transparence, produces a particularly fine effect.

53. RAWÊR. Limestone. Height 10 inches. Cairo, Museum, No. 6265.
From Rawêr's tomb at Giza. Fragment of a lifesize statue. The spiritualized face is formalistically related to the granite head of King Userkaf (Plates 50, 51).

54–55. KA-APER, PRIEST AND HIGH STATE OFFICIAL, KNOWN AS THE 'VILLAGE MAGISTRATE'.
Wood, Height 43 inches. Cairo, Museum, No. 140.

From his tomb at Saqqâra. The circumstances of its discovery make it doubtful whether it belongs to the Fourth or the Fifth Dynasty, but the latter is more probable. The name of 'Shêkh-el-beled', or village magistrate has stuck to this celebrated statue ever since the native workmen who excavated it so described it. It was found together with two other wooden statues of Ka-aper and the torso of a wooden female statue. The corpulence of the figure is in marked contrast to the youthful slenderness of form of one of the other statues in the round of this man. Over the wooden surface there was originally a thin layer of stucco, which has disappeared together with the colouring. The eyes, of quartz and other materials, are embedded in copper lids. Both feet and the forepart of the legs have been restored. The knotted stick (instead of the staff of rank) did not belong to the original. One of the earliest examples of the use of wood for a medium-sized Egyptian statue of a private individual.

56–57. GIRL GRINDING CORN. Limestone, painted. Height 14 inches and 12½ inches. Cairo, Museum, Nos. 114 and 818.
56. Described on the base as Ishat, in the service of the estate-owner Ur-ir-en.
57. The type is coarser, but the conception fresh and vivacious. One is reminded of the saying of a sage of the time: 'Good speech is more hidden than the green gem, yet one finds it in maids among the millstones.'
Similar figures of servants are frequently found surrounding the statue of their master in the statue chamber or Serdâb, providing him after death with the things he needed in life. They adhere less strictly to rule than the statues of their masters, the pose and draperies of which were governed by social conventions.

58–59. PORTRAIT OF AN UNKNOWN SCRIBE. Limestone, painted. Height 19½ inches. Cairo, Museum, No. 141.
From Saqqâra. The left hand holds the papyrus scroll, the right is ready to write. The colour of the body is orange-brown, that of the hair black. The eyes are inlaid in copper lids, which have now crumbled away; the eyeballs are of crystal, the whites of alabaster, a copper nail serving as pupil. The restrained, questioning expression is of great psychological charm, and the work of high artistic value. Works of this kind do not represent domestic scribes waiting on the orders of their master, but high officials conscious of their highly appreciated knowledge and skill, who desired to be thus immortalized.

60. AN OFFICIAL WRITING. Limestone, painted. Height 21 inches. Paris, Louvre.
From the tomb of the subject at Saqqâra. The skin is reddish-brown, the hair black. The eyes, as usual, are embedded in a copper surround and composed of alabaster crystal, black stone (pupil) and silver.

61–65. RANUFER, HIGH PRIEST OF MEMPHIS. Limestone, with traces of painting. Height of the figures: 73 and 70 inches. Cairo, Museum, Nos. 224 and 225.
From his tomb at Saqqâra. Colour of the body, light orange-brown, of the hair, black. Collar above shoulders painted. Inscriptions on the bases. The short hair of the statue on the left makes Ranufer appear older than in the right-hand figure with its strands falling on the shoulders. The difference of coiffure in funerary statues of one and the same person can be explained by the desire to give him the suitable coiffure or wig for every occasion. This was a very strict social convention in the East in olden days. In the left-hand statue Ranufer is wearing the usual apron turned back at the edge; in the right-hand figure, a short ceremonial apron with the ornamented part folded and decorative knots on the girdle. Both statues are among the best examples of Memphis statuary. The nose of the right-hand statue has been restored.

66–67. TI. Limestone with traces of painting. Height 78½ inches. Cairo, Museum, No. 229.
From his tomb at Saqqâra. A fresh and youthful nobility distinguishes this slightly over-lifesize portrait of the estate-owner and court official Ti. Traces of black colouring in the hair; the body was painted reddish-brown. Inscriptions on the base. The nose has been (not very skilfully) restored. Parts of the wig of small ringlets are not in their original state.

68–77. TOMBS OF THE FIFTH AND EARLY SIXTH DYNASTIES. The portraits reproduced in Plates 52–67, all, with the exception of the two girls in Plates 56 and 57, of high functionaries and in some cases at the same time priests, come from their tombs, or mastabas, at Giza or Saqqâra. As explained on p. 302, under the Fourth Dynasty there was no room in the mastabas for statues or reliefs of the deceased, since the practice of building sacrificial chambers and Serdâbs was abandoned. At the beginning of the Fifth Dynasty there was a change. The tombs of prominent personages became many-roomed buildings, though the external form of the traditional mastabas was retained. Amidst the massiveness of the undecorated and windowless whole, resembling a gigantic stone slab, the rooms necessary for rites and worship seem as if they had been hollowed out. The dominant element is not so much the room as the whole mass of solid stone. In the Serdâb, which usually adjoins the sacrificial chamber, we find the statue, or several portraits of the deceased. Only a little peep-slit allows the eye to see what is going on in the sacrificial chamber or elsewhere in the tomb. In the numerous rooms of the mastaba, however, his life is depicted in reliefs with all the joys of earthly existence, in order that they may be at the disposal of the deceased in the other world.

The following scenes from reliefs in three of the most important tombs at Saqqâra, belonging partly to the Fifth and partly to the early Sixth Dynasty, show examples of these varied pictures of human existence. Ground-plans of these three mastabas—all three on the same scale of reduction—will be found in Figs. 11–13. In the tomb of Ti, who was overseer of the pyramids of Neferirkarê and Ne-userrê and of the sun temples of Sahurê and his successors, the entrance consists of a spacious pillared hall. From this a subterranean passage leads to the burial chamber, while a long corridor gives access to the sacrificial chamber, adjoining which to the south is the Serdâb, which formerly contained three statues (those of Plates 66 and 67 were on its eastern side). The mastaba of Ptahhotep, the first of the priests of the pyramids of Asosi, Ne-userrê and Menkauhor, also contains the rooms dedicated to his son Akhethotep. The mastaba of the vizier Mereruka with its 31 rooms, includes the burial chambers of his wife Her-wadjet-khet and their son Meriteti.

68–71. TOMB OF TI AT SAQQÂRA. RELIEFS FROM THE SACRIFICIAL CHAMBER.
These mural reliefs are carved out of limestone. They show to a greater or lesser degree traces of painting.

68. TI WATCHING A HIPPOPOTAMUS HUNT.
On the North wall. Ti is in a boat which is traversing a papyrus thicket on the bank of an arm of the Nile. Amidst the foliage, a number of young birds in their nests, being

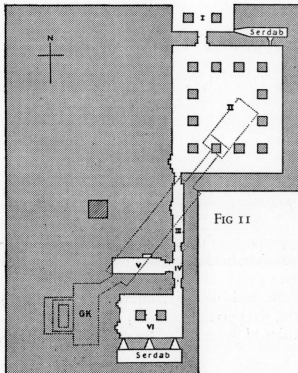

FIG II

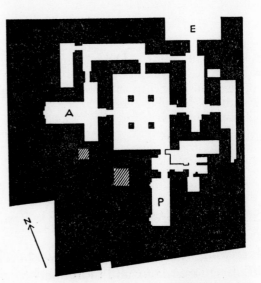

FIG. 12

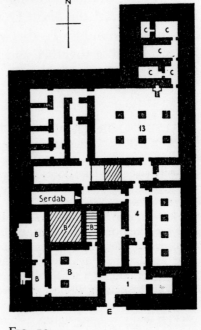

FIG. 13

FIGS. 11–13. Mastaba tombs of the Fifth and early Sixth Dynasties reduced on the same scale.—Fig. 11. Mastaba of Ti (width 110 feet, depth 143 feet). I: Entrance. II: Pillared hall; from this a subterranean passage leads to the burial chamber. VI: Sacrificial chamber containing the most celebrated reliefs (cf. Plates 68–71); adjoining it, the Serdâb, with the three peep-slits for the original three statues (cf. Plates 66 and 67).—Fig. 12. Mastaba of Ptahhotep (width 86 feet). Opening off the hall with its four pillars, to the south, is the sacrificial chamber of Ptahhotep (P); to the west, that of his son Akhethotep (A).—Fig. 13. Mastaba of Mereruka (width 68 feet). E: Entrance. In room 1, together with others, are the reliefs shown in Plates 76 and 77; in room 4, the relief showing Her-wadjet-khet (Plate 74); in the pillared hall, on the surfaces of the pillars, reliefs showing the figure of the deceased. On the north side is a sham door with a statue of the deceased. The rooms marked B are the portion of the tomb reserved for Mereruka's wife Her-wadjet-khet; those marked C, the portion reserved for his son Meriteti.

fed by their parents or protected against ichneumon or genets. Some of the birds are sitting on their eggs. In front of Ti's boat is another, the crew of which are harpooning hippopotami; a male hippopotamus turns round with open jaws, another is biting a crocodile. A young hippo is trying to climb on to its mother's back. In the small boat on the left, behind Ti's steersman with his pole, a man is angling for sheath-fish.

69. TI AND HIS WIFE NEFERHOTPES.
On the south wall. Ti, leaning on his long staff of office, and his wife Neferhotpes are watching game and cattle being brought in for sacrifice. The antelopes in the two upper rows are tethered to short stakes. The cattle are wearing ceremonial collars and their leads are attached to the under jaw. In front of Ti (on a level with his forearm) is a steward with an unrolled inventory scroll.

70–71. HERDS OF DONKEYS, RAMS AND CATTLE. Above: A herd of donkeys being driven over sheaves of wheat on the threshing-floor (eastern wall of the sacrificial chamber). Below: Top row: Rams being driven over the seed to tread it into the soil; behind the drovers, a man with a seed-bag. Bottom row: Cattle crossing a ford in the Nile valley. One of the naked drovers is carrying on his shoulders, to prevent it from drowning, a new-born calf, which is lowing and looking round at its mother who follows anxiously behind (north wall).

72. FROM THE TOMB OF PTAHHOTEP AT SAQQÂRA: PTAHHOTEP AT OFFERING TABLE. Limestone relief on the north wall of the sacrificial chamber. Painted. Lifesize. Ptahhotep is seated on a chair with lion's legs and stretches out his right hand towards the food on his table, while with his left he raises a ointment pot, on which

305

is written 'Finest festival oil', to his nose. In addition to the usual shoulder-collar and knee-length apron, he is wearing a leopard-skin, which is a symbol of one of his priestly offices. Under the chair an almost obliterated figure can be discerned. The obliteration of figures of relatives in consequence of quarrels is frequently found. Above the table, with its rows of peculiarly shaped objects, which might be loaves or cakes, an abundance of dead birds and other food-stuffs is depicted.

The close observation of nature is shown in the water-lilies on the right beneath the table, in which the two species native to Egypt are differentiated: the blue water-lily (*nymphaea coerulea*) with more slender calyx and bloom-fronds, and the Egyptian lotus (*nymphaea lotus*), in which these are broader. The latter species is not to be confused with the genuine lotus of India and Eastern Asia (*nelumbo nucifera*).

SIXTH DYNASTY (2423–2263): *Teti, Phiops (Pepi) I, Merenrê I, Phiops (Pepi) II, Merenrê II, Queen Nitokris (Neit-aqer).*
Increasing influence of local feudal families. Gradual disappearance of the superindividual coherence of life based on magic and more marked emergence of conscious individualism side by side with the idea of monarchy. Gradual splitting-up of the state organization.
The monarchs of the Sixth Dynasty, like those of the Fifth, built their pyramids on the edge of the desert near Memphis. To the west of the modern Saqqâra, the pyramids of Teti, Phiops I and II and Merenrê lie close together and not far away are the remains of pyramids of Seventh-Dynasty rulers, such as Ibi, etc.

73. FALSE DOOR FROM THE TOMB OF ATETI AT SAQQÂRA. Limestone, painted. Cairo, Museum, No. 239.
Unusually elaborate false doors with statues in the round of the deceased, are characteristics of private tombs during the Sixth Dynasty.
Ateti, known as Ankhires, is standing in the doorway leading to the kingdom of the dead, which, like the doors of real houses, is fitted with headpiece and round beams for rolling up the mats used to close doors. Above, in the niche, we see him on a relief tablet sitting at table, amidst hieroglyphs expressing wishes for his welfare. On either side of the false door he is shown in sunk relief wearing a wig of strands and a bulging apron, whereas the statue shows him with a wig of ringlets and ceremonial apron.

74–77. IN THE TOMB OF MERERUKA AT SAQ-QÂRA. Limestone reliefs with traces of painting.

74. HER-WADJET-KHET, WIFE OF MERERUKA.
East wall of Room 4. To the left of Her-wadjet-khet we see the leg and the lower part of the apron of the over-lifesize figure of her husband. She is wearing the simple dress of the period, supported by straps. On her shoulders is a broad collar. The head is surrounded by an ornamental fillet and round her left wrist she has an ornament consisting of hoops one above the other. She is enjoying the perfume of a blue water-lily.

75. PILLAR RELIEF OF MERERUKA. About lifesize; in the pillared hall forming the sacrificial chamber.
As a priest, Mereruka is wearing a leopard-skin, with apron and shoulder collar. In his right hand he is holding the long staff of rank, in his left the club-shaped sceptre.

76. A TRIP THROUGH THE PAPYRUS THICKET. Entrance hall, south wall. Standing in a light boat made of bundles of reeds, which is being propelled by four men, Mereruka seizes by the tail an ichneumon which is endeavouring to reach a nest of young kingfishers while their anxious parents flutter around. On the extreme left, another ichneumon (which in reality does not climb in this way) with its prey, a young bird. On the stems of the papyrus plants many kinds of birds are standing or sitting in nests. In the water are fish and hippopotami, one of the latter biting a crocodile.

77. HARPOONED HIPPOPOTAMI.
Entrance hall, north wall. Three hippopotami, to whose heads ropes are already attached, turn with open jaws towards the hunters approaching from either side in their boats and threatening them with other harpoons. From the mouths of the pachyderms project huge curved tusks, which as material for carvings were much-sought-after trophies. To the left the wall of papyrus stems in regular rows. In the centre, spawn-weeds, with frogs and locusts upon them, one of them erased.

78. KING PHIOPS I. Copper and other materials. Total height of the statue 70 inches. Cairo, Museum, No. 230.
From Hierakonpolis (Kôm-el-ahmar). The lifesize statue, like the smaller one of his son Merenrê found with it, is beaten out of copper plate; some of the parts have been cast. The pieces were riveted together and attached by copper nails to a wooden core. No other Old Kingdom metal statue hitherto found is as imposing as this. The crown is missing. The inlaid eyes give the face a fascinating vivacity, heightened even more by the incrustations of oxide.

79. URCHUU. Upper part of a limestone statue with traces of colouring. Height of the fragment about 14 inches. Cairo, Museum.

The surprisingly realistic and vivacious conception, which seems to rise above the hitherto prevailing convention, gives an idea of the tension and changes to which the Egyptian of the Sixth Dynasty—and perforce his sculpture as well—was exposed. Instead of the timeless dignity of expression found in the older works of sculpture, a novel class-consciousness becomes clearly evident.

After the all-too-long reign of Phiops II, who was succeeded by Merenrê and Queen Nitokris, the ever more rapid decay of long-revered institutions brought about a crisis, which led to a complete reversal of social relations and reduced Egyptian civilization to a primitive level. The collapse of state authority in the capital resulted in a social catastrophe, the extent of which becomes clear when we read the description of it given by Ipuwer in a work of the time.

In the midst of these upheavals, a Seventh Dynasty ruled in Memphis and an Eighth in Koptos or Abydos for several generations. The princes of Herakleopolis (Ahnâs), as the Ninth and Tenth Dynasties, carried on the tradition with ethical ideas of a new kind, and nurtured at their court a flourishing local culture, especially in literature, until, about 2040, they had to yield their place to the rising power of the princes of Thebes, who, with the Eleventh Dynasty, ushered in the Middle Kingdom.

THE MIDDLE KINGDOM

In the Nile Valley the traveller will seek in vain for well-preserved buildings from the Middle Kingdom period on their original sites. We know that there were plenty of them, for from the Delta to distant Upper Nubia traces of provincial capitals, temples and fortifications can be found, and like the rulers of the Old Kingdom, the mighty Pharaohs of the Twelfth Dynasty were buried in pyramids. But the condition of the pyramids at Dahshûr, Lisht, Hawâra and Illahun is typical of the fate which overtook the monuments of that memorable period, so important for the understanding of spiritual and historical development, not only in ancient Egypt. Built of bricks of modest dimensions, covered only on the outside with a facing of stone which nearly everywhere has crumbled away, they have been reduced to ruins and become shapeless mounds. The funerary temples belonging to them have been destroyed to such an extent that their sites are marked only by areas of ground strewn with debris.

We can measure the gravity of this loss when we read the descriptions of them written by those who visited them in ancient times or when we come across occasional fragments of buildings covered with beautiful bas-reliefs or decorative inscriptions. What the following rulers, foreign oppressors known as the Hyksos kings, did not destroy, was plundered by the later generations of the New Kingdom period, who in their fury to build and their ignorance looked upon existing structures as being no more than convenient stone-quarries. In the neighbourhood of Karnak, near the modern Luxor, which as the centre of the then flourishing cult of Amun contained many a royal monument dating from the Middle Kingdom, archaeologists have been able, after exhaustive labours, to reconstruct a little limestone chapel of Sesostris I, and other decorated portions of buildings, out of the stone structures into which at a later period they had been transformed. In the neighbouring temple zone of Medamud, French excavations have brought to light various architectural components decorated with beautiful reliefs, from a group of buildings of the reign of Sesostris III. At Medinet Maadi, on the South-west edge of the Fayûm, the desert sand has yielded up a much-damaged shrine of Ammenemes III, which was the focal point of a much later temple complex, while on the site of Iun, the ancient city of the sun (the modern Heliopolis, north-east of Cairo), a lofty obelisk erected to the glory of Sesostris I still stands—the oldest of the characteristic type that has hitherto been found. But all these are poor compensation for the loss of the great sanctuaries of that period at Tanis, Heliopolis, Krokodilopolis, Koptos, Thebes and elsewhere, and the extensive funerary temple of Ammenemes III—the famous 'labyrinth' described by classical travellers—in front of his pyramid at Hawâra.

At Der-el-Bahri near Thebes the funerary temple of Mentuhotep Nebhepetre, the most powerful member of the Eleventh Dynasty who succeeded in reuniting the kingdom after a long period of decline and thus inaugurated the second golden age of Egyptian civilization, is likewise no more today than a heap of debris that has been sorted out by archaeologists. The visitor has to consult the reconstruction drawings, if he wishes to obtain a clear idea of the imposing appearance of these structures, the earliest monuments of Middle Kingdom architecture.

We can form a better idea of the spatial conceptions of the period from the rock tombs of provincial princes. In the middle of Upper Egypt, and especially at Beni Hasan, El-Bershe, Mêr, Asyût and on the southern frontier near Assuân, half way up the cliffs running parallel to the river, we are impressed by the beauty and proportions of the façades and chambers hewn out of the rock. Unfortunately, of the slender columns and pillars which supported the roofs just as in free-standing buildings, very few have remained standing and undamaged, and the famous mural paintings, to which scholars owe much valuable information, are now very faded. The most recent of these structures, built by a community still under the patriarchal rule of a dynasty rising once again to power, are the graves of princes, grandiose in their architecture but unfortunately much destroyed, at Kau-el-Kebir, not far from El-Badâri to the south of the railway station at Abutîg. Sesostris III would appear to have put a drastic end to the reign of these 'nomarchs'.

The sculptural works of this period are scattered all over the world in famous museums, of which they are among the most treasured possessions—royal portraits of pure, severe design; heads of rulers full of lonely courage and disillusioned perception; sculptures revealing an understanding for the anatomical foundations of facial expression, hardly ever surpassed by earlier works and practically never by those of later periods of Egyptian art. From gigantic figures to tiny statuettes, every conceivable dimension is to be found, and almost invariably the artist's solution, whether it tends towards the typical or the individual, preserves its value even under the unfavourable conditions inevitable when such works are exhibited in the museums of large modern cities. The portraits of private individuals found in graves likewise surpass, with the simple grandiosity of their conception and their plastic treatment, the works of this kind produced in such surprising quantity during the following period of the New Empire. In the history of ancient oriental sculpture, no period has succeeded so well as the golden age of the Twelfth Dynasty in Egypt in the production of portraits which awaken the interest of mankind—an interest to which we of the present day feel ourselves intimately attracted, as if in them a part of our own problems had already been experienced and overcome.

ELEVENTH DYNASTY (2133–1992). A princely family from the neighbourhood of Thebes begins the reorganization of political affairs. After a struggle with the local princes of Herakleopolis, unification of various parts of the country is achieved, without at first eliminating the privileges of the feudal families.

The first rulers are Prince *Antef, Antef Sehertaui, Antef Wah-ankh*, and *Antef Nebtepnefer*. Starting from their provincial principality, they begin the work of 'unification of the kingdom'. This was completed by *Mentuhotep Nebhepetrê* (2060–2010), who changed his first names twice, so that for a long time it was believed that there were three monarchs named Mentuhotep. According to H. Stock, his three names can be explained by the fact that 'the reign of this monarch comprised various phases, from the inherited principality to his rule over reunited Egypt' (Otto). The final victory of this first Mentuhotep over Herakleopolis was achieved in 2040, so that the latter year really marks the beginning of the Middle Kingdom. With his successors *Mentuhotep Seankhkarê* and *Mentuhotep Nebtauirê* the Eleventh Dynasty comes to an end.

With the building of the funerary temple of Mentuhotep Nebhepetrê in the rock basin of Der-el-Bahri near Thebes a new era begins in architecture and the formative arts. This funerary temple, built close up against the rock wall behind it, is a combination of the rock tomb and the pyramid tomb. In its dimensions and the manner of its construction in stone, it is the only royal tomb of its kind.

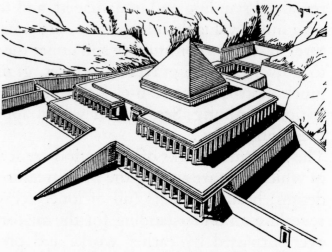

FIG. 14. Reconstruction of the funerary temple of Mentuhotep Nebhepetrê in the rock basin of Der-el-Bahri near Thebes. After *Koepf* 1955.

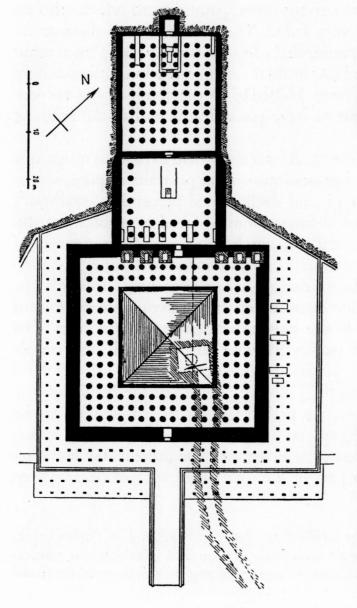

FIG. 15. Ground-plan of the funerary temple of Mentuhotep Nebhepetrê in the rock basin of Der-el-Bahri near Thebes.

This 'ground-plan' is really on three levels. On the south-east side, the lower level with its colonnade, intersected by the sloping ramp. Next, the level of the actual temple, with the colonnades surrounding it on three sides and, adjoining it to the north-west, the small pillared court and the hall hewn out of the rock, containing the holy of holies. The highest level corresponds to the pyramid (likewise shown on the 'ground-plan'). After *Naville* and *Hall* 1903–07.

The temple itself is built round a square base of stone. It was crowned by a comparatively small pyramid rising over 65 feet above base level. The whole plan was that of a rising pyramid. In front of the lower floor of the temple, which probably consisted only of rock, there was, on the south-east side, a colonnade. A sloping ramp led up to the next level, that of the actual temple. Colonnades like that on the lower level were built on the south-east, north-east and south-west sides of the temple. Its roof was supported by three rows (on the north-west side, only two) of octagonal, so-called protodoric columns. Six small chapels lay along the north-west side. Adjoining the temple was a smaller pillared hall, from which a shaft led to the burial chamber. The last room of all, with the holy of holies, was hewn out of the rock wall. Its roof is supported by eight rows of eleven columns each. A second burial chamber was built into the pyramid itself.

80–81. KING MENTUHOTEP. Sandstone, painted. Height 72 inches. Cairo, Museum, No. 287.
Found in a recess of the shaft known as Bab-el-hosân, forming part of the funerary temple of this king at Der-el-Bahri near Thebes. This undamaged massive seated figure was like a mummy wrapped in its bandages. The king, wearing the crown of Lower Egypt, is sitting enthroned in the attitude of Osiris, dressed in jubilee robes, on a plain cube-shaped seat with a high pedestal. The skin is olive-black, the robe whiteish, the crown dull red. On the same site other seated and standing statues of the king, coarser in their execution, were found. As the second consolidator of the kingdom, this monarch enjoyed considerable fame in the following periods and his tomb was the scene of one of the great Theban festivals, the 'beautiful festival of the desert valley'.

82. KING MENTUHOTEP SLAYING AN ENEMY. Limestone, with traces of colouring. Height 10½ inches; width of the whole relief, 20½ inches. Cairo, Museum.
From Gebelên, seventeen miles south of Thebes. The plate shows the right half of the relief. The king is shown slaying a Libyan chieftain in the traditional manner.—The fallen captive, held by his hair, has a feather symbolizing his nationality in his right hand. A fish is attached to the back of his girdle in the manner of a royal 'tail'. This could be interpreted in the sense that the activities of this mighty ruler and his great Twelfth-Dynasty successors were directed towards foreign conquests to a greater extent than was the case under the Old Kingdom.

83. Above: DETAIL FROM THE SARCOPHAGUS OF QUEEN KAWIT. Limestone with traces of colouring. Cairo, Museum, No. 623.
Below: SARCOPHAGUS OF QUEEN ASHAIT, shown in full length. Limestone with traces of colouring. Cairo, Museum, No. 6033.
Both these sarcophagi were found at Der-el-Bahri. In them, in wooden coffins, were buried Kawit and Ashait, the wives of King Mentuhotep. The reliefs decorating their sides are of a hard delicacy, somewhat coarsely expressive.
Above: *Queen Kawit*, seated on a chair, raises a drinking-cup to her mouth, holding a mirror in her left hand. A maid is tidying the ringlets of her hair, while in front of her a manservant is pouring liquid into a cup.
Below: *Queen Ashait* watching life on the royal estates.

TWELFTH DYNASTY (1991–1786): *Ammenemes I, Sesostris I (1971–1928), Ammenemes II, Sesostris II, Sesostris III (1878–1843), Ammenemes III (1842–1797), Ammenemes IV, Queen Sebekneferurê.*
Civilization flourishes anew under powerful, conscientious monarchs. Great activity in architecture under Sesostris I; re-attainment of full mastery in sculpture; notable achievements of craftsmen. The earnest ethical ideas of the time are reflected in the facial expression of the strikingly spiritualized statues of kings, as well as in the best private portraits. Warlike enterprises in Nubia and Western Asia, especially during the reign of Sesostris III. The court is transferred to the neighbourhood of the Central Egyptian oasis, the Fayûm. Royal pyramids are built between Memphis and the approaches to the Fayûm on the edge of the western desert plateau, e.g. those of Ammenemes II and Sesostris III at Dahshûr, of Ammenemes I and Sesostris I at Lisht, of Sesostris II and Ammenemes III at Illahun and Hawâra in the Fayûm area. At Heliopolis an obelisk of Sesostris I has been preserved, the oldest known example of this slender form of monument which afterwards became common.

84. UNKNOWN WOMAN. Wood and other materials. Height 3½ inches. Cairo, Museum, No. 4232.
Found at Lisht, near the pyramid of Sesostris I. The eyes were inlaid. The hair of the head, now incomplete, was carved from a type of wood different from that of the head and covered with a black paste in which little gold plates were stuck as ornaments. In execution and expression the face bears witness to a delicate artistic sensibility and in this respect may be compared with the beautiful, spiritualized portraits of women dating from the New Empire.

85. KING SESOSTRIS I. Limestone with traces of painting. Height 78½ inches. Cairo, Museum, No. 301.
Found together with nine very similar seated statues in a recess of the burial chamber in this king's pyramid at Lisht. The statue here reproduced is outstanding for the delicacy of its execution. The clenched right hand is holding a rolled-up cloth. The beard is delicately grooved. The raised eyebrows extending to the roots of the nose give the face a curiously tense expression.

86–87. RELIEFS ON THE THRONE OF TWO STATUES OF SESOSTRIS I FROM LISHT.
86. The falcon-headed Horus, and Set with his characteristic head of a long-eared animal, as national gods are tying a papyrus and lilies, the plant emblems of the two Egypts, round the hieroglyph meaning 'unite', on which the name of the king is shown between symbols of benediction.
87. The national gods (often called Nile gods), with robust limbs and pendant breasts, on their heads the plant symbols of Lower Egypt (papyrus) and Upper Egypt (lily), as representatives of Horus and Set and tying the respective plants round the hieroglyph meaning 'unit'. On the top of the latter the name of the king.

88–89. PRINCESS SENUI. Grey granite. Height 66 inches. Boston, Museum of Fine Arts.
From Kerma, in Nubia, where Senui's husband, Prince Hepdjefai of Siut, was governor during the reign of Sesostris I. This princess of an old and respected family is clad in a simple long robe and is holding a flower in her right hand. The high quality of the sculpture points to its having been carved in the court workshops in the capital, whence it must have been sent to the governor of this important southern outpost as a mark of special favour.

90–92. PILLARED TEMPLE OF KING SESOSTRIS I AT KARNAK. Limestone.
By utilizing the old, relief-covered limestone blocks which were subsequently used as filling in the pylon of King Amenophis III at Karnak, it was possible to reconstruct this processional temple. It was dedicated to the god Amun, identified with the ithyphallic god of fertility Min, and formed part of the sanctuary erected in honour of this god at Karnak. Flights of shallow steps on either side lead up to the interior, in which the sacred bark with the figure of the god was deposited. The disappearance of almost all Twelfth-Dynasty religious buildings makes this reconstruction, carried out by Henri Chevrier after careful research, all the more valuable.
92. Sesostris I Kheperkarê is conducted by Atum, the ancient god of the universe, who turns back towards the king to present him with life, into the presence of the ithyphallic chief god of ancient Thebes—Amen-Kamutef, the 'bull of his mother'. Above, as protecting divinities of Egypt, hover the vulture and the falcon, with symbols of life in their talons. The hieroglyphic inscriptions, beautifully carved in high relief, comprise, in addition to the description of the chief subject, the title and name of the king and prayers for his well-being.

93–98. PILLAR FROM A BUILDING OF SESOSTRIS I AT KARNAK. Total height 132 inches. Cairo, Museum.
This damaged pillar, of which two sides are here reproduced, comes from a temple erected on the occasion of a jubilee by Sesostris I in the sacred zone of Karnak. Fragments of its blocks were later utilized by Tuthmosis I to fill in the ground in one of his courts at Karnak. In quality of relief-work and beauty of execution these figured reliefs are on the same level as those in the king's pillared temple (Plates 90–92).

94. SESOSTRIS I AND THE GOD ATUM.

95 and 98. SESOSTRIS I AND THE GOD PTAH.
The features of the king and of the god are identical. Ptah, who was originally a Memphite god, but was also revered throughout the country, together with the local divinities, as the creator of all things and god of the arts, has the compact shape characteristic not only of him, but also of the gods Osiris, Min and Khôns. The king grasps his head and shares with him the breath of life. This silent, proud companionship of god and king, as expressed by Egyptian art, has a noteworthy dignity.

96 and 97. HIEROGLYPHS ON THE UPPER PART OF THE PILLAR.
In the rectangle beneath the falcon and the erect head and neck of the snake, the king's Horus name: 'Ankh-mesut' ('Life of births'), then, reading from top to bottom, other titles such as: 'Nesut bity' ('King of Upper and Lower Egypt'), 'Nefer Nuter' ('The good god'), 'Neb taui' ('Lord of the two lands'), and, placed as usual in a cartouche, his throne name 'Kheper-ka-rê', which means more or less: 'To create (Cheper=to become, to come into existence) is the essential force (Ka) of the sun god (Rê)'. Above, falcon and vulture hover as protecting divinities over the two countries. Other inscriptions express the hope that the ruler will be blessed with life (Ankh), endurance (Djed), good fortune (Uas) and health (Seneb), like the sun god for all eternity.

99. ROCK TOMB OF PRINCE SIRENPOWET I, SON OF SAT-KHENI, AT ASSUÂN.
The prince governed Elephantine during the reign of Sesostris I. The photograph shows the court and the façade of the tomb. On six columns supporting the roof of a hall, there were inscriptions and portraits of the occupant of the tomb. To the left of the door, on the back wall, a large figure of the deceased, followed by his servant carrying his sandals, and two dogs; next, cattle being led before the prince, who is spearing fish from a boat. On the right of the door, the deceased seen from behind, with his three sons behind him; above, women with flowers in a small pillared court.

100–101. IN THE TOMB OF PRINCE SIRENPOWET II, SON OF SATET-HOTEP, AT ASSUÂN.
The occupant of the tomb was a contemporary of King Ammenemes II. In the foreground of the tomb was an undecorated pillared court, in which, on the right, stood

the granite sacrificial altar. Further on there was a corridor with three niches on each side, in each of which, hewn out of the rock, was a statue of the deceased in the form of an Osiris mummy. At the end of the corridor, a small room with four columns and a niche, each of the back and side walls containing family portraits (in the middle, the deceased with his son; on the right, with his mother, Satethotep; on the left, with his son and wife).

100. Middle wall of the niche: Sirenpowet is sitting on a chair with lion's legs and stretches out his left hand towards the offerings which have been brought to him. Opposite him, his son with flowers. In the inscription, the name of the king enclosed within a cartouche.

102–104. KING SESOSTRIS III AT THE FEAST OF JUBILEE. Limestone with traces of colouring. Cairo, Museum.
From Medamûd near Karnak. Door-lintels from a building erected in the area of the temple of the god Monthu for a jubilee (Egyptian: Hebsed) festival. The king, clad in jubilee robes—wearing, on the right, the crown of Upper Egypt, on the left, that of Lower Egypt—is seated on his throne in a lightly-built chapel, while the symbols, with human arms, of the ancient capitals of Upper and Lower Egypt—on the left, Behdet (Damanhur); on the right, Nubt (Ombos)—offer him symbols signifying countless years of rule. From the bent arms of the symbols of the capitals hang hieroglyphic numerals the values of which increase according to their height, thus giving exaggerated expression to the wishes for the length of the monarch's reign. Below, on the left, the god Amun of Thebes; on the right, the falcon-headed god Monthu of Hermonthis, bringing wishes for 'all life and good fortune' to the newly enthroned king. Above, beneath the star-spangled sky, the disc of the sun, encircled with snakes, spreads its wings. Enframed in cartouches, the actual name of the king, Sesostris (=husband of the goddess Usret—'the strong'), and his throne name, Khakaurê ('Rising of the essential forces of the sun god').

105. KING SESOSTRIS III. Fragment of a head. Obsidian. Height 4 inches. Washington, National Gallery of Art (C. S. Gulbenkian collection).
Original location unknown. This deservedly famous head represents, I feel sure, Sesostris III and not, as is generally assumed, his son and successor Ammenemes III. The expression of the face cannot be adequately described. If the royal head-dress with the series of triple lines typical of the mature Twelfth Dynasty, did not prove that this is an Egyptian king, one might well believe that it was the head of a Renaissance Pope. In the sculptural mastery of the material, this little head of volcanic glass is also an outstanding masterpiece.

106. SPHINX OF KING SESOSTRIS III. Diorite. Height 17 inches, length 29 inches. New York, Metropolitan Museum of Art.
On the chest is the king's name. The lion's body is of the characteristic shape, but the face of the ruler is surprising in its highly individual effect as portraiture.

107. KING SESOSTRIS III. Dark-grey granite. Height of whole statue 66 inches. Cairo, Museum, No. 6049.
From Medamûd near Karnak. On the breast is an amulet, hanging from a necklace of pearls of various shapes. The arms and parts of the legs have been restored.

108–109. KING AMMENEMES III. Hard yellowish limestone. Height 63 inches. Cairo, Museum, No. 284.
This statue, which must certainly come from the funerary temple of this king, was found during the construction of a canal at Hawâra—the site of the 'labyrinth' mentioned by old writers and of the royal pyramids pertaining thereto—in the Fayûm. With its refined, quietly severe solemnity, this wonderful lifesize statue is one of the most important portraits of kings that ancient Egypt has bequeathed to us. On the breast, an amulet peculiar to this period hangs from a bead necklace. The size of the ears is noteworthy and probably due to deliberate artistic intention.

110. MANED SPHINX OF KING AMMENEMES III. Black granite. Length 72 inches. Cairo, Museum, No. 507 A.
From Tanis. This is the only one out of a total of four sphinxes of similar type found at the same place, of which the body is undamaged. The upper part of the head, the ears and parts of the face have been restored (cf. Plate 111 for properly restored ears). The strikingly large inscription on the high pedestal dates from the time of Ramesses II and gives his royal title and name. On the shoulder are traces of an obliterated king's name of the Hyksos period. The tense, concentrated strength of the body-lines is in conformity with the spirit of the time in which this sphinx was created.

111. MANED SPHINX OF KING AMMENEMES III. Greyish-black granite. Height of the Sphinx about 39 inches, length nearly 80 inches. Cairo, Museum, No. 507 B.
From Tanis. Of the four sphinxes found there this has the best-preserved features. In this special kind of sphinx, the face of the monarch is not, as is usual, enframed in the royal hood, but in the actual hair, formally stylized, of the lion's mane. Towards the end of the New Kingdom, a monarch had his title and name carved on the breast.

112–113. KA STATUE OF KING HOR IN ITS SHRINE. Wood. Cairo, Museum, No. 280.
From the tomb of this otherwise unknown king in the southern brick pyramid at Dahshûr. As the pair of arms on the top of the head shows, the statue represents the immortal essence (Ka) of the ruler incorporated in his body. The now naked body formerly wore a girdle and apron of a different material. The eyes are of quartz, alabaster and other substances and, as usual, are embedded in a bronze surround. The hands once clasped great sceptre staffs. The statue was found in the shrine shown in the reproduction.

313

The THIRTEENTH and FOURTEENTH DYNASTIES (1785–1680) comprised numerous monarchs, some of whom reigned only for brief periods. Among the more prominent, whose large and impressive statues have been preserved, we find the names of several rulers named *Sebekhotep*, and also *Mermeshau* (=general) and *Neferhotep*. The state was again involved in struggles between usurpers. Eventually Egypt was subjected to the rule of Asiatic intruders, whose princes, some of whom wielded considerable power, made the city of Avaris (later, under Ramesses, Tanis) in the eastern part of the Delta their capital. They are known as 'Hyksos', i.e. 'rulers of (foreign) Lands' in historical records. The 'Great Hyksos' (*Sewoserenrê Khian, Awoserrê Apophis, Nebkhepeshrê Apophis, Aasebrê* and *Aakenenrê Apophis*) form the FIFTEENTH DYNASTY (1730–1630) and the 'Lesser Hyksos' the SIXTEENTH DYNASTY (until about 1580). The native princes of Thebes at first ruled (together with princes of other Egyptian cities) as vassals of the foreign conquerors, and later as the independent monarchs of the SEVENTEENTH DYNASTY (1680(?)–1580).

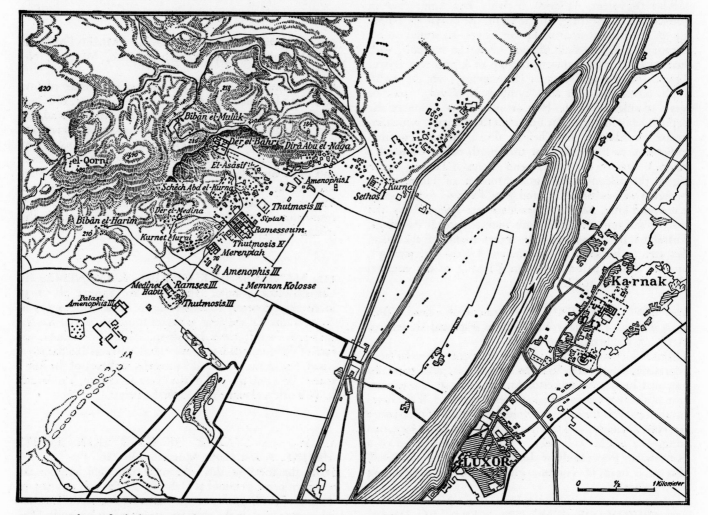

Fig. 16. Plan of Thebes. On the east bank of the Nile the modern towns of Luxor and Karnak; on the west bank, bordering on the cultivated zone, the Necropolis. For the sake of clarity, only the names of the monarchs are shown alongside their funerary temples; Bibân el-Harîm=Valley of the Queens' Tombs; Bibân el-Mulûk=Valley of the Kings' Tombs. Near the modern villages of Kurnet-Murai, Dêr el-Medîna, Shêkh Abd el-Kurna, El-Asasîf and Dirâ Abu'n-Naga lie the most important cemeteries of the Theban aristocracy.

Despite all the destruction of its ancient monuments, the landscape once dominated by Thebes of the hundred gates—its ancient Egyptian name was Weset—is nevertheless the real scene of the achievements of those generations who, after driving out the foreign rulers, extended the boundaries of the country and thus made Egypt a world power, and inaugurated a third golden age of their national civilization. Just as the Giza pyramid cemetery to us today represents the Old Kingdom, so does the world of monuments in and around Thebes conjure up before our eyes the New Kingdom: the age of enterprising, warlike kings, of the extension of Egyptian territory as far as the upper Euphrates, of the development in many directions of all the native creative forces. It was not until the Egyptians, by their conquests of Middle Eastern countries which had already reached the stage of a highly developed, conscious urban civilization, and the resulting need to enter world politics, had gained experience, that their talents came to full maturity and to the highest possible degree of realization. Nowhere in the Nile valley does the student of history see this so clearly as among the pillared halls, the temple courts and the cemeteries of Thebes, once a world-famous city full of pomp and glitter, whose ultimate fate the prophet Nahum predicted would also be that of the hated Assyrian city of Nineveh:

'Art thou better than populous No, that was situate among the rivers, that had the waters round about it, whose rampart was the sea, and her wall was from the sea? Ethiopia and Egypt were her strength, and it was infinite, Put and Lubim were thy helpers. Yet was she carried away, she went into captivity; her young children were dashed in pieces at the top of all the streets; and they cast lots for her honourable men, and all her great men were found in chains.'

As we wander through the immense ruins, we are reminded on every side not only of the conquest and sacking of Thebes by the cruel hordes of Assurbanipal, but also of later tribulations at the hands of Roman soldiers sent to suppress risings or of the fanatical followers of new faiths. Indeed, at times we cannot help thinking that the forces employed to achieve this mighty work of destruction were as great as those which contrived to erect this gigantic stone world, almost oppressive in its massiveness and power of effect, to the glory of their gods and kings.

From the early days of religious architecture under the New Kingdom, there has been preserved a small temple, restored in modern times, from the reign of Amenophis III, in the precincts of the Amun temple near the modern village of Karnak. The earliest large structure of the eighteenth dynasty is the terrace temple which Queen Hatshepsut, about 1490 B.C., had built by her gifted favourite Senenmut, in the Theban necropolis at the foot of the western cliffs of the rocky depression at Der-el-Bahri. This grandly

conceived structure, with its direct appeal to modern taste, and the sculptured ornamentation, fascinating in the play of its sparkling colours, produces upon the modern
beholder an impression of uplifting and gay harmony, such as is revealed only very
exceptionally by architectural monuments of the New Kingdom. In its musical charm
there is a regal feminine element, the fascination of which has not been dispelled by the
destructive efforts of the queen's bitter rival, Tuthmosis III.

This doughty conqueror and surprisingly able practical politician among the Pharaohs
of the New Kingdom left numerous monuments to his triumphs in the older part of the
Karnak temple area. The mighty transverse structure of his stone festival pavilion near
the old sanctuary bears witness to his military and diplomatic successes in Palestine and
Syria as eloquently as do the walls and columns of his halls of annals and the sweeping
contours showing the monarch slaying his arch-enemies on the walls of his two pylons.
A still greater tribute than the buildings commemorating victories or conquests are the
sober and factual descriptions of his campaigns carved on the stone walls of the
chambers.

The fruitful age of Amenophis III is commemorated not only by the colossal 'Memnon
statues' which are the only relics of his funerary temple, but also, and in a far more noble
manner, by that most solemn of all Theban temples which stands in the middle of
Luxor on the Nile promenade. The nobility of its lofty columns, the solemnity of its
broad second court and of the sacred chambers decorated with reliefs, leaves a lasting
impression on the mind and makes us regret even more the destruction of the funerary
temple and palace of this splendour-loving monarch, which once stood on the west side
of Thebes, close to the edge of the cultivated zone.

Where relics of that time are still found, they impress us with the dignity of their
conception and the skill of their execution. Though they may lack the energy and
freshness of early Tuthmosid works, they nevertheless reveal the assurance and self-
confidence of a proud and socially progressive community. Nowhere is this more
convincingly expressed than in the rock tombs of the great men of the time—for
example in the tombs of Khaemhet and Kheruef.

From the reign of Akhnaton the wanderer through the ruins of Thebes will find no
monumental relics. The remains of his sun sanctuary to the east of Karnak can barely
be traced amidst the sand; after the fall of the Aton rulers, King Haremhab used most
of the masonry for his own two pylons, which have partially collapsed, on the way
from the great Amun temple to the temple of the goddess Mut. Of the gigantic statues
of the heretic king, the best preserved have been removed from the ruined court of the
temple to the Museum of Antiquities in Cairo, where they can be seen together with
other interesting relics of the Amarna period.

With the exception of the terrace sanctuary at Der-el-Bahri, the festival temple of
Tuthmosis III and the Luxor temple, the most notable large buildings in Thebes date in
almost every case from the nineteenth and twentieth dynasties: Lovers of ancient Egypt
cannot help regretting that in particular the celebrated Ramesses II, in his zeal for

building, never lost an opportunity of imprinting his own ideas on older sacred buildings by building a court in front of them, or at least by covering them with his own inscriptions and statues. His exaggerated self-consciousness of his status as god-king frequently pushes into the background, in a most uncalled-for way, the more delicate and tranquil elements, even if it does not completely suppress them. Many of those who pay a flying visit to the so-called chief sights of the Nile Valley will carry home with them the wrong impression that in the achievements of the Ramesses epoch, with its squandering of material and labour, they have seen the most notable relics of the New Kingdom.

The will of the ruler—however popular the figure of the ruler may be—cannot put too great a strain on the national labour potential without paying the penalty. Nevertheless, however unsatisfactory the proportions of the various architectural components, however discordant the colossal statues of kings reduced to decorative elements empty of content, we must not let ourselves be blind to the grandiose effects produced by this exaggeration of will and achievement. The very obviousness of the presentation has a peculiar pathos. Whatever misgivings we may nourish in our hearts, it is a thrilling, unforgettable experience to penetrate into the forest of columns in the enormous hall of the Karnak basilica, to find ourselves face to face with the mighty pillar statues of the deified Pharaoh in the Ramesseum on the west bank, to feel, when we examine the walls of the well-preserved temple at Medinet Habu, in the building of which Ramesses III sought to rival his predecessor of the same name, whose influence was still strong, the reflexes of a historical period which has retained its greatness, or to find, preserved in the tomb of Sethos I, an abundance of coloured representations, in which the badly restored walls of the funerary temple near Kurna are lacking. The image of ancient Thebes would be incomplete without this extreme realization of all that was materially possible, under the sway of those strong-willed co-ordinators and consummators who are so often granted to great civilizations in the evening of their national history. But we must not take their world of monuments—still strikingly noble under Sethos I, but aiming rather at external effect and exaggerated demonstration of power under Ramesses II and III—as a yardstick for measuring the values of a national achievement which in reality underwent constant transformation over three thousand years.

The visitor who tires of temple halls, pillared corridors and gigantic statues, should betake himself alone to the tombs in the lonely cemeteries at the foot of the western hills. There, where the painter's brush so often replaced the sculptor's chisel, because the unsuitable nature of the limestone made sculptural relief impossible, he will find that which the great buildings could not offer him and that which alone makes the ancient world lovable—the charm and fascination of private existence, the intimacy of the family circle, festive social gatherings to the accompaniment of songs and the music of lutes, delicately limbed girls with antelope eyes and budding breasts beneath the folds of their semi-transparent robes, dancers, sowers, reapers, worshippers offering thanks to their god—expressed like a prayer with intimate and often very personal piety—and finally all that which, despite the contrast, is also a part of life—the funeral procession to the site of the 'eternal dwellings', the age-old lamentations and solemn rites of the mummy placed erect before the entrance to the tomb. And then the visitor should go to the lower end of the royal necropolis and let his eye rove over that site of which the history has at times been stranger than poetical fancy could imagine. He can enter the gates and corridors of that mysterious underworld in which the mightiest rulers of the New Kingdom were buried and finally, in one of the most modest of all these tombs once filled with treasures, gaze upon the peaceful image, glittering with gold, of the Pharaoh Tutankhamun, as he was just after he died—that magnificent outer coffin, which, the last treasure left in his tomb, still contains the mortal remains of the monarch who died so young.

Of the New Kingdom buildings and tombs scattered about in the Nile Valley between north of Thebes and the Sudan, some are rightly considered deserving of attention in view of their effectiveness or the unusual beauty of their artistic ornamentation. Two sanctuaries are particularly interesting: the temple erected by Sethos I on an ancient holy site at Abydos (the modern El-Baliana) and subsequently completed by Ramesses II, and the equally famous rock temple at Abu Simbel in Nubia, which Ramesses II's stone-masons carved out of the cliff fringing the valley near the bank of the Nile. The cycle of reliefs at Abydos, covering wall after wall with figures of which the original colouring has been partly preserved, is somewhat formal in character, with a coolness and objectivity which might almost be called academic, but one can never agree with those eminent critics who count them among the best created by old Egyptian sculptors of bas-reliefs. Similarly, though rough hands after herculean labour and the removal of whole sections of rocks carved the enthroned giants on the facade at Abu Simbel and the statues of kings nearly forty feet high, nevertheless all our reservations regarding this questionable attempt to rival the natural scenery of mountains disappear and are replaced not only by a feeling of historical amazement when we pass in front of these lonely giants and enter the lofty portal, dominated by the falcon-headed sun god in his niche. That which in other Nubian temples of Ramesses II, some of them likewise hewn out of the rock—Bêt el-Wali, Garf Husên, Es-Sebua and El-Derr—needs the support of the landscape and often disappoints because it is the work of provincial craftsmen, has here in the extreme south achieved a grandiose effectiveness, grandiose down to the sweep of the flowing contours of the reliefs.

EIGHTEENTH DYNASTY, First Phase, 1580–1450: *Ahmose (Iahmose)*; *Amenophis (Amenhotep) I* (1557–1530); *Tuthmosis I (1530–1520)*; *Tuthmosis II; Queen Hatshepsut (1511–1480)*; *Tuthmosis III (1504–1450)*.

Under the last Regents of the Theban Seventeenth Dynasty (*Sekenenrê Ta'a I and II, Kamose, Ahmose*) began the struggle for freedom which ended with the driving out and pursuit of the Hyksos and the re-establishment of the Kingdom of Egypt. From now on there was a powerful, warlike state with a standing army. Thebes became the capital and a world-famous city; Amun was fused with the sun god Rê and became the lord of heaven and of earth, the chief, 'imperial' divinity. Tuthmosis I conquered

Syria and Palestine, and Nubia as far as the Sudan. Under Queen Hatshepsut, aided by her chancellor Senenmut, there began an era of peaceful internal development, to the benefit of trade and the arts. With Tuthmosis III one of the most energetic and warlike kings of the New Kingdom ascended the throne. Suppression of rebellions on the part of leagues of cities in Palestine. Consolidation and thorough colonization of the Asiatic and Nubian provinces. A notable increase of wealth promoted a high standard of culture.

Of buildings of the early Eighteenth Dynasty, there have been preserved from the time of Amenophis I only the remains of his funerary temple at Thebes (near Dirâ Abu 'n-Naga) and the alabaster sanctuary at Karnak (Plates 115–117), while from the time of Tuthmosis I we have only the remains of his buildings in Karnak (Plate 118, pp. 343 ff.). A first great flowering of architecture and the formative arts began under Queen Hatshepsut, among whose buildings the terrace temple in Thebes (Der-el-Bahri) (Plates 119–125) takes first place. Under Tuthmosis III the artistic decoration of this temple was completed (though it is true that this was accompanied by the destruction of pictures and statues of Hatshepsut). We shall return to this king's buildings in Karnak (Plates 129, 136–139), when we discuss the temple zone in that city (pp. 343 ff.). Of particular interest in the history of architecture are the small, peripter-like temples of Tuthmosis III in Karnak and Medinet-Habu, as they anticipate to a certain extent the most usual form of the Greek temple.

114. ALABASTER SPHINX ON THE SITE OF THE PTAH TEMPLE AT MEMPHIS. Height 13 feet, length 26 feet.
Erected where it was discovered, in the palm-grove near the village of Mit-rahina; in 1953, it was provided with a new base. The work was long held to date from the time of Ramesses II, but stylistic features justify its attribution to the early Eighteenth Dynasty.

115–117. KARNAK. SANCTUARY FOR THE BARK OF AMUN, ERECTED BY AMENOPHIS I.
115. This alabaster chapel with its severe lines was re-erected by utilizing fragments which had been built into the third pylon and stands near the likewise re-erected bark sanctuary of Sesostris I (Plates 90–92), to the north of the great court of the temple of Amun.
116–117. Mural relief from the interior of the sanctuary of Amenophis I. The royal founder of the sanctuary is standing before the god Amun, who bestows everlasting life upon him with a sceptre. To the right, we see Amenophis again, here wearing (for the first time in works so far discovered) the so-called Blue Crown (Kheperesh, often incorrectly described as a 'war helmet'). The individual traits of the king's features are striking, especially the un-Egyptian, slightly hooked nose.
Amenophis I was deified together with his mother Ahmes-Nefertari and was much revered by the Egyptians. Later generations looked upon him as the protecting divinity of the Theban necropolis. After a feast in his honour, an Egyptian month was named 'the month of Amenophis'

(Phamenoth). In the laying out of his place of burial, Amenophis I was the first New Kingdom Pharaoh to separate the cult of the dead from the actual tomb, by erecting a (comparatively modest) funerary temple at the foot of the Theban mountain, at some distance from his rock tomb.

118. KARNAK. TEMPLE OF THE IMPERIAL GOD AMUN. FOURTH PYLON AND OBELISKS OF TUTHMOSIS I AND QUEEN HATSHEPSUT.
View towards the east from the ruined (third) Pylon of Amenophis III adjoining the great hall of pillars on the east. On the right, the obelisk of Tuthmosis I, which alone has remained standing of the two in Assuân granite that he placed in front of what was then the entrance to the temple. It is over 70 feet high, its base being 6 feet square. In the centre, the dedicatory inscription of Tuthmosis I; the lateral inscriptions were added by Ramesses IV and VI, the effect being spoiled by overcrowding of the surfaces. On the left, the remains of the (fourth) pylon erected by Tuthmosis I. Behind, the one obelisk still standing of the two erected by Queen Hatshepsut, 96 feet high, base 5 feet 4 inches square. It is adorned on each of its four sides with a vertical inscription containing figured representations in the upper part, showing Hatshepsut, Tuthmosis I and III sacrificing to the god Amun. The weight of the obelisk has been calculated to be 325 tons, whereas that of Tuthmosis I weighs only about 143 tons. The tips of the obelisks originally had caps of pale gold (electrum).—For the general layout of the temple in Karnak, see pp. 343 ff. and Figs. 30–31.

119–125. TEMPLE OF QUEEN HATSHEPSUT AT THEBES (DER-EL-BAHRI) (Figs. 17–18). The temple of Queen Hatshepsut was dedicated to the supreme god Amun, though parts of it were also dedicated to Hathor, Anubis and the sun god Rê-Harakhte. Last but not least, it also served for the funerary rites of the queen herself and her parents, Tuthmosis I and his second wife Ahmes.

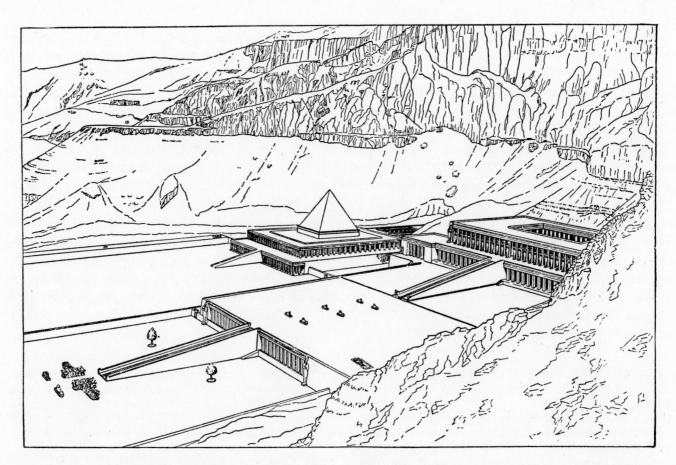

F<small>IG</small>. 17. Temple of Queen Hatshepsut at Thebes (Der-el-Bahri), from the north-east. In the background the funerary temple of Mentuhotep Nebhepetrê.—After G. *Steindorff* and *W. Wolf* 1936.

In his hatred for his rival of many years' standing to the royal throne, Tuthmosis III caused portraits of Hatshepsut to be obliterated or destroyed in this temple (and also in buildings erected by the queen at Karnak and elsewhere), but there were also political reasons for this act, namely the diametrically opposed attitudes of the two rulers. The twenty-two years of Hatshepsut's regency were a time of tranquil internal development and peaceful commercial missions, but at the same time it was during these two decades that the fruits of Tuthmosis I's successes abroad, which had done so much to strengthen Egypt's position as a future world power, were lost. Only after the death of Hatshepsut, was Tuthmosis III able to make good the damage and to recover what had been lost. A gifted and bold warrior, this king laid the foundations of Egypt's supremacy in seventeen campaigns, and this supremacy lasted until the days of Akhnaton.

The temple lies close up against the steep cliff of the western mountain, thus seeming to be halfway between the life of the city of Thebes in front of it and the mysterious world of death slumbering in the mountain behind. Approach to it from the cultivated zone was gained by an avenue of sphinxes leading to the gate of the temple courtyard planted with palm trees and vines (1 on the plan). From the court a ramp led up to the lower terrace (2 on the plan). In front of its supporting wall is a colonnade terminating the courtyard. An unfinished colonnade with chapels hewn out of the rock bounded its north-east side. This terrace ended in a colonnade in front of the supporting wall of the upper terrace (3 on the plan), access to which is provided by another ramp. The colonnade to the left of this ramp is dedicated to the representation of the expedition to the land of incense and myrrh, Punt (on the

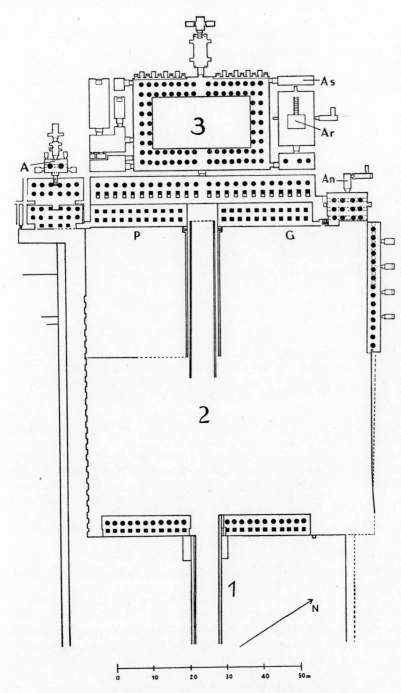

FIG. 18. Ground-plan of the temple of Queen Hatshepsut at Thebes (Der-el-Bahri). The 'ground-plan' actually comprises several levels. The lowest level is that of the temple courtyard (1). The next is that of the lower terrace (2), with the Punt colonnade (P) and the Hall of Birth (G), the Hathor sanctuary (A) and the Anubis chapel (An) with their vestibules. The topmost level is that of the upper terrace with the hall of pillars and the hall of Hatshepsut's statues lying before it, the holy of holies driven into the rock (in the centre), and the Hatshepsut funerary chapel in the west corner. As=the hall of Amun; Ar=the altar dedicated to the sun god Rê-Harakhte.—After *H. Ricke* 1950.

southern coast of the Gulf of Aden) (P on the plan), while the reliefs in the right-hand colonnade (G on the plan) have as their subject the divine birth of Queen Hatshepsut: how the god Amun, led by the god of wisdom, Thoth, approaches Queen Ahmes, who conceives the divine child; the confinement of the royal mother and the presentation by Hathor of the divine child to the supreme god Amun. On either side of the colonnades mentioned (G and P on the plan) lie those parts of the temple dedicated to Anubis and Hathor. To the north-west, adjoining the Hall of Birth, the chapel of Anubis hewn out of the rock (An on the plan), with a vestibule consisting of twelve sixteen-edged columns; to the south-west, adjoining the Punt colonnade, the sanctuary of Hathor, with two oblong rooms, some of the round columns in which have capitals in the form of the head of Hathor, and beyond these the chapel itself (A on the plan), consisting of three rooms with reliefs of exceptional beauty.

The upper terrace (3 on the plan) once had, above its supporting wall, a now almost completely destroyed colonnade, the ceiling of which was supported by an inner row of sixteen-edged columns and an outer row of colossal statues of Hatshepsut. A granite doorway led to the adjoining great hall, with two rows of columns round its centre. Along its north-west wall were alternately larger and smaller niches, the former once containing further statues of the queen. The holy of holies is driven deep into the rock. Adjoining the south-west corner of the great hall is the queen's funerary chapel, likewise driven into the rock, as are also its annexes. No better picture of the nobility of this temple can be given than that contained in the inscription on the relief showing Amun being led by Thoth to Ahmes, in the colonnade dedicated to the birth of Queen Hatshepsut:

321

Then came the glorious god
Amon himself, lord of the thrones of both lands,
when he had taken the form of her husband,
they found her resting in the beauty of her palace.

She awoke at the perfume of the god
and laughed in the face of his majesty.
Enflamed with love, he hastened toward her,
he had lost his heart to her.

She could behold him
in the shape of a god,
when he had come near to her.
She exulted at the sight of his beauty.

His love entered into all her limbs.
The palace was filled
with the sweet perfumes of the god,
all of them from the land of incense, Punt.

The majesty of this god
did to her all that he wished.
She gladdened him with her self
and kissed him.

119. THE TERRACE TEMPLE OF QUEEN HATSHEPSUT FROM THE EAST.
The temple, which has now once more been extensively restored, was dedicated to the imperial god Amun, but the goddess Hathor and Anubis, the god of embalming, also had their chapels therein. Other rooms were provided for the funerary rites of the queen and her parents, Tuthmosis I and Ahmes (Ahmose). The imposing group of buildings at the foot of the bare cliffs of the valley include part of the funerary temple of King Mentuhotep Nebhepetrê (visible on the left in the photograph).

120. TUTHMOSIS III AND THE GOD AMUN. Hall of Birth. Second row of columns, fourth column from the southern end.
The king is wearing the 'atef' crown adorned with horns and feathers, and a snake-entwined diadem fillet in his hair. His left arm is raised and with his right he holds the pear-shaped club, as he stands before the god Amun, who lays one hand on his shoulder. The figure of the god was obliterated by order of Akhnaton and superficially restored under Ramesses II.

121. PORCH OF THE ANUBIS CHAPEL AND HALL OF BIRTH.
View from the northern (unfinished) colonnade of the porch of the Anubis chapel, with its four rows each consisting of four sixteen-edged (protodoric) columns, and the Hall of Birth with its two rows of eleven columns each.

122. PAINTED MURAL RELIEF IN THE COLONNADE IN FRONT OF THE ANUBIS CHAPEL.
The vulture-goddess Mut, described in the inscription as mistress of the star-spangled heaven depicted above her, holds in her talons a signet-ring, the symbol of 'countless years'. Above, in a kind of puzzle of hieroglyphs, the name of Queen Hatshepsut; above the Ka-symbols a frieze of vipers standing erect, supporting on their heads the sun's

disc enframed by cows' horns. In front of the horns, alternately the symbol of 'endurance' and that of 'life'. The pictures beneath on this part of the wall were obliterated under Tuthmosis III by blows of the chisel.

123. THE QUEEN-MOTHER AHMES. Limestone, painted.
Hall of Birth, back wall. Queen Ahmes, wife of Tuthmosis I and mother of Queen Hatshepsut, is shown during her pregnancy. In the composition she is being led to her confinement by the ram-headed creator of mankind, Khnum, and the frog-headed goddess of birth, Heket. On the queen's head, the vulture hood, beneath which she wears her hair in long strands.

124. UPPER COURT WITH REMAINS OF THE HALL OF PILLARS.
The court lies right up against the wall of rock: its centre was once occupied by a great hall of pillars. Coptic monks, who in the early days of Christianity converted the temple into a monastery (Der-el-Bahri=northern monastery), inflicted considerable damage on the walls, which were once covered with reliefs depicting a festival procession. In the middle of the court, between the columns connected by parapets, the entrance to the holy of holies. In the north-west corner, on the right, the wall of the altar court with the door giving access to the hall of Amun. The western back wall of the court (running across the whole width of the photograph), contains a number of large and small niches with representations of Tuthmosis and Hatshepsut in the presence of divinities. In the larger niches, there were formerly statues of Queen Hatshepsut depicted as Osiris, of which only some of the lower parts have been preserved.

125. SANCTUARY OF HATHOR, MIDDLE CHAPEL: QUEEN HATSHEPSUT DRINKING FROM THE UDDER OF THE HATHOR COW.
The goddess Hathor in the shape of a cow was worshipped

as the protectress of the city of the dead, this being probably a survival of an ancient local form of cow-worship. In the ringlets of the queen's hair the protecting snake of the pharaonic office can be seen. Traces of colouring have been preserved.

126. SARCOPHAGUS OF QUEEN HATSHEPSUT: FRONT. Dark red quartzite. Cairo, Museum, No. 620.

From the queen's tomb in the Valley of the Kings' Tombs (Bibân-el-Mulûk) at Thebes. The sarcophagus has the same shape as that of her father Tuthmosis I, also in the Cairo museum. Enframed in inscriptions, Isis is kneeling on the hieroglyph 'nub' (='gold)') and lays her hand on that meaning 'ren' (='the ring of eternity').

127. QUEEN HATSHEPSUT. Limestone, Lifesize. New York, Metropolitan Museum of Art.

From Thebes (Der-el-Bahri). This seated statue has been reassembled from the body and throne, formerly in the State Museums in Berlin, and the partly damaged head found at Der-el-Bahri by American excavators. The head has been beautifully restored. The delicate rendering of the female form of the enthroned queen has a special charm.

128. KARNAK. TEMPLE OF THE GOD AMUN. TOP OF THE FALLEN OBELISK OF QUEEN HATSHEPSUT.

This fragment of the counterpart to the other obelisk still standing (Plate 118, left) now lies to the south of the pillared court of Tuthmosis I, near the northern edge of the sacred lake. The queen, with the Blue Crown on her head, kneels before the protecting god Amun. Above, beneath the star-spangled symbol of the heavens, the title and throne name of the monarch (Ma'atkarê='Just government of the world is the essential strength of the sun god'; the name Hatshepsut can be translated 'chief of noble women') and wishes for her welfare. The name ('Amen-Rê, lord of the heavens') and the figure of the god were obliterated under Akhnaton and restored at the beginning of the Nineteenth Dynasty; the obliterated portions can be clearly seen. This fragment of the obelisk can also be seen in Plate 216.

129. KARNAK. COURT AND FIRST HALL OF ANNALS OF TUTHMOSIS III IN THE TEMPLE OF AMUN.

View from the south-west part of the older court, also built by Tuthmosis III, towards the first hall of annals built within it. In the foreground, remains of two of the sixteen-edged papyrus-cluster columns, which formerly supported the ceiling of the court on the west and south sides. In the middle of the hall of annals stand two pillars of Assuân granite, on which the ceiling once rested. Both pillars are adorned with the plant emblems of Lower and Upper Egypt; the northern one with papyrus, the symbol for Lower Egypt, the southern with the 'lily', symbol of Upper Egypt.

Adjoining the first hall of annals to the south-east is the second hall of annals, with the chapel for the bark of Amun built in its centre. On the northern wall, in particular, of the second hall of annals, the long inscriptions have been very well preserved.

In these famous 'annals' of King Tuthmosis III, which 'represent a milestone in the history of Egyptian historiography' (E. Otto), the king's seventeen campaigns are commemorated, the first, the conquest of Megiddo, in considerable detail. Even though some of these campaigns were punitive expeditions rather than campaigns, they all had the same great aims—the Euphrates, the subjection of the hostile Mitanni kingdom and the quelling of the obstinate resistance on the Orontes of the prince of Kadesh, who was continually attacking Egypt with the help of coalitions of small Asiatic states. Kadesh was not finally subdued until the sixth campaign, and Mitanni not until the seventh.

In view of the prominence of the plant emblems of Egypt carved on the two pillars in the first hall of annals, a word concerning the so-called 'lily' symbolizing Upper Egypt is necessary. Obviously, from a geographical standpoint, one cannot talk of a lily in the strict botanical sense, i.e. a member of the genus lilium, which does not occur in Egyptian flora. A more correct description, also on account of the form of the smooth, knot-free stem, would be the opening bloom of one of the two water-lilies native to Egypt (*nymphaea coerulea* or *nymphaea lotus*), of whose four sepals, forming a cross, two, seen obliquely from the side, are used in the picture, with the bud of the as yet unopened bloom occupying the space between them. The name 'lily' is probably due to the fact that Anglo-Saxon Egyptologists were the first to mention this symbol and used the English term for Nymphaea (water-lily). If the two sepals depicted are shown curved less sharply towards the outside, this may be explained by the fact that the Egyptians after the time of King Zoser conceived the papyrus umbel as the curved line of a bell (Heinrich Schäfer) and that in depicting water-lily blooms on glazed composition cups, they tended more and more towards the shape of the papyrus bloom. In both cases, therefore, there is a tendency to depict a bell-shaped form, without regard to the natural shape, which was much stylized. It cannot be objected that water-lilies are native to both Upper and Lower Egypt, since, conversely, the same would be true of the papyrus, which is found from the northern coast of the African continent right down into the tropics, and is therefore not native to Lower Egypt alone.

130. QUEEN HATSHEPSUT. Detail from the top of the obelisk shown in Plate 128.

131. KING TUTHMOSIS III OFFERING SACRIFICES. White stone, resembling marble. Cairo, Museum, No. 428.

This little statue, only about 14 inches high, is of gentle, careful execution. It shows the king in the old traditional manner, kneeling and about to offer wine in two round bowls to some divinity. The rare stone must certainly have been considered a valuable material. The bridge of the nose seems to have been gone over again and made smoother.

132–133. KING TUTHMOSIS III. Hard, greyish-green slate. Height 6½ feet. Cairo, Museum, No. 400.

From Karnak. Among the numerous more or less well preserved statues of this great king, this standing portrait is noteworthy for the excellence of the carving and the portrait-like effect; it is a real triumphal monument. An obvious characteristic of the king is the short neck between the compact shoulders; the nose with its nobly bold sweep is very individual and the ear strikingly naturalistic. Tuthmosis III is here wearing the high conic crown of Upper Egypt. He is striding over nine bows carved on the base, the symbols of the nations subject to Egyptian rule.

134–135. KING TUTHMOSIS III. Hard greyish-green slate. Height 35 inches. Cairo, Museum, No. 404.
From Karnak. This little statue, showing the king in the pharaonic robes of the Old Kingdom, is also distinguished by the delicacy of its style and the masterly execution. In the clenched right hand, the stump of the 'staff of plenty' has been preserved, which is found in many forms in royal statues of the New Empire, though no convincing explanation of its real nature has ever been given. In front, on the buckle of the girdle, the king's throne name, Menkheper-rê (handed down by cuneiform inscriptions as 'Manakhpirija'), in the royal ring.

136. KARNAK. KING TUTHMOSIS III SMITING THE ASIATICS. Limestone relief on the south wall of the western tower of the seventh pylon.
The king, wearing the crown of Lower Egypt, seizes by the hair his conquered foes, who raise their hands begging for mercy, and makes a veritable bunch of them, strictly formal in its composition, while with his right hand he raises his club in the act of striking. Above, on the right,

the god Amun strides past. Below, in long rows, the names of the conquered foreign localities, each enclosed in a long oblong, out of which rises the upper body of an Asiatic captive of Semitic type, his arms bound behind his back.

137–139. CEREMONIAL TEMPLE OF KING TUTHMOSIS III.
143 feet wide and 52 feet long, this sandstone temple forms a transverse termination to the eastern portion of the temple complex at Karnak, opposite the site, now covered only with a few remains of buildings and rubble, of the religious edifices of the Middle Kingdom. Two rows each of twelve columns with capitals, which look like suspended bells and thus provide the only known example in large-scale architecture of the tent-pole form, support the roof of the middle nave, obviously conceived by the architect as a large ceremonial tent. The two lateral aisles were bordered on the outer side by low pillars corresponding to the columns. Together with the vanished outer walls, they supported, above a lower architrave, the pentagonal roof-stones, and on top of these are prolonged by upper columns. By this means the side-aisles are given the same height as the central nave. Light is admitted to them through window-like apertures between the upper columns. There must originally have been two other, lower aisles outside the existing two, covered by the above-mentioned pentagonal roof-stones and bounded by walls which today no longer exist. The position of the ceremonial temple within the complex of the temple of Amun can be seen in Figs. 30 and 31.

EIGHTEENTH DYNASTY, Second Phase, 1450–1372: *Amenophis II* (1450–ca. 1425); *Tuthmosis IV* (ca. 1425–1408); *Amenophis III* (1408–1372).
Progressive expansion of Egyptian power in conflicts with subject foreign peoples to the north and south; suppression of continual rebellions in the dominions; development of a genuine foreign policy. Increasing refinement of way of life and art forms as a result of the newly-acquired prosperity. Great achievements in architecture and sculpture, especially in the area of Thebes, but also at Memphis and elsewhere, as well as in Lower Nubia. Golden age of craftsmanship.
The architecture of the middle phase of the Eighteenth Dynasty culminates in the buildings erected by King Amenophis III. At Thebes, where the ruins of one of this king's palaces may still be seen, not far from the modern Medinet Habu, his great funerary temple was erected, further to the east. This was almost completely demolished during the reigns of late successors. Except for a few fragments, there remain today only the two colossal seated statues of the king which formerly flanked the entrance to the temple and as 'the Memnon colossi' were already famous in the days of classical antiquity (Plates 162, 163). On the east bank of the Nile, in the modern Luxor, the Amun-Mut-Khôns temple bears witness to the classical architecture of the reign of Amenophis III (Plates 158–161). In Karnak he built the now almost completely destroyed third pylon, which formed the western extremity of the buildings dating from the Tuthmoside period.

140. THEBES. IN THE TOMB (No. 100) OF REKHMIRE, Vizier under Tuthmosis III and Amenophis II. Long hall, right wall. Two portions of one of the numerous painted registers adorning the wall.

Festival scenes are depicted in both excerpts. Ladies kneeling in pairs, with water-lilies in their hands and heads anointed with myrrh, receive from their maids at the beginning of the festival perfumes, trinkets and other objects of value. Girl musicians inaugurate the festival by playing on harps, lutes and hand-drums, while others clap their hands.

141. THEBES. IN THE TOMB (No. 56) OF USER-HÊT, Secretary to King Amenophis II. Long hall, left wall. From a chariot drawn by two stallions, Userhêt is shooting arrows from his bow at the game of the semi-desert: gazelles, hyenas, hares etc. The vegetation of the country-side is schematically indicated by flowering shrubs. The reins are wound round the hunter's body, while quivers full of arrows hang at his back and on the body of the chariot. No inscriptions have been inserted between the perpendicular strokes beneath the picture.

Plates 140 and 141 show tomb paintings from the Theban necropolis. Later, in Plates 146, 147, 150, 151, 164 and 175, similar paintings will appear. A few words on the general arrangement of Theban rock tombs are therefore necessary.

The basic form of Theban rock tombs from the Eighteenth to the Twentieth Dynasty can be visualized from the following description. A forecourt, generally square-shaped, made by levelling the slope of the hill, was the place in which the first funeral rites were celebrated. From this a door led into a transverse oblong room, the vestibule or transverse hall. In its left wall there was normally a false door, on the right wall the tombstone of the deceased. Then came a more or less long and narrow hall, from which access was gained to the ritual chapel with seated statues of the deceased and his family. Beneath this chapel lay the burial chamber, access to which varied according to the design—in some cases it was a vertical shaft, in others a sloping corridor or steep stairs. The walls of the transverse and long halls were often decorated with paintings showing work in the fields or hunting scenes, to ensure supplies of food for the dead, and others depicting the joys and amusements of festive hours. The variety of these scenes is incomparable. That in some of these tombs limestone reliefs, originally coloured, were installed instead of the ordinary paintings on a stucco surface (Plates 152–153, 166–174), shows the care with which the tombs of important personages in Thebes were fitted out. In the rock cemeteries near the modern villages of Shêkh Abd el-Kurna, Dêr el-Medîna, El-Asâsif, Kurnet-Murai and Dirâ Abu'n-Naga, several hundred tombs of well-to-do private individuals and high officials can still be seen, Not all of these tombs have the arrangement given above, though this is the commonest and, one might say, the typical layout. In the tomb of the vizier Ramose (Fig. 20), the design is much more elaborate and extensive. One of the deviations from the normal type is, for example, the tomb (No. 85) of Amenemhab, an official at the court of Tuthmosis III, with a small pillared hall in place of the transverse oblong vestibule, while the adjoining 'long hall' has the form of a cross. Of a special type is also the tomb (No. 96 B) of Prince Sennufer, superintendent of the gardens of the temple of Amun under Amenophis II. In this case a steep stairway leads past the vestibules to two underground rooms, painted to resemble vineyards and with elaborate decoration on their walls, and thence to a transverse rectangular antechamber and an almost square pillared hall.

142–143. HATHOR AS GODDESS OF THE DEAD IN THE SHAPE OF A COW. Sandstone, painted, Length 88 inches. Cairo, Museum, No. 445.
From Thebes. The group was found in the small chapel, with barrel vault and coloured mural reliefs, in the cliff adjoining the temple at Dar-el-Bahri. As the chapel was built by Tuthmosis III, it might be thought that the group pertained to him, but in a cartouche on the papyrus cluster the damaged figure of a king in front of the cow is stated to be Amenophis II. Between the horns of the goddess-cow, above the sun's disc wreathed with serpents, rise two lofty, stylized feathers. In accordance with Egyptian relig-ious teaching, she emerges from a papyrus thicket, indi-cated by a few stems with alternately open and closed umbels, which lie close to her neck and head-dress. On the wall beneath the cow's body, we see the king kneeling to drink from her udder.

144. WOODEN COFFIN OF QUEEN MERIT-AMUN.
Over-lifesize. Height of the face up to the head-dress $13\frac{1}{2}$ inches. Cairo, Museum, No. 6150.
From the queen's tomb in Thebes (Der-el-Bahri). Merit-Amun was a daughter of Tuthmosis III and at the same time the wife of his son and successor Amenophis II. The huge outer coffin of cedarwood is a masterpiece of Theban craftsmanship. The facial expression, especially round the mouth, is of a striking delicacy. The inlaid eyes are of black

and white stone, the edges of the lids, the eyebrows and the cosmetic lines, of dark-blue glass. The depressions of the originally gilded hair are filled with a blue grit. On the upper part of the body on the lid of the coffin a feather pattern has been incised, to which is contrasted, on the lower part of the coffin, a delicate pattern quite differently stylized. The forearms are crossed on the breast; the clenched hands grasp a papyrus sceptre and amulets, signifying 'green' and 'fresh'.

145. KING AMENOPHIS II OFFERING SACRIFICES. Granite, Cairo, Museum, No. 448.

From Karnak. The kneeling ruler offering sacrifices to some divinity is, despite the excellence of the carving, essentially of more conventional conception than the known statues of his father Tuthmosis III, in which the features generally have a marked element of portraiture. The idealized type of a New Kingdom Pharaoh has here reached a new stage of development.

146. THEBES. IN THE TOMB (No. 69) OF MENNA, superintendent of agriculture and steward of the country estates under Amenophis II. Long hall, right wall.

On either side of a papyrus cluster, with a waterway leading up to it, Menna is shown with members of his family in reed boats. On the left, he is killing a bird with a kind of boomerang; on the right, he is spearing two fish. Below, the Nile, depicted by means of a zigzag pattern, teems with waterfowl, fish and water-lilies. In the boat on the left a naked girl bends down to pluck a water-lily. The faces of some of the figures were deliberately obliterated in ancient times.

147. THEBES. IN THE TOMB (No. 52) OF NAKHT, priest of Amun and court official under Amenophis II. Transverse hall, left end-wall.

Festival scenes in several pictorial registers.
Upper register: A blind harpist. Behind him, six ladies in festival attire with a maid. They hold water-lilies in their hands, and the second lady from the right is letting her neighbour smell a mandrake (love-apple).
Middle register: Three guests at the feast, also holding water-lilies. In front of them vases and bowls on trestles, a large jar of ointment, flowers and grapes, as in a still-life.
Lower register: On the right, three female musicians with a harp, a lute and a double-flute.
The lumps on the heads have hitherto generally been explained as being lumps of ointment which, as they melted, scented the hair, shoulder-collar and robe. But probably they are a more direct reference to the fact that the use of myrrh on this occasion was lavish. Cf., in this respect, the large bowl of myrrh in Plate 150.

148–149. KING TUTHMOSIS IV AND HIS MOTHER QUEEN TIO. Granite. Height 43 inches. Cairo, Museum, No. 503.

From Karnak. The fact that the king is wearing a ringlet wig adorned with cobras and holding a symbol of life in his hand, is unusual. He is embracing his mother with his left arm. She is wearing a vulture hood over hair falling in long strands.

150–151. THEBES. IN THE TOMB (No. 38) OF DJESER-KA-RE-SENEB, who served under Tuthmosis IV as 'counter of corn'. Transverse hall, right end-wall.

150. PREPARATIONS FOR A FESTIVAL.

A maid, with a fillet in her hair, wearing a necklace and an ornamental girdle, is arranging the hair of a lady who sits before her on a low chair with lion's legs. A second maid is bringing a necklet of blooms and water-lilies. Behind her, jugs covered with vine-leaves and a large bowl of ointment, on trestles.

151. THE DAUGHTERS OF THE DECEASED.

The foremost daughter, who is already married and 'mistress of a house', is offering a necklet to her father, while the other daughter holds a little bowl full of intoxicating liquor. In front of the daughters a vase of water-lilies on a stand; behind them, jugs on stands, covered with vine-leaves. Below, a woman playing the harp. The charm, distinction and freshness of social conditions at that time come to life in these vivacious figures.

152, 154–155. THEBES. IN THE TOMB OF KHERUEF, chamberlain of Queen Tiy, wife of King Amenophis III.

This tomb, discovered not very long ago, is, like that of Kha-em-hêt, decorated with mural reliefs of exceptional beauty. They confirm in a striking manner the long-held opinion as to the high degree of civilization existing at that period.

152. KING AMENOPHIS III AND QUEEN TIY.

The occasion is a jubilee festival and King Amenophis III is sitting on his throne, holding his crook-shaped sceptre and a fan, with the 'blue crown' on his head. The throne is a high bench in a flimsily built chapel, the roof of which is supported by small pillars with flower capitals. Behind him, with a folding queen's fan and a symbol of life in her hands, sits Queen Tiy, his chief wife, with a diadem and the high crown of a goddess on her head. Her throne is richly adorned with figures: on the arm-rest, Pharaoh in the shape of a lion is trampling on an enemy; between the lion's legs of the throne are the conquered arch-enemies of Egypt, an Asiatic and a Negro, combined with the hieroglyph meaning 'unite'. In comparison, the king's throne seems simple. The back consists of a Horus falcon embracing the ruler with its wings. On the roof is a frieze of cobras and rows of pendent grapes. The feet of the royal couple rest on box-like hassocks. Below, enframed in oblongs, are the names of conquered localities; out of each oblong rise the head and shoulders of a prisoner, with his hands tied behind his back. Here and there are traces of colouring.

154–155. PRINCESSES CARRYING SACRED VESSELS.

These slender, truly regal maidens, in their close-fitting, but at the same time flowing, robes, are daughters of King

Amenophis III; they are about to consecrate the scene of their father's jubilee by pouring water from sacrificial vessels. On their ringlets, from which a wide strand of hair hangs down at the side, they wear a curious, undecorative headdress. Between the four pairs and in front of the leading pair are other sacrificial jars on wooden stands.

153. THEBES. IN THE TOMB (No. 57) of KHA-EM-HÊT, who, as 'superintendent of the barns', was a high official under Amenophis III. Near the entrance.
Kha-em-hêt, with hands raised, is praying to the sun god. On his wide collar he wears a double gold chain with links shaped like lentils. Such chains are often found in tomb reliefs of the period, and, as representing gifts from the king to trustworthy officials and functionaries, they had a special significance.

156. AMENHOTEP THE WISE, SON OF HAPU, IN HIS YOUTH. Grey granite. Cairo, Museum, No. 459.
From Karnak. This sage, who was later revered as a god and had his own temple in the Theban necropolis, was one of the highest officials and superintendent of buildings under Amenophis III. He was allowed to erect portrait-statues of himself in the temple of Amun at Karnak. He is here shown writing, his head bent in thought.

157. AMENHOTEP THE WISE, SON OF HAPU, IN HIS LAST YEARS. Grey granite. Height 56 inches. Cairo, Museum, No. 461.
The work is based on a type of sage dating from the end of the Middle Kingdom, revived on this occasion for reasons which have not been explained. The features of this highly respected adviser to the king produce a striking effect of portraiture.

158-161. LUXOR. AMUN-MUT-KHÔNS TEMPLE.

The idea of this temple, dedicated to the imperial god Amun, his wife Mut and their son Khôns, the moon god, goes back to Amenophis III, under whose reign the most important portions were built.
In view of the fact that the north-eastern portion of the temple dates from a later period, we will begin by describing the parts erected by Amenophis III according to the original plan, which included the large 'second' court (C) and the building adjoining it to the south-west, the actual temple of Amun.
In the north-east part of the temple, there was first a hall of pillars (with side-rooms along its end-walls), which during the Early Christian period was converted into a church. Adjoining it, were two smaller halls, each with a ceiling borne by four columns (the back of these was later transformed into the sanctuary of Alexander the Great [S]). Then followed a fourth, transverse, oblong hall with two rows each of six columns, and lastly the holy of holies, its ceiling likewise borne by four columns. On either side of this middle line of pillared halls were chapels, the first of these on the east side being the 'hall of birth', with mural reliefs depicting the marriage of Queen Mutemwia and Amun and the birth of King Amenophis III. Cell-like rooms on the north-west and south-east flanks of the complex must have been used for storing ceremonial robes and vessels.
From the great court (C) a pronaos with four rows of eight columns led to the first hall of the temple. On the remaining three sides of the court were colonnades with two rows of pillars. According to the original plan, the court was to have been terminated at the north-east end by a pylon. Before this had been completed, the royal architect altered his plan and began to build an imposing pillared hall, of which only the seven pairs of central columns, 52 feet high with capitals in the form of open papyrus umbels, were completed (B). It is impossible to tell whether this projected hall of pillars was to have had columns all of the same height, or whether, by raising the height of the middle nave, it would have had the form of a basilica, like the later large pillared hall in Karnak.
The building of the temple was not resumed until the reigns of Kings Haremhab and Ramesses II. Under the latter the large 'first' court (A) and the pylon, the colossal statues and the obelisks were completed. To conform with the direction of the Nile, the axis of this court had to be at an angle of 7° East, as is the case with the axis of the small temple from the time of Tuthmosis III near the northern end of the court. Colonnades, each of two rows of pillars, surround all four sides of the court.
An avenue of ram-sphinxes led from the door of the pylon to the imperial sanctuary in Karnak, ending at the triumphal (tenth) pylon of Haremhab.

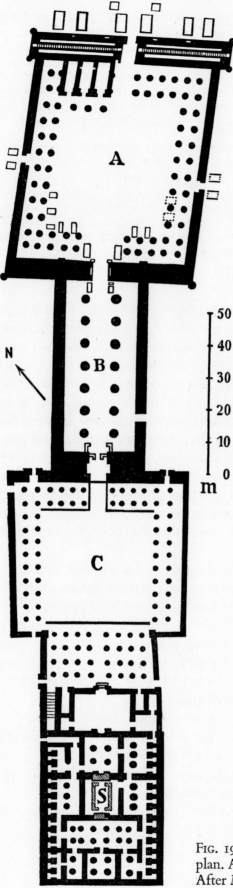

50
40
30
20
10
0
m

N

158. NORTHERN PART OF THE TEMPLE AREA.
In the background on the left, the pylon, consisting of two towers of stone blocks flanking the lofty gateway, their transverse walls enframed by astragals and terminating at the top in hollow fluting. Of the two obelisks which once stood before the gateway, only one remains and this can be seen in the picture; the other has, since 1836, adorned the Place de la Concorde in Paris. In front of the pylon towers were colossal royal statues.—Adjoining the pylon came the 'first' court built by Ramesses II with double rows of columns; then the large colonnade with seven pairs of 52-feet high columns, occupying the centre of the picture, with capitals in the form of open papyrus umbels. The abacus and architrave on top of each of these have been preserved. The walls, now to a large extent destroyed, of this pillared hall were decorated with reliefs by King Tutankhamun, showing the celebration of the great New Year festival in Thebes. His name in the inscriptions, however, was later replaced by that of Haremhab.

159. PORCH OF THE TEMPLE FROM THE WEST.
On the left of the picture, the last columns of the double colonnade on the north-west side of the second court; on the right, the porch of the temple. In both of these, the columns were in the form of papyrus clusters, the capitals consisting of clusters of papyrus umbels in bud form.

160. VIEW OF THE LARGE 'SECOND' COURT FROM THE NORTH.
On the left and extreme right of the picture, the colonnades of the south-east and north-west sides. At the end of the court, the pronaos or vestibule of the actual temple.

161. THE COLONNADE AND LARGE 'SECOND' COURT FROM THE EAST.
In the foreground on the right, part of the wall surrounding the first court.

162–163. THEBES, THE MEMNON COLOSSI.
The two colossi, which as now preserved are 63 feet high, against an original height (including the crowns which are no longer there) of 68 feet, represent Amenophis III. They formerly adorned the entrance to the king's funerary temple. This temple was almost completely demolished under the later Pharaohs and erected elsewhere in another form. Each colossus is hewn out of a single block of stone from the neighbourhood of Heliopolis. Amenophis III is sitting in each case on a cube-shaped throne. On the sides of the thrones, beneath the king's names and titles, are figures of the two national gods, with the plant emblems of Lower and Upper Egypt encircling the hieroglyph meaning 'unite'. On the northern colossus (on the right of the

FIG. 19. Luxor. Amun-Mut-Khôns Temple. Ground-plan. After *Daressy* in *B. Porter* and *R. L. B. Moss* 1929. After *N. de Garis Davies* 1941.

picture) on the king's left stands his mother, Mutemwia; on the right, his wife Tiy. A third figure, between the legs, has been destroyed. This northern colossus is the famous 'singing colossus' of the ancients, visited at the time of the Roman emperors by numerous travellers, among them the Emperor Hadrian and his wife Sabina. On certain days, shortly after sunrise, a sharp ringing noise could be heard. As a result of restoration in the reign of Emperor Septimius Severus, the colossus lost the ability to emit sounds.

According to legend, the singing sound was the lament of Memnon, the Ethiopian killed by Achilles during the Trojan war, who at sunrise greeted his mother Eos.

164–174. TOMB OF THE VIZIER RAMOSE AT THEBES.

The extensive tomb of Ramose, who was vizier and governor of the capital during the last years of the reign of Amenophis III and the first of that of Amenophis IV, later known as Akhnaton, was built at the beginning of the reign of the latter monarch, then still residing in Thebes. As a result of the removal of the court from Thebes to the newly founded city of Akhet-aton, the tomb was left unfinished.

In front of the tomb was a courtyard, the irregular shape of which is due to the presence of other, earlier tombs nearby. A short and narrow corridor leads from this courtyard to the principal hall, the roof of which is supported by four rows each of eight papyrus-cluster columns (now for the most part destroyed, but in part replaced by imitations). From the south-west corner of the main hall, a long underground corridor leads down to the burial chamber, at a depth of 55 feet, which consists of a vestibule and other rooms, never used. Adjoining the main hall and on the same level, is a smaller, long hall with eight papyrus-cluster columns, and after this a small room with niches. These last two rooms are undecorated, only the mural pictures and reliefs in the main hall having been completed.

The tomb was discovered by Villiers Stuart in 1879, and in 1904 it was partly restored by Sir Robert Mond and fully cleared between 1924 and 1927. It is of particular artistic interest because the decoration of its main hall is partly in the noble, refined style of the reign of Amenophis III, during the last years of which Ramose became vizier, and partly, in sharp contrast, in the completely different manner introduced under Amenophis IV, later known as Akhnaton.

On the south wall of the tomb, in two superimposed registers (Plates 164 and 165) are mural paintings depicting the funeral procession of the inmate of the tomb.

The east, or entrance, wall is covered with the celebrated reliefs, of which the most important are reproduced in Plates 166–174.

On either side of the entrance in this east wall, Ramose is shown offering sacrifices. On the left, he is making gifts to the gods in the presence of his wife and members of his household; on the right, he is making an offering to the sun and is followed by twelve youthful assistants, in three ranks; the three young men in the middle rank are noteworthy for the beauty and delicacy of execution.

The remainder of the north part of the entrance wall shows the use of consecrated oil and salves and the purification of Ramose (Plates 166 and 167), while the southern half, in addition to Ramose's offering to the sun, shows, in two rows, the 'festival in the house of bliss', built in the city of the dead. This is a sacred, ceremonial banquet, in which Ramose and his wife Merit-ptah take part, together with their nearest relatives. In these paintings, most of the personages seen in the upper row are repeated in the lower. Plates 168–173 show the left and middle portion of the lower row of reliefs, the two parts which have been best preserved.

Let us first consider the relief in Plate 168. On the left is Keshy, chief huntsman of Amun, with an unnamed personage behind him; then comes May, a cavalry officer, with his wife Werel behind him. May and the unidentified figure hold bunches of water-lilies in their hands. Next come the parents of Ramose (Plates 169, left, and 170), first his mother Apuya, 'the darling of the gods,' and then his father Neby, chief herdsman of Amun in the northern zone and superintendent of the granaries in the Delta. Separated from him by a pile of foodstuffs and water-lilies, we see Ramose's brother Amenhotep, one of the highest officials and chamberlain of the king's court in Memphis with his sceptre of rank, the double row of gold discs round his neck, i.e. the gold of praise, and behind him his wife May, first lady of the court and favourite of the queen. These two were the parents of Ramose's wife Merit-ptah (Ramose's brother was thus his father-in-law as well). At the right end of the lower row of reliefs is the less well preserved (and for this reason not reproduced) relief showing Ramose blessing the meal and his wife Merit-ptah. There follow Ramose's brother and his wife with their daughter Merit-ptah between them. The relief in the upper row is similar.

On the west wall are reliefs and preliminary sketches for reliefs, some of them in the style of Akhnaton and including interesting scenes in which Akhnaton and his wife Nefertiti present Ramose with gold medals, the gold of praise and other objects in gold, and also receive the homage of foreign ambassadors.

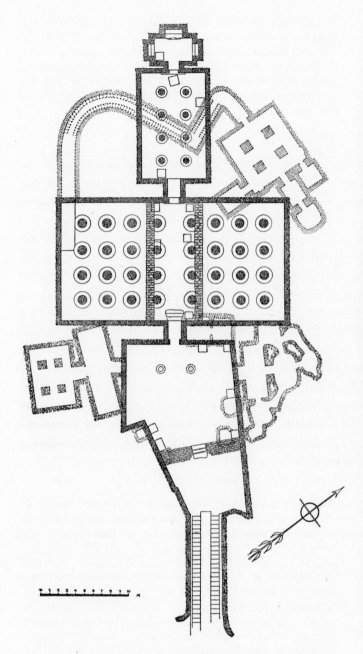

FIG. 20. Tomb of the Vizier Ramose at Thebes. Ground-plan of the main hall of the tomb.—After *N. de Garis Davies* 1941.

164–165. MURAL PAINTING ON THE SOUTH WALL: THE FUNERAL PROCESSION OF RAMOSE.

The lower half of Plate 164 shows, in two parts, the funeral procession occupying the whole breadth of the south wall of the main hall. The top part of the plate shows the rear portions of each of the two registers into which the procession is divided; the lower part of the plate shows only the lower register of the procession. The following description begins at the head of the processions and continues from right to left.

Of the two registers, the upper one with its larger figures is the less well preserved: bearers of offerings, men marching with ceremonial solemnity, draught oxen before a symbol which is being carried on a sledge, the funerary shrines with the symbols of Osiris and Isis, also drawn on sledges and with projecting parts of funerary barks, on which stand the goddesses of death, Isis and Nephthys, with priests and mourners behind them. Lower band: the rites at the moment when the mummy is placed erect at the entrance to the tomb, standing and crouching female mourners, bearers of offerings with papyrus stems, a group of standing women whose laments rise to the funerary shrine, men carrying tomb accessories, symbols of rank and jugs, and lastly a number of distinguished mourners in white robes reaching to below their knees.

166–167. FROM THE NORTH WING OF THE EASTERN ENTRANCE WALL: THE CEREMONIAL PURIFICATION OF RAMOSE.

Ramose, carrying the symbols of his rank and wearing the great chain of office with the heart symbol is being sprinkled with water by two servants, from the vessels prescribed for the ritual of purification.

168–173. RELIEFS SHOWING GUESTS AT THE FEAST.

In each of these figures type and personality are wonderfully balanced. The faces, cut as sharply as gems, filled with a latent sensuousness which is nevertheless in none of them lacking in spirituality, stand out against the incomparable wealth of the framework and ornamentation. In the sublime beauty of these noble couples the perfection of a civilization is proclaimed. The enchantingly expressive world which we have here before our eyes represents the achievement of a goal. Later, Akhnaton's artistic revolution took a completely different road. But those who have a feeling for art will always consider this achievement as one of the most perfect artistic realizations of humanity.

168. KESHY AND AN UNNAMED PERSONAGE, MAY AND HIS WIFE WEREL.

169. RAMOSE'S PARENTS AND HIS BROTHER WITH HIS WIFE MAY.

170. THE PARENTS OF RAMOSE, NEBY AND APUYA.

330

171. RAMOSE'S BROTHER AMENHOTEP WITH HIS WIFE MAY.

172. MAY, WIFE OF RAMOSE'S BROTHER.

173. RAMOSE'S BROTHER AMENHOTEP.

174. ONE OF THE YOUTHFUL ASSISTANTS OF RAMOSE AS HE OFFERS GIFTS TO THE SUN. The youth here reproduced and his two companions (who form the middle rank in the group of twelve youths) reveal an unusual beauty in the treatment of line and modelling. Robust virility is combined with all the charm and lovableness of youth.

EIGHTEENTH DYNASTY, Third Phase, 1372–1314: *Amenophis IV—Akhnaton*. From 1377 to 1372, Co-regent with his father Amenophis III; sole ruler from 1372 to 1358. *Tutankhamun* (1358–1349); *Ay* (1349–1345); *Haremhab* (1345–1314).

Affirmation of a spiritual and artistic trend, sporadic manifestations of which had occurred under Amenophis III, but which was uncompromisingly asserted by Amenophis IV—Akhnaton, who by the use of consequential theological methods, imposed a monotheistic religious doctrine, despite the resistance of the priests of Amun, whose power had grown to be a menace. Aton, the divine personification of the sun's disc, creator and preserver of life, is proclaimed the one and only god. Obliteration of figures and names of other gods, especially those of the family of Amun, closing of their temples, spoliation of their priests. Transfer of the capital to Central Egypt, to the newly-founded city of Akhet-Aton, near the modern el-Amarna. Almost total loss of Egyptian dominions in Hither Asia. Corruption and misrule prevail.

After the death of Akhnaton, his son-in-law Tutankhaton ascends the throne when still a mere boy. He recognizes once again the old imperial gods, one form of recognition being the changing of his name to Tutankhamun, and transfers the capital back to Thebes. On his death at the age of about eighteen, he was buried by the priest Ay, who later became king but ruled for only four years, in the tomb which Ay had prepared for himself. The tomb was disturbed soon after the burial, but the thieves were interrupted before they could complete the robbery. Since then the treasures remained undisturbed in this tomb until their recent discovery made them famous throughout the world.

The complete restoration of the old religion and temples, the definite disavowal of the heretic Akhnaton and his doctrine and the extinction of his capital Akhet-Aton took place under Haremhab, commander-in-chief of the army and governor of the realm, who became king after the death of Ay. During his reign a drastic reform and reorganization of the state administration was carried through. The recovery of Egypt's lost position in Asia began with this king, who in this respect inaugurated the foreign policy of the Nineteenth Dynasty.

Nothing has been preserved of the buildings erected by Akhnaton in his new capital at Akhet-Aton (near the modern el-Amarna). All we know of the plan of the great Aton temple and of the royal palace has been learned in the course of excavations and from reliefs in the tombs hewn out of the mountain close to the city. For the history of architecture the remains of the capital which have been excavated and reconstructed are of considerable importance.

175. THEBES. IN THE TOMB (No. 181) OF THE SCULPTORS NEBAMUN AND IPUKI, active during the reigns of Amenophis IV—Akhnaton and Tutankhamun. Transverse hall, left wall.

Above: FUNERAL CEREMONY AT THE ENTRANCE TO THE TOMB.
In front of the tomb, the upright, decorated mummy is being purified by priests who sprinkle water upon it and also perform the ritual of the 'opening of the mouth'. In front of the mummies, the heads and shoulders of which, in accordance with custom, are covered with portrait masks, while tall bunches of flowers stand before them, crouch mourning women, who stroke the bandaged feet of the deceased. The larger of the two figures has scratched her breast and is strewing earth over her head.

Below: MOURNERS AT THE FUNERARY SHRINE.
Women and menservants are bewailing their loss, by laying their hands gently on the funerary shrine, adorned with papyrus stems and standing on a wooden sledge, which men are waiting to draw to the tomb by means of the rope attached to it. From the shrine protrude the prow and

331

stern of a funerary bark, on which are small figures of Isis and Nephthys, the tutelary goddesses of the dead.

176–177. AMENOPHIS IV, LATER KNOWN AS AKHNATON.
Reddish-brown sandstone, with traces of colouring. Height of the completely preserved statue about 13 feet. Cairo, Museum, Nos. 6015, 6016.
From the pillared court of the Aton temple, which the king erected on the eastern edge of the Karnak area. The court was adorned with a number of these over-lifesize statues, of which the two reproduced are the best preserved. It is noteworthy that on these statues the name Amenophis was not altered after the completion of the reform and the change of the king's name to Akhnaton, nor was the forbidden word Amun obliterated, as was the case elsewhere. The style introduced by this ruler, which is at the same time fascinating and decadent in its effect, did not long retain this exaggeratedly pointed form.

176. Beneath the king's headdress, instead of the usual lappets, are two pendent bands of plaited ringlets. In his hands are the crook-shaped sceptre, held tight against his body, and the ceremonial flail. On the arms, on separate tablets, the names of the sun god Aton, enclosed in royal cartouches.

177. On his head the king wears the double crown on top of the purse-shaped hood with cobra. The sceptre and flail are crossed on his breast. The cut of the fashionable royal apron enframes and intentionally stresses the slightly bulging belly. On the arms and breast, on separate tablets, the names of the sun god Aton; on the girdle, below the navel, the titles and names of the king, who is here still called Amenophis.

178–179. QUEEN NEFERTITI. Brown quartzite, with traces of colouring. Height 13 inches. Cairo, Museum, No. 6206.
Found in 1933 in a house at Akhet-Aton, the modern el-Amarna, in the course of excavations carried out by the Egypt Exploration Society. The back of the head must certainly have been covered by a hood of another material. Marks of the point of the chisel can be detected all over this unfinished work and many of them have not been sufficiently eliminated. The eyebrows, edges of the lids and headband are indicated by black colour.—This is a fascinating addition to the known portraits of the queen, bearing witness to the high and lasting standard achieved by the leading sculptors in the court workshops at Akhet-Aton.

180. KING AKHNATON. Limestone. From a group 31 inches high. Paris, Louvre.
On the king's right was Queen Nefertiti, whose hand rests on his back. In his right hand the king is holding the crook-shaped sceptre and the flail. The almost feminine lines of the breast are characteristic of the new official style.

181. QUEEN NEFERTITI. Limestone, painted. Height about 20 inches. Berlin-Dahlem, formerly in the State Museums at Berlin, No. 21,300.
From the model-store of the sculptor Tuthmosis at Akhet-Aton. This bust, famous all over the world for its beauty, is merely a workshop model, though it is true that it is very carefully executed. The experimentally inlaid eye consists of a piece of rock-crystal on a flat paste of black wax. The cap over the crown is hardly ever found except in figures of Nefertiti.

182. KING TUTANKHAMUN. Grey granite. Almost lifesize. Cairo, Museum, No. 457.
From Karnak. The extremities of the nictitant muscles of the two collar-bones are plastically emphasized in accordance with the artistic tradition of Akhet-Aton. Some have claimed to deduce from the features that the king suffered from lung-disease. This assumption, which cannot be proved, has obviously been influenced by the fact that the king died at a very early age, and perhaps also by the results of the anatomical examination of his mummy, which showed that he was of very frail build.

THE TOMB OF KING TUTANKHAMUN AND ITS TREASURES

The tomb of King Tutankhamun was not originally intended to be at the place where the eighteen-year-old king, after reigning for nine years, was buried. During his lifetime the construction of a tomb for him was begun on the western edge of the Valley of the Kings' Tombs. After the premature death of the young monarch, the priest Ay, who succeeded him and had evidently already been granted the privilege of building a tomb for himself in the Valley of the Kings' Tombs, offered his tomb as a burial place for the dead king—that tomb which is now known to all the world as the tomb of Tutankhamun. For himself Ay later completed a tomb which had originally been intended for Tutankhamun.

Access to the little tomb of Tutankhamun, consisting only of a few rooms, is gained from the eastern side by a flight of steps ending in a corridor. This leads to a vestibule lying at right angles to it, adjoining which is the actual burial chamber. In addition there are other rooms, at the western end of the vestibule and at the eastern end of the burial chamber.

The burial chamber, barely 21 feet long and only 13 feet wide, contained wooden chests enclosed within each other and covered with gilded stucco, decorated with scenes from the underworld and funeral texts. The outermost chest was so large (21½ feet ×14 feet) that a space of only 20 inches was left between it and the wall of the burial-chamber. In the innermost of the four chests was the sarcophagus of yellowish crystalline sandstone with pink granite top. Its sides are covered with religious pictures and texts. At its corners four goddesses carved in relief protect the dead king with their wings. This sarcophagus contained three mummy-coffins shaped like the human body: an outer one of wood covered with stucco and richly gilded; a middle one, likewise of wood, with gold and glass inlays and a footplate of thin gold plate (Plate 186); and an innermost one of solid gold weighing about 250 pounds (Plates 184, 185). All three coffins rested on a wooden bier. In the innermost gold coffin lay the king, with a diadem round his brows, amulets, pectorals and a number of other valuable ornaments. The head of his mummy was covered by a mask of solid gold (Plate 183) and his body was clothed in his state robes.

The four chests, the inner and middle coffin, together with the gold mask and the other ornaments, are now in the Cairo museum, but the open sarcophagus and the outermost of the three coffins with the king's mummy are still in the original burial chamber in the Valley of the Kings' Tombs.

The celebrated treasure of Tutankhamun, which is now all together in the Cairo museum, was found partly in the above-mentioned vestibule and partly in the treasure-room. In the side-room were ceremonial vessels and oil and wine jars. At the originally walled-up entrance to the burial chamber stood, as watchers, two life-size statues of the king walking (of wood, covered with black lacquer and partly gilded), with the club in his right hand and the ruler's staff in his left.

183. GOLD MASK OF KING TUTANKHAMUN. Height 20 inches. Cairo, Museum (Tutankhamun Collection, No. 220).

This lifesize mask is a masterpiece of goldsmith's work from the Theban court. On the royal hood, the emblems of the twin kingdom: the head of the vulture goddess of El kab and the cobra of Buto. The stripes on the hood, as well as the eyebrows and the eyelids, are inlaid with lapislazuli-coloured glass. The eyes are of white calcite and very dark obsidian. A wide, richly decorated collar covers the chest and ends on the shoulders with two falcon heads. The chiselling of the beard holder shows that this was plaited. On the base on which the mask is mounted is a double chain of gold discs of various shades. It was found round the neck of the mask.

184–185. GOLD COFFIN OF KING TUTANKHAMUN. Height of whole coffin 73 inches. Cairo, Museum (Tutankhamun Collection, No. 249). (Photograph taken from mirror held above glass.)

This third and innermost of the three coffins, which are symbols of the king's consubstantiality with Osiris, contained the mummy with its gold mask (Plate 183) and the rich offerings. It is made of solid 22-carat gold 1 to 1⅛ of an inch thick. On the headcloth, as royal emblems of protection, are the head of the vulture goddess of El kab and the cobra of Buto. Both goddesses embrace with their wings the body of the monarch; the feathers consist of delicate inlay work adorned with cut semi-precious stones—cornelian, lapislazuli and turquoise. In his hands crossed on his breast the king carries the crook-shaped sceptre and the flail, the age-old insignia of priestly kingship. The eye-

brows, eyelids and beard-holder are inlaid with lapislazuli-coloured glass. On the front of the neck is a double chain of lentil-shaped discs of natural gold, crimson-tinted gold and blue glass. On the surface of the body a delicate feather-pattern is engraved, terminating at the bottom of the coffin with a line of characters along the edge. The collar and bracelets with their stone inlays complete the decoration of this, the richest of all the royal coffins that have come down to us.

186. FOOTPLATE OF THE MIDDLE COFFIN OF KING TUTANKHAMUN. Wood, gilded. Height 19 inches, total length of the coffin 78 inches. Cairo, Museum (Tutankhamun Collection, No. 222).

The middle of the three coffins reproducing the form of the king is carved out of wood, faced with stucco, gilded and adorned with elaborate glass inlays, imitating red jasper, lapislazuli and turquoise. The figure of the goddess Isis is engraved on the gold outer side of the footplate. She is kneeling on the hieroglyph meaning 'gold', a broad collar with pendants and lace, and stretches wide her winged arms in a gesture of protection. The text surrounding the goddess, continued below in transverse lines, promises the dead king protection against all his enemies.

187–189. GOLD-PLATED WOODEN COFFER FROM THE TOMB OF KING TUTANKHAMUN. Wood, gilded. Height 19 inches. Cairo, Museum (Tutankhamun Collection, No. 14).

This little wooden coffer in the form of a chapel stands on a sledge covered with silver. It has a door with two wings, which could be closed with ebony bolts. In the coffer there was a support on which a statuette must originally have stood. The gold-plate is engraved with delicate reliefs depicting with charming simplicity incidents from the daily life of the youthful royal couple.

190-191. THRONE OF KING TUTANKHAMUN. Cairo, Museum (Tutankhamun Collection, No. 1).

The wooden throne is covered with gold-leaf and with multi-coloured inlays of glazed composition, glass and stone. The legs are carved in the shape of lion's legs; on the front legs, at the top, are lions' heads of chased gold. The arm-rests consist of protecting goddesses in the form of winged serpents, wearing the double crown of the Egyptian kings on their heads and embracing the names of the king—and thus his person—with their wings. His name is here given as Tutankhaton, but on other parts of the throne the form used is Tutankhamun. Between the struts supporting the arm-rests are six cobras carved in wood, gilded and decorated with inlays, with crowns and sun-discs. Their heads are of violet glazed composition, the crowns of gold and silver, and the sun's discs of gilded wood. The space between the legs and the stays joining them was filled with delicate trellis-work symbolizing the union of Upper and Lower Egypt—the plant emblems of the two countries entwined about the hieroglyph for 'unite'. The golden plant emblems were torn off in ancient times by cemetery thieves and only the hieroglyphs for 'unite' remain.

The back depicts the hall of a palace with pillars in the form of bunches of vegetation, with a frieze of royal cobras at the top. The sun (Aton) casts down its life-giving rays, ending in hands. The king is sitting on an upholstered lion's-leg throne, and on his ringlet wig adorned with a diadem is the threefold 'cluster' crown entwined with serpents. Broad streamers hang from his neck and from the ornamental apron. In front of him stands the queen with a lofty crown of feathers and a long pleated robe (with coloured inlays in the bands of her scarf). Like the king, she is wearing a wide collar adorned with blooms. In her left hand she holds a small salve-cup with a stem and she lays her right hand on the collar of her husband, probably in order to spread perfume upon it. Behind the queen is a stand with floral decorations.—On the back of the throne a papyrus thicket with aquatic birds in relief is depicted.

192. BACK OF KING TUTANKHAMUN'S CEDAR-WOOD CHAIR. Cairo, Museum (Tutankhamun Collection, No. 3).

Like the throne in Plates 190-191, this beautifully carved chair has lion's legs and here too the gold-plated ornaments representing the plant emblems of Egypt were torn off by cemetery thieves. On the back, above, in chased gold plate, the winged sun. In the middle, the god of eternity, Heh, is kneeling on the golden collar symbolizing gold, holding the symbols for 'a hundred thousand years of reign' in either hand; on his head, the sun's disc, entwined as above, by two cobras, while on his right arm hangs the symbol for 'life'; to the right and left of his head, vertical lines of writing giving the king's throne name and birth name. On either side the royal god Horus with the double crown; below, within a framework, the name borne by

the king as Horus.—The inscriptions carved on the framework of the chairback contain numerous complimentary titles and names of the ruler.

193. LID OF A CHEST FROM THE TOMB OF KING TUTANKHAMUN. Cairo, Museum (Tutankhamun Collection, No. 1189).

The lid is curved like the roof of a chapel and fitted with a large knob, round which and round a second knob on the chest the cord closing it was once wound. The wood is inlaid with ivory, showing in the middle field, in delicate flat incision, Tutankhamun with his wife Queen Ankhesenamun in the garden of a palace. The king, looking little more than a boy, leans on a staff and raises his left hand. His girl wife stands before him, offering him bunches of papyrus and water-lilies, while other bunches are shown behind the two figures. The curious plaited coiffure of the queen has a conical top with two royal serpents and a cone (of myrrh?). The frieze beneath shows two kneeling maidservants gathering other flowers and mandrakes for the royal couple. A wide ornamental border surrounds the picture, terminating on the outside with coloured compartments separated from one another by four light-coloured strips.

194. LID OF A RECEPTACLE FOR THE INTESTINES OF KING SEMENKHKARÊ. Alabaster. Cairo, Museum.

From a tomb in the royal cemetery at Thebes, sometimes believed to have been that of Queen Tiy or of Akhnaton, since the latter's name occurs on the foundation-stone offerings. In the burial chamber a royal sepulture with the usual four jars for the separately buried intestines was found. As the names of the little more than twenty-year-old buried man have been completely obliterated, it is impossible to identify him with certainty, but he was most probably Akhnaton's son-in-law and co-regent Semenkhkarê, who must have died young. According to the custom of the time, the lids of the intestines holders consisted of portrait heads of the deceased, above wide collars, so that they produce the effect of portrait busts. The style is that of the mature art of Akhet-Aton. The wig is such as was usually worn by distinguished personages in those days; the space on the forehead, hollowed out to take a royal cobra, was probably made later. The eye, inlaid with some special material, has crumbled away; the eyebrow is filled with a coloured paste. Various traces of colouring.

195. LID OF A RECEPTACLE FOR THE INTESTINES OF KING TUTANKHAMUN. Alabaster, coloured. Cairo, Museum (Tutankhamun Collection, Nos. 437-440).

Four such lids have been preserved, which fitted into four holes in an alabaster receptacle for intestines; these contained the embalmed internal organs of the monarch enclosed in little coffins reproducing the form of the king. A comparison with the slightly older lid in Plate 194 reveals an over-refinement of style. The eyes, eyebrows, mouth, nose and nostrils are painted or outlined with colour, as are also the neck with its two small folds, the band on the forehead and the royal emblems—vulture's head and cobra. The bottom of the lid, which fitted into the jar, has been blackened by salve-oil.

196–197. PRIEST OFFERING SACRIFICE AND MUSICIANS. Limestone. Height 23 inches. Leiden, Rijksmuseum van Oudheden.
From the tomb of Pa-aten-em-heb near Saqqâra. During the first excavations at Amarna, the tomb of a man of the same name was discovered. As he was a military leader, it is possible that his tomb was transferred to Memphis at the same time as that of General Haremhab and that he is identical with the inmate of our tomb. As regards date, the tomb near Saqqâra from which this beautiful relief comes, belongs to the reign of Tutankhamun; the style of relief has an evident resemblance to that of the reliefs in Haremhab's tomb. On the left, the shaven priest wearing a panther skin is scattering water over the table and at the same time burning incense in the censer held in his left hand. Behind him kneel a blind harpist and an oboe-player. The finely modelled head of the harpist appears to be very individual, but in fact is typical of such representations of blind harpists. Above, hieroglyphs, flowingly and firmly carved, in vertical lines separated by strokes.

198–199. HAREMHAB. Grey granite. Height 46 inches. New York, Metropolitan Museum of Art.
From Memphis. This work dates from the time when Haremhab was still the highest state official under King Tutankhamun. He is shown as a scribe. His left hand grasps a papyrus scroll, on the unrolled part of which rests the right hand which held the rush pen. On the thigh near the left hand, the ink-shell. The writing on the scroll consists of a hymn of praise to the god Thoth. Over the left shoulder according to ancient custom were hung the writing materials; on the right forearm is a little picture of the god Amun, chiselled in sunk relief.

200–203. FROM THE TOMB OF HAREMHAB NEAR SAQQÂRA. The Memphis tomb of this powerful military leader and subsequent ruler was furnished with unusual artistic refinement, but unfortunately has been completely ruined owing to the plundering of its artistic treasures in recent times. We do not even know its exact location. Fragments of magnificent mural reliefs are distributed among the museums of Leiden, Vienna, Berlin, Bologna, Brooklyn, etc. It is possible that the granite statue of Haremhab with a papyrus scroll, in New York, also came from this tomb.

201, 203. GENERAL HAREMHAB DECORATED BY THE PHARAOH. Limestone with traces of colour. Height of the wall portion 35 inches. Leiden, Rijksmuseum van Oudheden.
From the tomb of Haremhab near Saqqâra. The important state functionary who afterwards became king, is joyfully raising his arms as he beholds the decoration bestowed upon him by King Tutankhamun. His head has been anointed with myrrh; his shoulders are overladen with gold chains of honour. The royal uraeus was added later on his forehead. He is surrounded by jubilant followers; three bowing servants offer him other donations. In the centre, towards the left, two soldiers are doing homage; above, bowing court officials with flails as symbols of their office.

200B. PARADE OF PRISONERS OF WAR. Limestone with traces of colour. Height 31 inches. Leiden, Rijksmuseum van Oudheden.
From the tomb of Haremhab near Saqqâra; continuation to the left of the scene reproduced on Plate 201.
Egyptian guards, of whom the foremost kneels in homage, lead up pairs of prisoners belonging to various Asiatic peoples, each pair bound with ropes. The prisoners are handcuffed; the Semites wear long robes and head bands, and have beards. In the top row can be seen the lower portions of the bodies of Egyptian officials and the legs of numerous horses in agitated movement.

200A, 202. PARADE OF PRISONERS OF WAR. Limestone with traces of colour. Height 31 inches. Leiden, Rijksmuseum van Oudheden.
From the tomb of Haremhab near Saqqâra, continuation to the left of the scene reproduced on Plate 200B.
Groups each consisting of two Egyptian guards and two handcuffed Asiatic prisoners. The nationality of the various foreigners is cleverly characterized in their faces. On the left is a woman, with two children in a cloth slung over her back.

204. THE GOD KHÔNS. Grey granite. Height 102 inches. Cairo, Museum, No. 462.
From the Khôns temple in Karnak. This beautiful figure, which must certainly have been dedicated by King Tutankhamun and shows his boyish features, has been reassembled from fragments. The arms, the lower parts of the thighs, the forepart of the left foot and the pedestal have been partly restored. As the son of Amun and Mut, the youthful god—probably at one time a local divinity known as the 'Wanderer'—is holding, after the manner of kings, a flail and a crook-shaped staff and, in addition, in his right hand a sceptre, made up out of the symbols for life, endurance and welfare. A large lock of plaited hair, ending in a curl, falls from behind the right ear to the shoulder. The roll-shaped chain characteristic of this god hangs over the wide collar on the breast. Here the chisel of a great master, after the collapse of Akhnaton's doctrines, has produced a figure of one of the old Theban gods in the spirit of mature Amarna art.

205. THE GODDESS MUT. Limestone. The part preserved is over lifesize. Cairo, Museum, No. 456.
From Karnak. As wife of the king of the gods, Amun, the goddess wears on her head on top of the vulture hood the high double crown. The work is one of a colossal group of four probably dating from the reign of King Haremhab. Perhaps the features of this maternally smiling face were inspired by those of Queen Mut-nodjmet, Haremhab's wife. The vivacity which the artist has obviously striven to achieve, and in fact has achieved, by means of the broad mouth with its extremities rising in a smile and the corresponding modelling of the cheeks, is rarely found in Egyptian sculpture in the round. The masses of hair beside both ears and other portions of this fragment are due to modern restoration.

206. MAIA AND MERIT. Limestone. Height 60 inches. Leiden, Rijksmuseum van Oudheden.

The court official Maia and his wife Merit, who served the god Amun as a singer, are seated side by side on a bench with lion's legs, which has been only partially finished. Merit embraces her husband with her left arm and he holds in his left hand a folded napkin. A water-lily bloom has been incised on the woman's headband and hangs down over her forehead. The nobly conceived group gives a good idea of the high standard of social culture during the mature Empire period. The coiffure and the style of dress came gradually into fashion during the reign of Amenophis III and remained unaltered, except for a few variations, until the end of the New Empire. The single figures of this couple reproduced in the following plates formed part of the same tomb furnishings. Probably from the cemetery near Saqqâra.

207. MAIA. Limestone, Height 75 inches. Leiden, Rijksmuseum van Oudheden.

Maia is seated on a chair with lion's legs, holding a napkin in his clenched left hand; on his head he is wearing the delicately curled man's wig fashionable at that time. Cf. the description of the group in the preceding plate.

208-209. MERIT. Limestone. Height of complete seated statue 63 inches. Leiden, Rijksmuseum van Oudheden.

Seated on a chair with lion's legs, the outlines of which are in part only roughly blocked out, in ceremonial, highly fashionable attire and wearing an exaggeratedly long ornamental wig, Merit, as a temple singer, is holding before her breast a symbol of the cult of the goddess Hathor (Menit)

with the rolled chain pertaining thereto. The strands of the wig have been left unexecuted at the top.

210. THE VALLEY OF THE QUEENS' TOMBS (BIBÂN-EL-HARIM) ON THE SOUTHERN EDGE OF THE THEBAN NECROPOLIS.

At the bottom, in the centre, the (modern) entrance to the tomb of King Ramesses II's chief wife, Queen Nefertari-mi-en-Mut (cf. Plates 246 and 247). The path on the left leads to other Nineteenth- and Twentieth-Dynasty tombs of queens and princes.

211. VALLEY OF THE KINGS' TOMBS NEAR THEBES.

'Bibân el-Mulûk', the gateways of the kings, is the modern Egyptian name for this valley with its grandiose scenery, in the Western Mountains near Thebes. Dominated by the natural rock pyramid of the summit of El-Qorn ('The Horn'), with its stern precipices and masses of boulders, the valley lies beneath the hot rays of the sun. In tombs, some of them very extensive, driven over 650 feet into the heart of the mountain and to depths of almost 325 feet, lie the Pharaohs of the Eighteenth, Nineteenth and Twentieth Dynasties. In the picture, on either side of the cleared floor of the valley, the entrances to several tombs can be seen: on the extreme left, that of the tomb of King Sethos I, the finest of all those in the royal cemetery; on the extreme right, the gateway to the tomb of King Ramesses VI, in front of which is the tomb of Tutankhamun. In ancient days, the Greek geographer Strabo described forty of the tombs here as 'worth visiting'. Now over sixty are known, but only seventeen of them are open to visitors.

Chronologically, the series of tombs at Bibân el-Mulûk begins with that of King Tuthmosis I and extends to the end of the Twentieth Dynasty. The great majority of the buried personages are kings, but among them we find the tomb of Queen Tiy, wife of Amenophis III and mother of Akhnaton. Occasionally officials of high rank were also allowed to build tombs for themselves in this valley. The extreme western arm of the valley is called Gabbanêt el-Kurûd, and here, among others, are the tombs of King Amenophis III and King Ay.

In contrast to the pyramid tombs in which kings were usually buried down to the beginning of the New Kingdom, the royal tombs of Bibân el-Mulûk are corridors hewn in the rock. They were intended only for the sarcophagus and the offerings. For the funerary ceremonies in memory of the kings, temples were built in the Theban plain, on the boundary line between the cultivated zone and the desert mountains.

The construction of royal tombs varies considerably in details, but as regards the whole, certain rules can be observed. From the entrance, three corridors normally lead one after the other to the lower level. Small rooms are sometimes found leading off these corridors, or niches for the articles needed by the deceased. Often in the middle of the corridors we find deep shafts, the primary purpose of which was to prevent the entry of tomb thieves, but which also served to catch water that had seeped down. In the simplest kind of tomb, there is then a vestibule leading to the principal chamber. In more elaborate tombs, however, there are often several such vestibules before we reach the principal chamber, the roof of which is generally borne by pillars. In this chamber, generally in a slight depression in the floor, lies the royal sarcophagus. The principal chamber, too, often has small rooms leading off it.

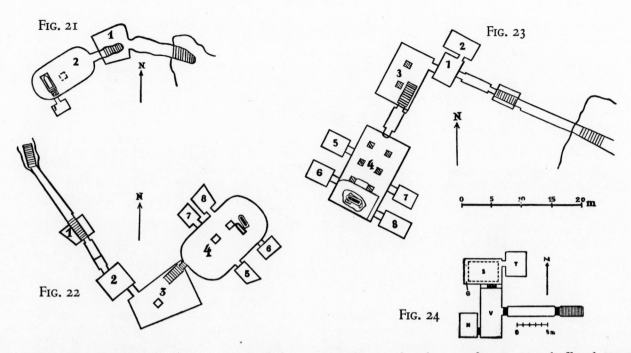

FIG. 21. Tomb of King Tuthmosis I.—1. Vestibule. 2. Sarcophagus chamber.—After *G. Steindorff* and *W. Wolf* 1936.—FIG. 22. Tomb of King Tuthmosis III. The entrance to this tomb lies very high up in a steep ravine. Access is gained by a steeply sloping corridor, a flight of steps and a shaft about 16 feet deep. 3. Vestibule, with a list of 741 divinities and demons. 4. Sarcophagus chamber with two pillars. 5–8. Side-rooms.—After *Rovet*.—FIG. 23. Tomb of King Amenophis II. Steep stairs and corridors leading to a great depth. 1. Shaft, at the bottom of which is a chamber (2). 3. Vestibule. 4. Burial chamber with deep-lying 'crypt', in which is the sarcophagus. 5–8. Side-rooms.—After *G. Steindorff* and *W. Wolf* 1936.—FIG. 24. Tomb of King Tutankhamun. Fig 24 is drawn to the same scale as the other tombs shown, in order to emphasize its smallness.

Figs. 21–27, all drawn to the same scale, show how the dimensions of the tombs may vary. By far the longest tomb is that of Queen Hatshepsut, with a total length of 693 feet and corridors leading down to a depth of 315 feet. The shape of the room containing the sarcophagus is in many cases a transverse oblong. In many tombs, however, e.g. in those of Tuthmosis I (Fig. 21) and Tuthmosis III (Fig. 22), the transverse section reminds us of the shape of royal cartouches. Noteworthy in older tombs is the change of direction of the axis, as exemplified in Figs. 21–23 of the tombs of Tuthmosis I, Tuthmosis III and Amenophis II. The tomb of Amenophis III and the unfinished tomb of Tuthmosis IV even show in their general design a double change of direction, the first shaped like an S and the second turning off at the same angle. The greater part of the length of the above-mentioned tomb of Queen Hatshepsut is occupied by corridors twice interrupted by flights of steps. These run more or less in the shape of a half-oval terminating at the further end in the vestibule. From this another flight of steps leads to the burial chamber, the roof of which is supported by three pillars and from which three smaller rooms lead off. From the end of the Eighteenth Dynasty it became customary for the axis to run in one straight line from the entrance to the burial chamber, as can be seen in Figs. 25–27 in the plans of the tombs of Sethos I, Merenptah and Ramesses III.

According to the ancient Egyptian idea, during the night the dead king travelled through the underworld in a boat together with the sun god. The walls of the burial chambers were accordingly decorated with pictures and texts intended to describe this voyage and to help the king on his way. These pictures and texts in the tombs are based on works of the ecclesiastical literature dealing with the world to come.

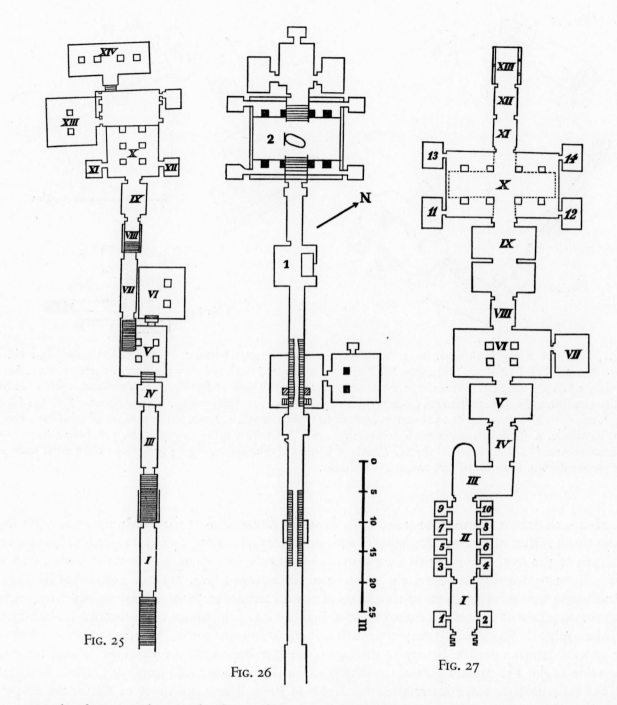

FIG. 25

FIG. 26

FIG. 27

FIG. 25. Tomb of King Sethos I. The finest of the kings' tombs with important reliefs and paintings. I–III: Corridors and flights of steps. On the walls of II: Isis (Plate 213) and Nephthys. IV–VI: Vestibules. In VI, preliminary sketches for reliefs drawn on stucco (Plate 214). VII and VIII: Corridors. In VIII, representation of the ceremony of 'opening the mouth'. IX: Vestibule. Reliefs showing Sethos before the gods of the dead. X: Sarcophagus chamber. On the pillars, pictures of the kingdom of the dead; at the back formerly stood the alabaster sarcophagus now in the Soane Museum in London. XI and XII: Side-rooms. XIII: Sacrificial chamber. XIV: Unfinished room.—After *Weigall* and *Carter*.—FIG. 26. Tomb of King Merenptah. 1: Vestibule. 2. Pillared hall with middle aisle covered with barrel-vaulting. Here is the sarcophagus, on the pink granite lid of which is the figure of the king lying on a mattress.—After *B. Porter* and *R. L. B. Moss* 1927.—FIG. 27. Tomb of King Ramesses III. X: Pillared hall in which was originally the king's sarcophagus. The sarcophagus is now in the Louvre, Paris, the lid at Cambridge.—After *Lefébvre*.

The *Book of that which is in the Underworld* consists of twelve parts, the underworld being conceived as divided into twelve caverns corresponding to the twelve hours of the night. In each of these is a river, along which the ram-headed sun god and his attendants travel in the sun ship, bestowing light and life on all around for a short while. Monsters, demons and spirits, crowding on the banks, greet the sun god as he passes and hold off his enemies.

The journey of the sun god through the twelve parts of the underworld is similarly described in the *Book of the Gates*. Between the various parts of the underworld were fortified gateways, the guardians of which were gigantic serpents, whose name the dead king had to know. Two serpents vomiting fire and two gods protected the entrance and greeted the sun god.

The hymn in praise of the sun god occurs originally in the *Hymn to Rê*. On entering into the underworld the deceased had to call the sun god by his seventy-five names. The hymn is found only in the first two corridors of the tomb.

The manner in which the sun god speaks in the presence of the spirits and monsters of the underworld is explained in the book of *The Sun-God's Journey through Hell*.

The use of the first three texts mentioned above can be clearly seen in the tomb of Sethos I, in which we also find reliefs and pictures showing the king in the presence of the various divinities of the dead, and also pictures inspired by an earlier legend of mankind's fear of the sun god. In most cases, however, it is the first three collections of spells mentioned above that inspire the texts and pictures throughout the tomb.

NINETEENTH DYNASTY (1314–1200): *Ramesses I* (1314–1312); *Sethos I* (1312–1298); *Ramesses II* (1301–1235); *Merenptah; Sethos II; Siptah; Iarsu* (1234–1200).

TWENTIETH DYNASTY (1200–1085): *Setnakht* (1200–1198); *Ramesses III* (1198–1166); *Ramesses IV–Ramesses XI* (1166–1085).

The new royal family, who came from Lower Egypt and evidently ascended the throne at the wish of Haremhab, were not in any way related to the royal line of the Eighteenth Dynasty. Their founder was Paramessu, the son of a military family, who under Haremhab combined all the highest offices in his own person and after Haremhab's death ascended the throne without encountering any opposition, taking the name of Ramesses I. His son was Sethos I and his grandson Ramesses II.

For urgent political reasons the military and political centre of gravity was transferred to Lower Egypt. Tanis-Avaris, the old Hyksos city, became the political capital. Only in this way could the country safeguard its connection with the Mediterranean world. From the cultural point of view Thebes retained its leading position.

The reconquest of Egypt's position in Asia, begun at the end of the Eighteenth Dynasty under Haremhab, was successfully completed. The adversaries of Egypt emerged from this conflict as partners on an equal footing and reached agreement by means of a far-seeing peace treaty—the oldest peace treaty which has come down to us in its original text. Increasing prevalence of Asiatic influences.

In the last quarter of the thirteenth century B.C., important migrations of peoples began in the Mediterranean area. The 'maritime' nations began to menace Egypt from the north. Despite his victories, King Merenptah was unable to check the steady infiltration of Libyans into the Nile Delta.

Ramesses III at length gained a decisive victory over the fleet and army of the encroaching Mediterranean peoples. Under the various kings of the Ramesside dynasty who succeeded him a gradual decline of royal power began, accompanied by increased influence of the priests of Amun. Politically the country was split into two areas centred on Thebes and Tanis. The Pharaohs resided for most of the time in the north, but continued to be buried in the Valley of the Kings' Tombs near the ancient and holy southern capital at Thebes.

Under Ramesses I and the art-loving Sethos I there was great activity in architecture. In Karnak began the construction of the great pillared hall in the area of the temple of Amun (Plates 226–229); in Abydos that of the king's funerary temple (Plates 216 and 217) with its celebrated cycles of reliefs, which have been perfectly preserved and in beauty rival those in his tomb at Bibân el-Mulûk (Plates 212–214). An unprecedented burst of activity, both as regards the number of buildings and their dimensions, followed during the reign of Ramesses II. The completion of the great pillared hall at Karnak (Plates 226–229) of the Amun-Mut-Khôns temple in Luxor (Plates 239 and 240), the buildings at Tanis and Memphis (among the latter the colossus of Mit-rahina, a part of which has been preserved and is reproduced in Plate 242), the funerary temple at Thebes (generally known as the Ramesseum, Plates 220–226), the Memnonion at Abydos, the rock temple of Abu Simbel, are only some of the king's most striking creations during his reign of 67 years. From the time of Ramesses III we will mention here only the grandiose, completely preserved funerary temple at Medinet-Habu at Thebes (Plates 248 and 249).

212–214. THEBES. VALLEY OF THE KINGS' TOMBS. IN THE TOMB OF KING SETHOS I.

212. KING SETHOS I OFFERING WINE TO A DIVINITY IN SPHERICAL JUGS.
From the vestibule (IX), at the entrance to the third hall of pillars. Limestone with traces of painting.

213. THE GODDESS ISIS, sister and wife of Osiris. On the over-lifesize head of the goddess is the symbol denoting her, a throne, of which the lower part is visible.—Opposite Isis, on the right wall, is her sister Nephthys, goddess of the dead.—From the left wall of the second flight of steps (II). Limestone with traces of colouring.

214. KING SETHOS I BEFORE MAAT, goddess of truth and righteousness. Maat, the embodiment of that law and order which it was the king's duty to ensure, is holding up to the ruler the symbol of 'life'. The large feather projecting from the band round her hair is her attribute of 'eloquent'.—Design and draughtsmanship, in their sureness and nobility of conception, reveal the hand of a master. —From the second pillared hall (VI), on the first of the two pillars.

215. THEBES. IN THE TOMB (No. 51) OF USER-HÊT, who under Sethos I was chief priest of the Ka (essential strength) of King Tuthmosis I.
In the detail reproduced we see Userhêt's mother Tawosret and his wife Hatshepsut. Under a fig tree teeming with birds the two women, together with the deceased, are preparing to drink the liquid which the tree goddess is pouring into their raised cups. They are wearing head-bands and collars of flower-petals stuck side by side on a papyrus foundation, ornamental bracelets, ear-rings, and cones of myrrh on their long wigs. Their features, with the large eyes and delicate noses, are highly attractive. Their cheeks are tinged with red.—In recent times this wonderful picture, like all the others in this tomb, has suffered considerable damage.

216–225. TEMPLE OF KING SETHOS I AT ABYDOS.
This temple, known since the days of the Greek geographer Strabo as the Memnonion, was re-excavated in 1859. It is built partly of limestone and partly of sandstone. Its walls, with their valuable reliefs, are of fine limestone.

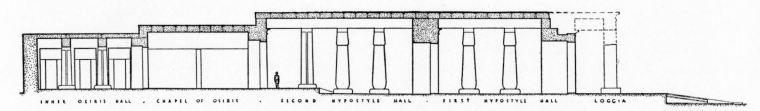

INNER OSIRIS HALL · CHAPEL OF OSIRIS · SECOND HYPOSTYLE HALL · FIRST HYPOSTYLE HALL · LOGGIA

FIG. 28. Longitudinal section of the Temple of King Sethos I at Abydos.
The longitudinal section begins on the right with the ramp leading from the second court to the colonnade (here called a 'loggia') and passes through the centre of the two hypostyle halls, the Osiris chapel and the inner Osiris hall. In the back wall of this, which is shown, are the doorways leading to the three small chapels dedicated to Horus, Sethos-Osiris and Isis.—After *Alan H. Gardiner*, Chicago 1933.

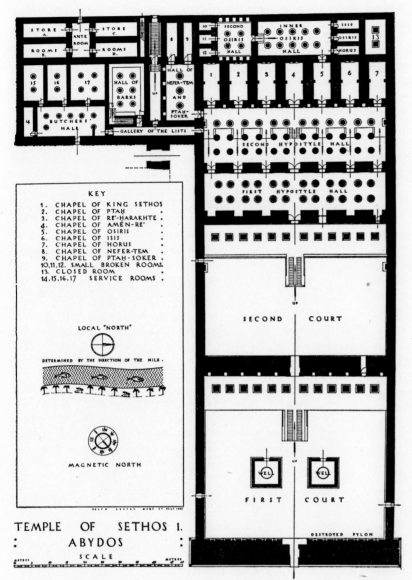

TEMPLE OF SETHOS I.
: ABYDOS :
SCALE

FIG. 29. Ground-plan of the Temple of King Sethos I at Abydos. After *Alan H. Gardiner*, Chicago 1933.

216. COLONNADE ON THE SOUTHWEST SIDE OF THE SECOND COURT.

The middle of the colonnade, which consists of twelve square columns, is between the first and second columns on the right of the photograph. The sunk reliefs on the columns show King Ramesses II in the presence of various divinities. He continued the construction of the temple after the death of his father Sethos, but the decorations he added are of much coarser execution.

217. VIEW OF THE SECOND COLONNADE, from a point near the north corner.

The photograph shows an angle of the north-east wall and affords a glimpse of the three rows each of twelve columns supporting the roof. Whereas the columns of the first two rows, slightly conical towards the tops, have so-called 'closed capitals' with abacus, those of the back row, which stand on a step-like elevation running right through the colonnade, are so-called 'tree-trunk' columns, with the abacus on the top of

the cylindrical shaft without an intervening capital. One of them can be seen in the photograph next to the foremost column. Above each abacus is an architrave running parallel to the shorter walls of the hall, and this in turn supports the roof.

218 and 222. HALL OF NEFERTEM AND PTAH-SOKER.

View, from the south, of the north-west wall, which adjoins the king's sanctuary.

218. KING SETHOS I OFFERING INCENSE AND GIFTS TO PTAH-SOKER,

the funerary god of the Memphis necropolis, who in one of the reliefs is wearing the high conical crown with feathers on the sides which is characteristic of the god Osiris. King Sethos appears in various forms of headgear. In the relief on the left (cf. Plate 222) he wears the customary royal hood (chat), in that on the right the blue crown.

341

219. A KING AND A PRINCE CAPTURING A BULL. In the room leading off the hall of Nefertem and Ptah-Soker; north-west wall. The bull is to be sacrificed to the wolf-headed funerary god Upuaut of Siût (Lycopolis). Ramesses II has thrown a lasso over the horns of the skinny animal, while the prince endeavours to restrain it by twisting its tail. The king is wearing the crown of Lower Egypt with streamers and above him hovers the protective falcon holding in its talons the symbol of eternity, from which 'life' and 'welfare' descend upon the monarch. This vivid picture in sunk relief dates from the reign of Ramesses II. From the cartouche on the relief it is clear that the king is Ramesses II. The prince must therefore be one of the latter's sons.

220. SETHOS-OSIRIS AND THE GOD THOTH. With his right hand the ibis-headed god of learning and writing offers the symbol 'life' to King Sethos, who wears the 'cluster' crown and carries the crook-shaped sceptre and flail and is thus identified with Osiris. In his left hand Thoth carries the plant emblems, entwined with cobras, of Upper and Lower Egypt.

221 and 225. CHAPEL OF ISIS: KING SETHOS I BRINGING OFFERINGS TO THE GODDESS. To the enthroned goddess, who holds the symbol 'life' in her right hand and that for 'welfare' in her left, the king offers loaves of bread, slices of meat, dead ducks, grapes, figs and pomegranates.

222. KING SETHOS I BEFORE THE GOD SOKER. With his left arm Sethos raises the handle of the censer, which terminates in a falcon's head and an incense cup, held in a little hand, from which the fumes of incense are rising. With his right arm he is pouring water from a ritual jug over a bunch of water-lilies on a stand. On the side of Soker's throne is the symbol of the unity of the two Egypts, and on the pedestal beneath it the symbols of 'life', 'welfare' and 'endurance', arranged in groups on the symbol 'all', so that it is possible in each case to read 'All endurance and welfare' or 'All life and welfare'. The falcon-headed Soker holds in his left hand the symbol of 'life', which he offers to the king.

223. CHAPEL OF RE-HARAKHTE: THE KING BEFORE THE UNIVERSAL GOD ATUM. The king, here shown with a purse-like headdress, stretches out his hands towards the double crown of the universal god of Heliopolis, who offers him the symbols of life and welfare.

224. THE GODDESS ISIS. The goddess, wearing the vulture hood and a headdress encircled with cobras, horns and the moon's disc, holds in her left hand a ritual sistrum in the form of a handle and a mask of Hathor, above which is a little shrine flanked by spring-shaped clappers with a small figure of Horus and two little lions' heads. In her other hand she holds the counterpoise amulet of Menit, one of her attributes, as it was one of Hathor's, with a bead necklace.—In the whole composition, the son of Isis, Horus, stands before her, without a crown, but wearing a panther-skin and collar, and with a long strand of hair hanging down from his ringlet coiffure. He is offering incense to the mummy-like figure of Sethos-Osiris, who is holding his crook-sceptre and flail, on his head a crown of horns, feathers, royal cobras and sun's discs.

The ground plan of the temple reveals a peculiar design, due to the fact that the temple and its seven chapels had to serve for the worship of the deified King Sethos I, Ptah the divine creator-god of Memphis, the sun god Rê-Harakhte, the supreme god Amun, the god of death Osiris, his wife Isis and their son Horus. The plan becomes all the more complicated in that it comprises, in addition to the temple proper with its seven chapels, a south-east wing with rooms dedicated to still other gods, or at all events connected with the temple services.

A pylon, facing north-east, which has fallen into ruin, led to the likewise destroyed first court. This was terminated on its south-west side by a colonnade on a slightly higher level, to which access was gained by means of a ramp. On the same level as this first colonnade was the second court, from which another ramp led up to the platform on which all the rest of the temple buildings were built.

The complex of the actual temple begins with a second colonnade, which at the same time forms the termination of the second court (Plate 216). In the original state, seven portals led from this colonnade to the first hypostyle hall. On solemn occasions processions passed through these seven apertures, which gave access to the chapels of the deified king and the six other divinities mentioned above. By the time of Ramesses II the six lateral portals had already been walled up, only the middle one remaining open. The first hypostyle hall after the colonnade consisted, as regards depth, only of two rows of papyrus-cluster columns with bud capitals. But, as is so often the case in Egyptian architecture, the transversal development was far more elaborate. Each of the rows consists of twelve columns. Standing close together in pairs, they provided seven passages for processions. The same applies to the second hypostyle hall, except that this consists of three rows of columns (Plate 217), of which the first two have the same form as those of the first hypostyle hall, whereas those of the third row are 'tree-trunk' columns without capitals and with a round disc as base. This last row of columns and the adjoining rooms of the temple stand on a step-like elevation of the ground. In the wall separating the first hypostyle hall from the second are seven doorways, corresponding to the original seven doorways in the entrance wall.

After the second hypostyle hall come the seven chapels mentioned above. In each of these is a bark of that divinity for the worship of whom they served. Reliefs (Plate 223), some of them with the colouring well preserved, adorn the walls of all these chapels. In the nobility of their style they rival those of the north-west wall of the second hypostyle hall and the exceptionally beautiful reliefs in the three small lateral chapels of the inner Osiris hall.

Behind the above-mentioned row of seven chapels, we pass through a door in the back wall of the Osiris chapel into a series of rooms occupying the whole width of the south-west side of the temple, these rooms being dedicated in particular to the worship of Osiris. To the north-west of the middle hall with its ten columns are three little chapels dedicated to Isis, Sethos-Osiris and Horus. The magnificent reliefs, with their colouring still well preserved, comprise scenes showing Sethos-Osiris before the god Thoth (Plate 220), Sethos before Isis (Plates 221, 225), Sethos-Osiris before Isis and Horus (detail in Plate 224), and others. Each of these scenes is enframed in its own false chapel, richly decorated.

South-eastern wing: From the second hypostyle hall we pass into a large hall dedicated to Ptah-Soker, funerary god of Memphis, and Nefertem, the lotus god and son of Ptah. Another door leads from the second hypostyle hall into the gallery of kings, containing lists of the kings of Egypt from Menes to Sethos. From here we enter a narrow corridor (with relief of the king and a prince capturing a bull, cf. Plate 219) leading to a flight of steps and then into a six-pillared hall with benches for the presentation of offerings. Of the remaining rooms we need only mention here the butchers' hall, where animals were sacrificed.

Behind the temple to the south-west lies the so-called Osireion, which is not the tomb of Osiris, but an elaborately furnished false tomb of King Sethos I. The king was actually buried in the Valley of the Kings' Tombs, but the fact that he also wanted to have a tomb here bears witness to the religious significance of Abydos.

One of the oldest cities in Egypt, Abydos had been, during the First and Second Dynasties, the burial place of the monarchs and highest dignitaries of the kingdom. It was in the immediate neighbourhood of Abydos, on the hill of Umm el-Ga'ab, that the tomb of Osiris, lord of the West, was supposed to be, despite the fact that his cult had originated in the extreme north of the country, in the Delta. This was also the burial place of the First and Second Dynasties, and to be buried near it, had been the wish and the will of pious Egyptians in all parts of the country ever since the Sixth Dynasty. 'To find one's last resting-place near the tomb of Osiris, or to have one's remains sent there for a time to be consecrated, or at least to recommend oneself by means of a cenotaph or a tombstone to Osiris, lord of the underworld, was considered as the height of good fortune' (G. Steindorff).

226–229. KARNAK. TEMPLE OF THE IMPERIAL GOD AMUN.

226. VIEW FROM THE SOUTHERN SIDE OF THE SACRED LAKE TOWARDS THE MAIN PART OF THE TEMPLE AREA. On the right, the remains of the palace of the Tuthmosid kings, with the obelisk of Tuthmosis I. In the centre, the great pillared hall of Kings Sethos I and Ramesses II.

On the left rise the towers, which were never finished, of the first pylon, the main gateway to the whole area. Above the northern corner of the embankment wall of the sacred lake can be seen the memorial stone placed there by Amenophis III, with the sun god Khepri in the shape of a beetle.

227. SOUTHERN PORTION OF THE GREAT HALL OF PILLARS, SEEN FROM THE ARCHWAY OF THE FOURTH PYLON. Of the great hall, the middle one of three main aisles (on the right of the photograph) can be seen, and adjoining it, the southern main aisle. This is bounded on the left by lower pillars with bud capitals. Above them are the architrave and cornice, as well as an upper wall with large windows filled with stone latticework, which admitted light to the middle aisles.

Then, to the left, the southern side-aisles, finished under Ramesses II, which are separated from one another by a row of pillars with bud capitals, seven of them being visible in the photograph. In the foreground, the obelisk of Tuthmosis I.

228 and 229. IN THE GREAT HALL OF PILLARS,

LOOKING UPWARDS AND DOWN THE AISLE. Both photographs were taken from approximately the same point in the transept between the northern and southern entrances to the hall of pillars.

At the extremity, the bud-capital pillars of the innermost of the six northern side-aisles, then similar pillars forming the boundary of the northernmost of the three main aisles. Above the architrave and cornice on the tops of these pillars can be seen the northern upper wall with its windows. Then comes a pair of the pillars with papyrus-umbel capitals which flank the middle one of the three main aisles. Behind, in the photograph, the architrave, cornice and upper wall with latticed windows of the south end of the southernmost of the three main aisles. The reliefs on the pillars of the main aisles and the northern side-aisles date mostly from the reign of King Sethos I, but later Ramesside monarchs also had their names inscribed here.

In contrast to other large temples, built more or less in conformity with a uniform plan, the temple of Amun in Karnak is an epitome of architectural ideas and buildings, some of them going back as far as the Middle Kingdom Twelfth Dynasty, and others dating from as late as the Ptolemaic period.

The original complex was a Twelfth-Dynasty creation, but only a few relics of it have come down to us. The actual Middle Kingdom temple, which occupied an area of 50 square yards, has now almost completely vanished. Only the space it originally occupied can now be identified. A sanctuary for the sacred bark of Amun dating from the time of King Sesostris I (Plates 90–92), which had no direct connection with the temple (see below), has now been reassembled.

After the expulsion of the Hyksos, the ambition of the Seventeenth-Dynasty kings was to continue to add to the original complex, all the more so since Amun had then become the imperial god and his temple a national sanctuary.

All that exists in Karnak today from the time of King Amenophis I is the little alabaster sanctuary reassembled from fragments (Plates 115–117). Like the above-mentioned sanctuary from the reign of Sesostris I, it was re-erected at the spot where the wall from the east wing of the seventh pylon towards the fourth pylon was afterwards built.

The building activity during the reign of Tuthmosis I can be clearly followed. It consisted in enclosing the whole of the Twelfth-Dynasty temple complex within a uniform wall, terminating at its western end in the so-called fourth pylon (the number merely denotes its place in the series of pylons starting from the western end and has nothing to do with the order of their construction). In front of the gateway of this pylon were erected two obelisks, one of which is still standing (Plate 118). To them Tuthmosis III added two others, which, however, have not been preserved. To the east another pylon was added, the fifth.

In the space between these two pylons, on either side of the passage between the gateways of the fourth and fifth pylons, Queen Hatshepsut erected two obelisks, the largest to be found in Karnak. The northernmost (Plate 118) is still standing, while a large fragment formerly belonging to the southernmost now lies near the sacred lake (Plate 226). In the intervening space Tuthmosis I had already built a pillared court with wooden columns. In its later form, this pillared court with its statues (in niches along its west side) dates from the reign of Tuthmosis III.

The first pylon facing south was the eighth, built by Hatshepsut, thus providing access to the temple of Mut, the goddess wife of Amun, in the southern portion of the temple area. This eighth pylon is the oldest of the four pylons, resembling triumphal arches, on the way to the shrine of Mut erected in the

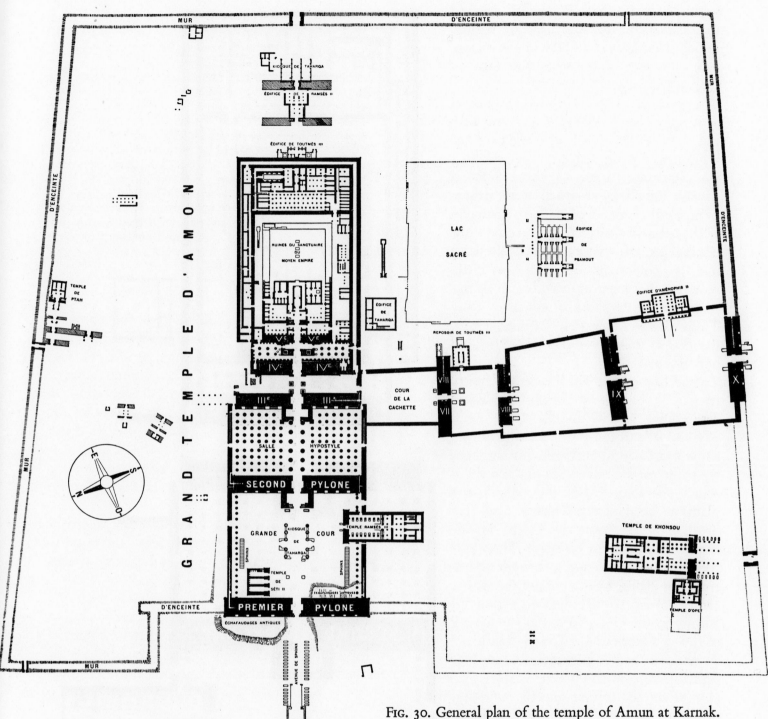

FIG. 30. General plan of the temple of Amun at Karnak.
After *Henri Chevrier* 1936.

southern portion of the Amun temple area. Obviously it must have already existed in the early years of
the Eighteenth Dynasty, even if the temple of Mut which we now know was not built until the reign
of Amenophis III.

The so-called apartments of Hatshepsut lie immediately to the west in front of the Twelfth-Dynasty
temple. What is still standing today, however, is probably only the northern and southern wings of a
complex of buildings, the centre portion of which was later transformed by Tuthmosis III into the

345

second hall of annals. It may be assumed that the shrine for the bark of Amun, which occupies the middle of the second hall of annals, dates from the time of Queen Hatshepsut.

The space between the above-mentioned apartments of Hatshepsut and the fifth pylon of Tuthmosis I was filled by the buildings of King Tuthmosis III. Starting from the west, there were two pillared courts, joined by a small sixth pylon. Whereas the western court had colonnades with statues of Osiris running round three of its sides, the eastern court (Plate 129) had a colonnade of papyrus-cluster columns. Between the two halves of this court lies the first hall of annals of King Tuthmosis III (Plate 129). Adjoining it on the east is the above-mentioned second hall of annals.

To the east of the old Twelfth-Dynasty temple Tuthmosis III built his five-aisled ceremonial temple in the form of a pavilion (Plates 137–139) and adjoining it a few more rooms and halls, among them the room on the lower part of the walls of which the king caused the animals and plants to be depicted which he had had brought from Syria to Egypt in the twenty-fifth year of his reign. These pictures, with their loving treatment of animals and plants, form a counterpart to the careful observation of nature which we admire in the Hall of Punt in the temple of Queen Hatshepsut at Der-el-Bahri.

A uniform wall, beginning beside the fourth pylon, surrounds the whole complex of the old temple and the buildings of the period from Tuthmosis I to Tuthmosis III. The wall was probably built by

FIG. 31. The temple of Amun at Karnak. After *Henri Chêvrier* 1936. 1. Ceremonial temple of Tuthmosis III.—2. Apartments of Hatshepsut and second hall of annals.—3. First hall of annals and courts of Tuthmosis III.—4. Obelisks of Hatshepsut and pillared court built by Tuthmosis I and Tuthmosis III.—5. Obelisks of Tuthmosis I and Tuthmosis III.

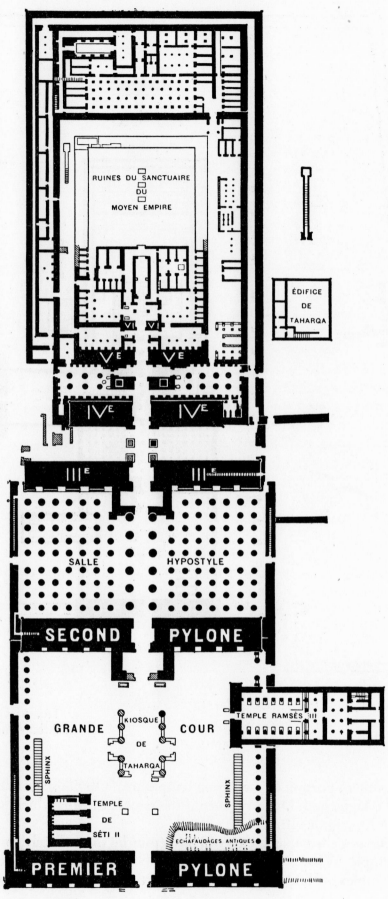

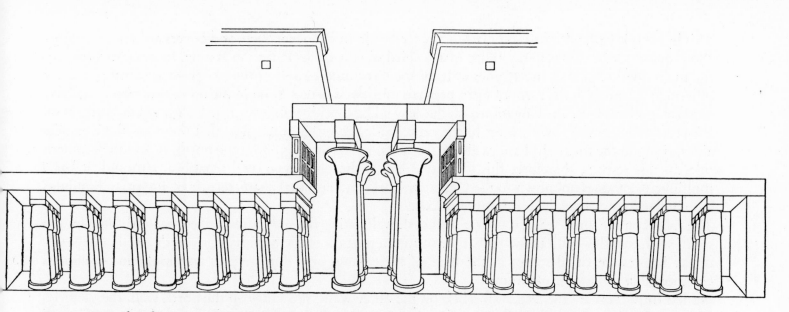

FIG. 32. Temple of Amun at Karnak. Transverse section of the great colonnade of Kings Sethos I and Ramesses II, at the point of intersection with the north-south transept, with view of the western entrance.

Tuthmosis III, who also constructed the sacred lake, on which the bark of Amun floated during solemn festivals. Parallel to the outer side of the wall mentioned runs an external perimeter wall with reliefs of Ramesses II on those parts of it that have been preserved. Beyond its eastern side lies the sanctuary dedicated to the funerary cult of King Tuthmosis III and Queen Hatshepsut, with colossal statues of the royal couple and six standing statues of the king as Osiris.

Among the other buildings erected by Tuthmosis III at Karnak is the little Ptah sanctuary on the north side of the temple area, which was enlarged during the Ethiopian and again during the Ptolemaic periods, and also the peripteral chapel near the east wing of the seventh pylon.

This seventh pylon, on the front and back walls of which are reliefs exalting the king's victories (Plate 136), forms an imposing counterpart to the eighth pylon previously erected by Queen Hatshepsut.

From the early part of the middle phase of the Eighteenth Dynasty we have only the ruins of a small temple of Amenophis II, adjoining the east wall of the court, between the later ninth and tenth pylons. Amenophis III built the large third pylon, thus continuing the line running west to east formed by the fourth, fifth and sixth pylons.

Outside the temple area, a few hundred yards to the south, Amenophis III also built the temple of Mut, in all probability to replace an older sanctuary. From this temple an avenue of sphinxes led to that eighth pylon which Queen Hatshepsut had had erected as a gateway to the approach to the temple of Mut and to which Tuthmosis III added the seventh pylon further to the north. To the south of these two pylons, under King Haremhab, the so-called ninth and tenth pylons were built, thus completing a fourfold row of pylons along the path taken by processions on their way from the temple of Mut to that of Amun.

The west façade of the above-mentioned third pylon built by Amenophis III (into the core of which were incorporated the fragments of the sanctuaries dating from the time of Sesostris I (Plates 90–92) and Amenophis I (Plates 115–117), which were demolished in the reign of Tuthmosis III and have now been reassembled) and the east façade of the still larger second pylon built by Ramesses I, form the eastern and western limits of the large pillared hall, dating from the time of Ramesses I, to which Karnak owes its fame and which ever since ancient times has been proclaimed one of the 'wonders of the world'.

347

This hypostyle hall, with its 140 pillars, is 335 feet wide and 169 feet deep, and covers an area of roughly 5800 square yards, that is to say more than a third of that of St. Peter's in Rome. Its construction is in the main due to Sethos I and Ramesses II. In the two middle rows of the 78-feet-high centre aisle, the pillars have capitals in the form of open papyrus umbels, whereas those of the other fourteen rows have papyrus-bud capitals. Prolongations of the low pillars, with windows filled with stone-latticework between them, in the rows nearest to the centre aisle, give the impression that there are three middle aisles, rising in the form of a basilica above the seven lateral aisles on both the northern and the southern side. In this respect, therefore, this hypostyle hall is the prototype of the basilica, although it has a multiplicity of aisles unknown to the Christian world and also that characteristic of Egyptian buildings —a median axis shorter than its transverse axis.

The reliefs on the inner walls, those on the north wall dating from the time of Sethos I and those on the south wall, together with the whole of the southern portion of the hypostyle, from that of Ramesses II, depict impressive ritual scenes in the lives of these kings and thus give us an insight into religious ceremonial in the temple of Amun.

No less important are the historical reliefs on the outer walls, showing, on the north wall, the victories of Sethos I and on the south wall those of Ramesses II over the inhabitants of Libya and Palestine, and in particular the struggle against the Hittites. Perhaps the most impressive of all are those showing the young king's campaign against the Hittites and the battle of Kadesh.

Ramesses II had with him but a fragment of the four corps with which he had started to march towards the Orontes, when he found himself opposed by the whole Hittite coalition, and it was due entirely to the king's personal bravery and determination that the battle did not result in the defeat of Egypt and the collapse of the country. Even though the Kadesh poem carved on the right wing of the outer southern wall is written with the pathos characteristic of the time and perhaps exaggerates the king's achievement, nevertheless it conveys in a most moving manner the spiritual anguish of a hero deprived of almost the whole of his army and surrounded by countless enemies, who, feeling himself alone and abandoned, turns to his divine father Amun in his need and prays:

> What then, my father Amun? Can it be that a father has forgotten his son? I call to thee, my father Amun. I am in the midst of strangers whom I know not. All the nations have banded together against me. And I am alone and no other is with me.
> My soldiers have abandoned me and not one of my charioteers turned his head to seek me. If I cry after them, no one of them hears me.
> But I call and see that Amun is better for me than millions of footsoldiers and hundreds of thousands of charioteers, better than ten thousand brothers and children who stand together as one man.
> The work of many men is as nothing; Amun is better than they. I have come here obedient to the thoughts of thy mouth, Amun! And I have not departed from thy thoughts.

The end of the long war against the Hittites and the peace-treaty concluded by Ramesses II in the twenty-second year of his reign with the young Hittite king Hattusilis III is described in a monumental inscription (a translation of the original, incised on silver in cuneiform characters) on the outer wall to the east of the south gate of the hypostyle at Karnak (and also in the king's funerary temple). Both rulers understood that it was impossible for one of them to gain a decisive victory over the other, one reason being the great distance separating their respective kingdoms. Both understood, too, that danger was threatening from nearer at hand, for the Hittites from Assyria, and for the Egyptians from the west, and that the struggle against these dangers would absorb all the energy of their peoples for generations to come.

The great pillared hall was not finally completed until the Twentieth Dynasty.

In the southern portion of the great court, between the second and the first pylons, the latter, an unfinished erection of the Ethiopian Period, being the last pylon to be erected, stands the temple of Ramesses III, while in the north-west corner is a small temple of Sethos II. Later, under the Ethiopian Taharka (689–663), the colonnade with its twenty-one tall pillars was erected in the centre of the great court.

In front of the first pylon and leading up to it are the remains of the avenue of ram-headed sphinxes which originally extended as far as the second pylon and formed part of the sacred road running from the pylon of the Amun-Mut-Khôns temple in modern Luxor to the temple of Amun in Karnak. The ram sphinxes lie on chapel-like bases, resting their horned heads on statues, standing between their lion's paws, of King Ramesses II, who was responsible for the construction of the whole avenue. This sacred road passed through the whole of the city of Thebes on the eastern bank of the Nile. The city was so large that its four- and five-storied houses stretched from the modern Luxor to what is now the small village of Karnak.

Ptolemy III Euergetes (247–222) built on this avenue an arch which formed the entrance to the walled Karnak temple zone. Beyond this a row of sphinxes, erected by the last Ramesside king, Ramesses XI, led to the Khôns temple, which was begun by Ramesses III, but was not completed until the reign of Ramesses XI, while small sanctuaries were added to it during the Ptolemaic period.

FUNERARY TEMPLES OF THE KINGS IN THE THEBAN NECROPOLIS

At the beginning of the Eighteenth Dynasty, a novelty was introduced into the procedure of the cult of dead kings which had a decisive influence on the form of the Theban necropolis. This was the separation, introduced under Amenophis I, of the tomb itself from the place in which the funerary rites were celebrated. It is true that this first king of the Eighteenth Dynasty was the only one of his line who built his tomb, not in the Valley of the Kings' Tombs, but in the mountains behind the modern Dirâ Abu'n-Naga near his funerary temple and that the latter, compared with later works, is only a modest edifice, but it was nevertheless during his reign that a definite separation of the tomb from the funerary temple took place and that great series of funerary temples was inaugurated which resulted in the erection of ever larger and more magnificent funerary temples on the steep slopes of the mountains to the west of Thebes.

It should be noted that these Theban temples were primarily temples of the god Amun and that their use for the funerary cult of the kings was only a secondary purpose.

In this connection it must also be mentioned that the New Kingdom kings obviously had no objection to having their palaces in the immediate neighbourhood of their funerary temples. This is true at all events of Ramesses II and Ramesses III, traces of whose palaces can be seen in immediate proximity to the first courts of their temples.

It is not possible for us to discuss all the Theban funerary temples here. As examples of such temples on the grand scale we will describe those of Ramesses II and Ramesses III, a further reason for choosing these two being that they were built according to a uniform plan and have been comparatively well preserved, and thus give an idea of the general arrangement of large Theban funerary temples under the Nineteenth and the early Twentieth Dynasties.

FUNERARY TEMPLE OF KING RAMESSES II, KNOWN AS RAMESSEUM

The ruins of this temple (Fig. 33) are still surrounded by extensive brick buildings (Plates 232 and 233), which had platforms on top of their roofs and were obviously used as dwelling-houses, stables and store-rooms. The cartouche stamps on their bricks prove that they too were erected during the reign of Ramesses II.

349

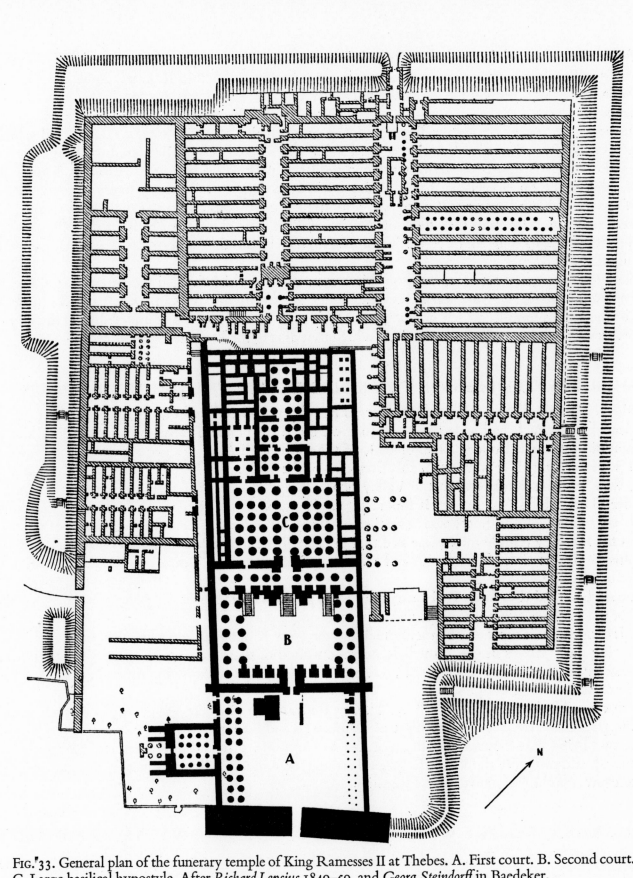

FIG. 33. General plan of the funerary temple of King Ramesses II at Thebes. A. First court. B. Second court.
C. Large basilical hypostyle. After *Richard Lepsius* 1849–59, and *Georg Steindorff* in Baedeker.

350

The temple complex began on the south-east side with a huge pylon 217 feet wide. Its outer façade has now completely crumbled away, but on the side facing the adjoining first court there are still reliefs depicting, in particular, the campaign against the Hittites which the king undertook in the fifth year of his reign.

Of the first court only portions of the pylon-like north-west wall have been preserved. The colonnade formerly in front of the south-west wall formed at the same time the façade of the adjoining royal palace. On the side of the north-west wall facing the court the reliefs show the battle of Kadesh (below) and the festival of the harvest god Min (above), which was celebrated when the king ascended the throne.

The second court (Plate 234), which followed immediately after the above-mentioned wall, had colonnades on both its right and its left sides (on the shafts of the columns are reliefs of the king offering sacrifices). Along its front and back walls were pillars with statues of the king as Osiris, and by the north-west wall (Plate 235) two colossal seated figures of the king in black granite, the remains of which give an idea of the grandeur and nobility of their style. Another row of pillars to the north-west, together with the pillars already mentioned, supported the ceiling of the pronaos, to which three ramps led up. Behind is the front wall of the great hypostyle hall, the first of the series of apartments dedicated to the cult of Amun and the funerary rites of the king.

This great hypostyle hall, like that at Karnak, is built in the form of a basilica. The higher pillars of the two middle rows have open papyrus-umbel capitals, while the lower pillars of all the other rows have bud capitals. On top of the architraves of the two innermost rows of lower pillars is a pillared wall (with window-openings). This makes the height of the two aisles to right and left of the centre aisle the same as that of the latter (Plate 237), so that in all there are three higher aisles with two lower aisles adjoining them on either side (Plate 236). With eight pillars in each of the transverse rows and six leading into depth, the transverse axis of the hypostyle is longer than the longitudinal. The same is true of the three smaller halls adjoining the middle part of the great hypostyle hall, each of which has four columns in the transverse axis and two in the longitudinal. The first of these three apartments has a ceiling with astronomical designs. A fourth apartment with only four pillars concludes the series of rooms along the median axis. The small rooms to the left and right have been to a great extent destroyed.

FUNERARY TEMPLE OF KING RAMESSES III (Figs. 34–39)

The arrangement of the rooms and the general plan of this temple have evidently been modelled on those of the Ramesseum. A first pylon, facing south-east and well preserved (Plate 248), gives access to the first court. To the south-west of it is a hall supported by eight pillars with open papyrus capitals, which also serves as a vestibule to the royal palace behind it; to the north-east is another hall with its ceiling borne by seven Osiris pillars. Between the first and second courts is the lower second pylon. On the south-west and north-east sides of the second court were colonnades with bud-capital pillars. To the south-east of the second pylon was a pillared hall, and to the north-west, on a higher level, the pronaos, with Osiris pillars on its façade and a centre row of columns. After this came another basilical hypostyle, with three higher middle aisles and two lateral aisles on either side, followed by two transverse oblong rooms each with eight pillars and then a square hall, the roof of which was borne by four columns. On either side of these three rooms were smaller apartments. The temple, of which the parts surrounding the two courts are well preserved, contains an abundance of reliefs which are important from the historical and artistic point of view.

Of particular interest are the preserved portions, on the south-east side, of one of the two high gates forming part of the perimeter wall of the temple area. This gate, with the various indentations of its 70-feet high towers flanking the entrance, encloses the space in front of the portal like a pair of pincers

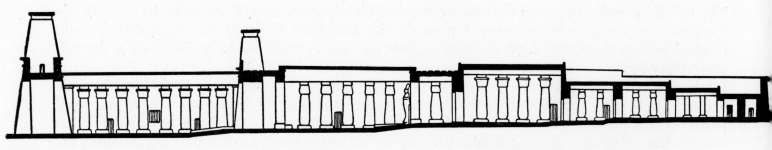

Fig. 35

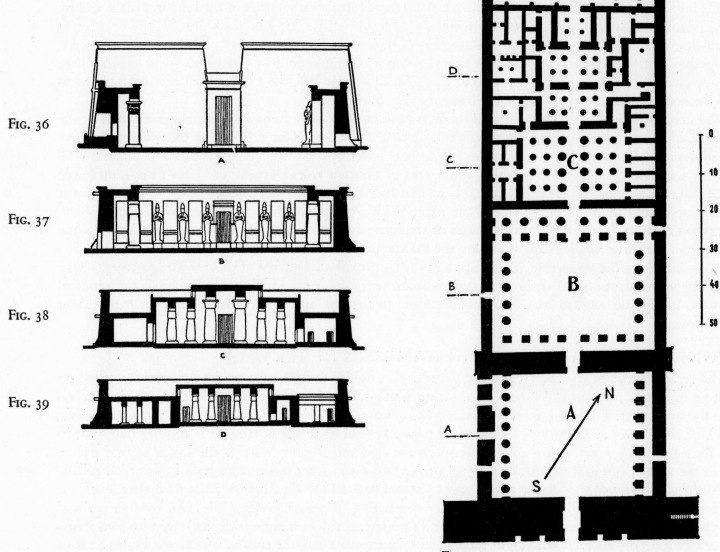

Fig. 36

Fig. 37

Fig. 38

Fig. 39

Fig. 34

Figs. 34–39. Funerary temple of King Ramesses III at Thebes (Medinet Habu). Fig. 34. Ground-plan of the temple. A. First court. B. Second court. C. Great hypostyle hall.—Fig. 35. Longitudinal section of the temple.—Figs. 36–39. Transverse sections of the temple. In Fig. 34 the lines marked A to D show the positions of the cross-sections of Fig. 36=A, Fig. 37=B, Fig. 38=C and Fig. 39=D.—After *Uvo Hoelscher* 1934.

and resembles the door of a Syrian fortress of the Migdôl type. It was designed more as a monument to the Syrian campaigns undertaken by the king and his ancestors than for any strategical purpose. The two towers combine to make a uniform architectural element two stories high, and from the decorations on their walls it would seem that the king and his harem resided in the rooms inside them.

As in the case of the Ramesseum, the king's palace adjoined the temple area and could be reached from the first court. The Pharaoh could watch the ritual processions from a platform above the southwestern colonnade of the first court.

230–237. THEBES. FUNERARY TEMPLE OF KING RAMESSES II, KNOWN AS THE RAMESSEUM.

230–231. KING RAMESSES II. Granite. From Karnak. Height 76 inches. Turin, Museo di Antichità.
Reassembled from fragments without major additions. Fragments of a second corresponding statue are in the Cairo museum. The king, wearing 'blue crown' ornaments, carries the crosier on his right shoulder. He is wearing a robe with fine folds and an apron; the unequal length of the sleeves gives the upper part of the body, when seen from the front, an irregular outline which is in contradiction with its plastic origin. In the left foreground, on a throne, the little figure of his wife; on the right, one of his sons. Beneath the soles of the king's feet, nine bows, symbolizing his power over the nations.

232. GENERAL VIEW OF THE FUNERARY TEMPLE AND ENVIRONS OF THEBES AND LUXOR, seen from the high-lying tomb (No. 78) of Haremhab, one of King Tuthmosis IV's generals. The photograph shows the whole of the walled area of the temple, most of the space being occupied by store-rooms. In the middle distance the cultivated zone with the houses of Luxor on the banks of the glistening Nile; on the horizon, the mountains of the eastern desert.

233. VIEW FROM THE NORTH OF THE TEMPLE AND THE RUINED STORE-ROOMS.
The pylon, once 220 feet wide, which originally formed a monumental gateway, is now a ruin and much of the first court has also been destroyed. In the photograph, running from left to right, can be seen the second court, of which the colonnades originally flanking the north-east and south-west sides have been destroyed except for a few pillars, whereas the pillars with statues of Osiris on the south-east side and those on the north-west side have been better preserved (cf. also Plates 234 and 235). Separated by a destroyed section, there follows the pillared hall, for the most part preserved, which, like that at Karnak, has the form of a basilica (cf. Plates 236 and 237). The store-rooms visible in the foreground were built of sun-dried mud bricks.

234 and 235. THE SECOND COURT.

234. VIEW FROM THE SOUTH-WEST, showing the two rows of pillars with statues of Osiris. On the extreme right, the remains of a fallen colossal statue of Ramesses II, carved out of Assuân granite. The figure must have been a magnificent piece of work. Its total height was probably 57 feet and its weight about 100 tons.

235. VIEW FROM THE SOUTH-EAST. In the foreground on the right the back row of pillars with statues of Osiris, standing on a slightly raised terrace. Behind these, the great pillared hall, the middle and north-eastern main aisles of which can be seen, while to the left of these the original south-east wall of the hall obstructs the view of the south-western side-aisles.—On this wall there are reliefs in three registers. Below: The king's eleven sons. Left centre: The king is led to the temple by Atum and Mont. Right centre: The king kneeling before the three principal divinities of Thebes; behind him, Thoth. Above: The king offering sacrifices to Ptah (left) and incense to Min (right). In the court the head and the lower parts of a seated statue of Ramesses II, in black stone, can be seen. Much of the original plaster has been preserved.

236. GENERAL VIEW OF THE TEMPLE FROM THE WEST.
On the extreme right the ruins of the fallen colossal statue of Ramesses II and the second court with its Osiris pillars. To the left of this, stretching right across the photograph, the actual temple building, with the three high main aisles of the great pillared hall and, in front of these, the two south-western side-aisles (the pillars of the innermost of these are still standing); lastly, the small pillared halls. In the foreground, ruins of other store-rooms.

237. THE GREAT PILLARED HALL, middle and north-eastern main aisles. The original roof-slabs are still on the architraves. In the foreground, the bases of two pillars inscribed with the name of Ramesses II.

238. THE THEBAN NECROPOLIS SEEN FROM THE FUNERARY TEMPLE OF KING RAMESSES II. At the foot of the mountain range culminating in the long-revered peak of El Qorn, lie sand-covered tomb mounds and the villages of Kurnet Murai and Shekh Abd el-Kurna. On the extreme right, high up on the slope, can be seen the openings in the façades of Middle Kingdom tombs.

239 and 240. THE AMUN-MUT-KHÔNS TEMPLE IN LUXOR. SEEN FROM THE FIRST COURT OF KING RAMESSES II.

239. VIEW FROM THE NORTH. The first court, 185 feet long and 166 feet wide, has not yet been completely cleared, as the mosque of the Mohammedan saint Abu'l-Haggâg still stands in the north-east corner. Originally it had colonnades on all four sides, the architraves and roof-slabs of which were borne by 74 papyrus columns with closed capitals. Between the columns stand enormous standing statues of Ramesses II; two seated statues, of which one has been preserved, stood on either side of the entrance to the great colonnade of Amenophis III.

240. COLOSSAL STATUE OF KING RAMESSES II IN THE RIGHT HALF OF THE SOUTH-EAST COLONNADE.

On the king's head there was formerly a crown, hewn out of a separate block, which has not been preserved. The 'staffs of plenty' in his hands have ends like circular seals. On the front of the girdle and apron, the king's names. Close to the king's advancing left leg, stands his wife, Queen Nefertari-mi-en-Mut, with an ornamental wig reaching to her breast and a lofty crown of feathers; her right hand is laid gently on her husband's calf. On the lower part of the pillar on the left (belonging to the south-western colonnade) above the stylized plant symbols of Egypt, the king's subjects symbolized by a crouching lapwing with human arms raised in prayer, worshipping the name of the king placed above the symbol for 'gold' and enframed in the royal cartouche, with the solar disc above it. On the pillar in the centre of the photograph is Amun Kamutef, identified with Min, and behind him Isis. On the column to the right, a figure of Amun in relief can be seen.

241. LOWER PORTION OF A COLOSSAL STATUE OF KING RAMESSES II IN THE RIGHT-HAND PORTION OF THE SOUTH-EASTERN COLONNADE.

Assuân granite. Just as in her statue in the round on the socle behind the leg of the colossal statue of Ramesses in Plate 240, the 'great king's wife' Nefertari-mi-en-Mut is here seen in deep relief on the connecting wall joining the thrust-out leg of the statue to the rear column. Here, in addition to the vulture hood on her head, she also has the crown of feathers with horns and the sun's disc. On the pillar to the left, also shown in the plate, King Ramesses II can be seen offering sacrifice to Amun.

242. MIT-RAHINA. COLOSSAL STATUE OF KING RAMESSES II FROM THE SITE OF THE PTAH TEMPLE IN MEMPHIS.

This limestone statue was 42 feet long before the loss of its legs. It now lies in a mud-brick building.

The delicately but at the same time firmly treated features, with the long, finely-balanced nose and smiling mouth have the characteristics of portraiture. They radiate some of that personal charm of the 'Good God', who once again directed the strength of Egypt to the achievement of a great aim and covered the Nile valley, from the Delta as far as Nubia, with enormous buildings and sculptures. Above the collar, there hangs, from ornamental ribbons, a breast tablet in the form of a chapel, bordered at the top by a frieze of cobras. In the middle of this, beneath the solar disc entwined by two cobras, is the king's throne name: Woser-maat-rê Setep-en-rê: 'Strong is the just regime of the sun god; the chosen one of the sun god.' Turning towards the name within the framework of the chapel are Ptah and Sekhmet, the great divinities of Memphis.

243-245. THE GREAT TEMPLE OF ABU SIMBEL.

We do not know what induced Ramesses IV to build at this point in southern Nubia, not far from the second Nile cataract, a large temple for the cult of Amun-Rê, Rê-Harakhte, Ptah and himself, as well as another sanctuary for the goddess Hathor and his deified wife Nefertari, all hewn out of the rock. There was no lack of open land in the neighbourhood, on which it would have been possible to build free-standing edifices in the traditional manner. If it was just the pleasure he took in carrying out this daring self-imposed task, then we must admit that the task was accomplished in a most imposing style. The usual complex of rooms is more or less inserted in the rock. Four colossal statues of kings, each of them about 40 feet high, with hood and double crown, tower in front of the façade. The upper part of the body of the second colossus on the south side has collapsed. Above the entrance is a standing statue of the falcon-headed sun god, sculptured in the round, so that it seems to stand in a niche, worshipped by the kings carved in relief on either side, who dedicate to the god a statue of the goddess of truth. Above, a frieze of baboons with hands raised in prayer runs to the point first illuminated by the rising run; beneath is a hollow groove with the first names of Ramesses II, figures of Amun and Harakhte and a dedicatory inscription. Between and at the sides of the thighs of the colossi are round portraits of members of the royal family and falcon gods.

The longitudinal axis of the whole complex runs almost exactly from east to west; the early-morning sun shines upon the holy of holies. The interior of the great rock temple measures about 70 yards from the threshold to the back wall of the last apartment. We first enter the Great Hall of Pillars, corresponding to the first courtyard surrounded by roofed halls in free-standing sanctuaries. On either side four columns appear to be supporting the roof and on them stand statues of the king nearly 32 feet high, holding the insignia—crosier and flail—on the breast. The statues on the north side have the double crown, those on the south side the crown of Upper Egypt. The ceiling of the middle aisle has paintings of flying vultures, those of the side-aisles, of stars. The reliefs on the walls, well preserved also as regards the colouring, are in part of great historical interest. Four treasuries and store-rooms lead out of the great Hall of Pillars, then comes a room with four pillars, from which three doors give access to a transverse apartment, out of which apertures lead to the last three rooms. Of these the middle room, the most imposing, is the holy of holies. The support for the sacred bark is hewn out of the rock; on the back wall we see damaged figures of Ptah, Amun, Rê-Harakhte of Heliopolis and the royal founder, who was the divine patron of the Nubians.

In front of the sanctuary is an open space, also hewn out of the rocky ground and protected by old brick walls against the infiltration of sand; from this an ancient staircase and a ramp lead up to the entrance terrace.

246-247. IN THE TOMB OF QUEEN NEFERTARI, CHIEF WIFE OF KING RAMESSES II.

The position of the tomb in the Valley of the Queens can be seen in Plate 210. It was explored in 1904 by an Italian research expedition. The paintings in this unusually impressive though not very large tomb are executed in light relief on a stucco ground.

246. FIRST ROOM. VIEW FROM THE NORTH-EAST CORNER.
On the projection from the south wall on the left, Osiris stands with the fetishes of the god of the dead, Ame-wet, in his shrine. On the west front of this same projection, the goddess Selket, with the scorpion attribute on her head.

In the east recess behind this, the goddess Isis with cow's horns and the moon disc (she is leading the queen, cf. Plate 247). In front of her on the south wall, to the left of the door, the sun god Khepri, identifiable by the dung beetle (*ateuchus sacer*, the so-called scarab) on her head. The ceiling is conceived as a nocturnal sky with painted stars.

247. FIRST ROOM, EAST RECESS. QUEEN NEFERTARI LED BY THE GODDESS ISIS.
Isis has on her head the cow's horns and moon disc, from which a cobra hangs down. On her breast is a rolled chain with a counterpoise amulet (Menit) visible between her back and her arm; in her left hand she holds her divine sceptre. Queen Nefertari, dressed according to the fashion of the time, is wearing the lofty crown of feathers of a god's wife on top of the vulture hood. The hieroglyph texts read as follows: 'Words, spoken by Isis: Come, great king's-wife Nefertari, beloved of Mut, justified (i.e. without fault, literally: true of voice), that I may show thee thy place in the sacred (the next) world', and 'The great king's wife and mistress of the two lands, Nefertari, beloved of Mut, justified before Osiris, the great god'.

248–249. THEBES (MEDINET HABU). FUNERARY TEMPLE OF KING RAMESSES III.

248. THE TEMPLE SEEN FROM THE SOUTH.
The photograph gives a good idea of an ancient Egyptian temple, with in this case a large first pylon and a lower second pylon, the whole surrounded by a wall topped with fluting and provided with gates which make it impossible to see into the building from the outside. In the left foreground, the ruins of the king's palace adjoining the temple.

249. KING RAMESSES III HUNTING.
External back wall of the left tower of the first pylon. Above is a prince, shooting arrows from a chariot at desert animals: oryx antelopes, cow antelopes and wild asses. Below, King Ramesses, wearing the blue crown, in his chariot, hunting wild oxen. In his hunter's zeal, he is standing on the shaft of his flimsy chariot, and holding a bow in his hand, at the same time aiming with a long lance at a bull, which is trying to escape into the reeds bordering the river. Two other hunted bulls are in their death agony. These wild cattle are aurochs (*Bos primigenius*), which were found at that time in North Africa. The two hunting chariots are well provided with quivers full of arrows. Below, above the line of large hieroglyphs giving the names and titles of Ramesses III, a group of seventeen armed men with bows, lances and shields; one of them is carrying a coil of rope on his shoulder. In front of the armed men, a pond full of fish.

The first millennium B.C., which is also the last of real pharaonic civilization, makes a deep impression on the visitor today with its last great temples, built during the Macedonian-Greek domination and in part under that of Rome.

In Upper Egypt there is no lack of architectural monuments dating from the period of restoration under foreign and native rulers which followed upon the fall of the New Kingdom, but the most typical monuments of the late period, in particular those of the talented twenty-sixth dynasty, which strove to revive the old splendour, and of the nationalistic thirtieth dynasty, were undoubtedly those which were erected in the old provincial capitals of Sais, Mendes and Sebennytos. These, like the mighty complexes of buildings at Tanis and Bubastis in the Delta, have crumbled away. Constantly exposed to the depredations of invading armies, the flat, arable zone with its high level of subsoil water and its liability to floods, combined with a stormy history, was a region unsuited for the preservation of the monuments of former ages.

All the more imposing, on the other hand, are the temples erected in Upper Egypt by the Ptolemies and the Emperors and preserved until our own times—at Dendera, Esna, Edfu, Kom Ombo and Philae. A senile mania for preservation covered almost every inch of their walls with religious pictorial motives, figures and texts, even pillars and architraves being used for inscriptions, and as a result nothing has remained of that free and venturesome spirit which distinguished the older compositions. Nevertheless, both the designs of the architects and the skill of the stonemasons are deserving of respect. In the double sanctuary at Kom Ombo, the division into two parts by means of an ideal axis running through the building is a notable solution of a special problem. The wealth of forms in the flowered capitals is as astonishing as the sureness in the filling of the surfaces. And who can resist the picturesque charm of the ruined temple at Kom Ombo with its delicate reliefs or the impressive power of the sanctuary at Edfu, as completely preserved from the pylon to the holy of holies as if the winged sun god were still worshipped today.

From the Ethiopian domination down to the days of the last native kings before the coming of Alexander, the architecture of the Late Period continually produced notable works. In the midst of sham antique or purely conventional works of frigid conception with an expression of empty niceness we find unexceptionable creations, more than worthy of admiration. There are portraits of old men of striking profundity, which for all their restraint afford a glimpse into the innermost recesses of the soul. And lastly there are the figures of animals from the reign of Nectanebos, full of dignity and majesty, which combine a clear derivation from the creations of the New Kingdom with an interesting expression of their own times.

The full thousand years of the Egyptian Late Period with its constantly changing conditions and its variety combined with fidelity to old traditions has been judged and evaluated in a spirit of idly contemptuous generalization. Here is a fruitful field for future research. What remained to the people of the Nile Valley, after three golden ages of immeasurable productivity, was enough to give the Greeks a creative impulse and, through the striking late works of the Memphis school of portraiture, to inspire the portraitists of the Hellenistic art of Rome.

After the reigns of the by no means unimportant last Ramesside rulers, priests of Amun ascended the throne in Thebes, while at Tanis in the Delta an independent kingdom was founded. The kings of the Twenty-second Dynasty were descended from leaders of Libyan mercenary troops. In the year 926 B.C. Sheshonk I—the biblical 'Shishak'—conquered Jerusalem. The first royal tombs were built at Tanis and Thebes began to decline in importance. The Delta city of Bubastis became the capital.

TWENTY-FIRST DYNASTY (1085–950): Thebes: *Hrihor; Pankhi; Pinodjem I; Mahasarta; Menkheperê; Pinodjem II; Smendes;* Tanis: *Tentamun; Psusennes I; Amenemope; Siamon; Psusennes II.*

TWENTY-SECOND (BUBASTIDE) DYNASTY (950–730): *Sheshonk I; Osorkon I; Takelothis I; Osorkon II; Sheshonk II, Takelothis II; Sheshonk III; Pemu.* At the same time there also ruled:

TWENTY-THIRD DYNASTY (817(?)–730): *Pedubastis; Sheshonk IV; Osorkon III; Takelothis III; Amenrud; Osorkon IV.*

TWENTY-FOURTH DYNASTY (730–715) (Sais): *Tefnakhte, Bocchoris (Bakenrauf).*

The Twenty-fifth Dynasty was based on a native Nubian kingdom of which the capital was Nápata, founded about 750 by King Kashta. About 725 the Nubian king Piankhi invaded Egypt and the rule passed into the hands of his line. There was a deliberate revival of the great ancient Egyptian tradition. About 670 the Assyrians under Asarhaddon attacked Egypt.

Under the capable rulers of the Twenty-sixth Dynasty there was a carefully planned restoration of the old cultural greatness. The crafts flourished again. In morals and customs there was a return to olden days, together with close contacts with the rising Hellenism. Sais, in the Delta, became the capital.

TWENTY-FIFTH (ETHIOPIAN) DYNASTY (715–656): *Kashta; Pankhi; Shabaka; Shabataka; Taharka; Tanatamun.*

TWENTY-SIXTH DYNASTY (Sais) (663–525): *Psammetichus I; Necho; Psammetichus II; Apries; Amasis; Psammetichus III.*

In 525 B.C. the Persian King Cambyses, son of Cyrus I, conquered Egypt, and there followed the period of Persian domination. In the meantime, between 404 and 341, various patriotically-minded native princes asserted themselves and left noteworthy monuments behind them. There was a revival of sculpture based on New Kingdom models. Herodotus visited Egypt about 445 B.C. and wrote description of the condition of the country and its cities.

TWENTY-SEVENTH DYNASTY (FIRST PERSIAN PERIOD) (525–404): *Cambyses; Darius I; Xerxes; Artaxerxes; Darius II.*

TWENTY-EIGHTH DYNASTY (404–398): *Amyrtaeus.*

TWENTY-NINTH DYNASTY (398–378): *Nepherites; Muthis (?); Psamuthis; Hakoris; Nepherites II.*

THIRTIETH DYNASTY (378–341): *Nektanebos I (Nekhtnebef); Teos; Nektanebos II (Nekhtherkhêt), Khababash.*

SECOND PERSIAN PERIOD (341–332): *Artaxerxes III, Okhos; Arses; Darius III, Kodoman.*

250. UPPER PORTION OF THE TOMB OF THE VICEROY MENTUEMHÊT, IN THE WESTERN MOUNTAINS NEAR THEBES.
View from the east of the pylon-like front of the tomb, built of bricks of Nile mud.—In the background the rocky valley of Der-el-Bahri, dominated by the sacred mountain of El-Qorn, the summit of which rises above the mountain chain like a pyramid.

251. THE VICEROY MENTUEMHÊT. Grey granite. Height 53 inches. Cairo, Museum, No. 935.
From Karnak. Mentuemhêt was a faithful supporter of the Ethiopian regime. He came from a family of Theban priests, and held the title of 'fourth prophet' of Amun. Under the Nubian kings he rose to the high office of governor of the district of Thebes, and in addition he was mayor of Thebes and chief superintendent of the priestly princesses of Amun. The statues of him that have been preserved show him in his later years.

252. THE PRIEST PEDIAMENOPET. Granite. Height 12¼ inches. Wiesbaden, formerly in Berlin.
A late example of the so-called 'cubic squatter' type. The subject, seated on the ground, his robe crushed between body and thighs, seems as if encased in a cube. Petamenophis, who has his forearms crossed in front of his knees, is noteworthy for the marked naturalism of his features. On his robe, in front, he is shown in high relief in the apron dress of the pyramid period, praying to Osiris.

253. HEAD OF THE STATUE OF A PRIEST. Granite. Paris, Louvre.
A new tendency in sculpture, becoming more and more marked after the Ethiopian domination, asserts itself in this astounding portrait, which appears to violate all the Egyptian rules of form. Hellenistic influence has been suspected, but there is no real reason why this work should not be considered as purely Egyptian. Statues which are known with certainty to date from the Twenty-fifth or Twenty-sixth Dynasty, like the astonishingly realistic, corpulent Irigadiganen and the squatting Harwa in Cairo, prove that such ideas of formal construction were beginning to assert themselves at the beginning of the Late Period.

254. THE 'GREEN' HEAD OF A PRIEST. Greywacke. Height 8½ inches. Berlin, No. 12500.
From Memphis. The most important example, probably dating from about 400 B.C., of a group of heads with individual colouring, which it is not possible to date with certainty, and at the same time one of the best examples of the formal clarity of late Egyptian sculpture. The wrinkles, with a true Egyptian delight in ornamental severity of line, are incorporated in the form. Round the ears, a new interest in the observation of nature, hardly ever to be discerned in earlier works, becomes apparent.—The body belonging to the statue, as is unfortunately the case with all works of this group, has not been preserved.

PTOLEMAIC PERIOD

In 332 B.C. Alexander the Great occupied Egypt without meeting resistance and was hailed as the liberator of the country from the Persian yoke. Under his successors of Macedonian origin to the throne, and in particular as a result of the efforts of the first talented and far-seeing Ptolemaic sovereigns, Alexandria became the most important centre of Hellenic culture in the Mediterranean basin. As later under the Roman emperors, temples were erected in Egypt in the old manner, or were renovated and extended, and adorned with obelisks, statues and murals, while the cult of the old Egyptian gods continued to be celebrated. On the other hand, as a result of increasing Greek immigration, Hellenic customs, learning and art asserted themselves more and more.

After Alexander the Great's conquest of Egypt and the instalment after his death of the Ptolemaic kings of the Lagid dynasty, Egyptian architecture flowered once again—and for the last time—on the grand scale. It was not until the second century of the Christian era that building activity in ancient Egypt definitely came to an end.

Thanks to a wise and tolerant policy, the Ptolemaic kings and the Roman emperors who assumed the government of Egypt in the year 30 B.C. were able, although they were aliens in an alien land, to show their Egyptian subjects that they were worthy successors of the Pharaohs. By building temples and making donations to sanctuaries, and in particular by rebuilding and extending temples and religious sites which had been revered for centuries, they won the approval of the still powerful priesthood and the love and respect of pious Egyptians.

Despite the fact that the capital had been removed in 332–331 to the newly founded seaport of Alexandria, whereby the focal point of the country was transferred to the extreme north, the scale of building activity during these centuries in Upper Egypt shows the attention paid by the rulers to that part of the country, which for more than a thousand years had been the centre of the Pharaonic kingdom. Subsequent destruction in the areas of the northern cities and districts, such as Memphis, Crocodilopolis (Arsinoe), the capital of the Fayûm, and also in the Delta, was so extensive that we can only form an approximate idea of the buildings of the period. What has been preserved in Upper Egypt, however, is a glorious page in the history of architecture during these last centuries before the Christian era. Names such as Edfu and Kom Ombo, Dendera, Esna and Philae recall to our mind the last days of the glory of ancient Egypt. 'Even if this last period did not produce any really new ideas in architecture, it must be noted to its credit that these later architects continued to cultivate and consolidate the old traditional forms with great understanding and feeling for beauty' (Alexander Scharff).

Since the buildings at Philae are now for most of the year hidden beneath the water of the reservoir and the temples at Esna and Dendera, apart from the fact that they have not been completely preserved and in parts remained unfinished, are identical in many respects and especially in their fundamental design with the well preserved temple at Edfu, we shall limit ourselves to describing the temples at Edfu and Kom Ombo, the latter being particularly interesting on account of its ground-plan and the twofold cult to which it was dedicated.

THE TEMPLE OF HORUS AT EDFU, erected on the site of an earlier sanctuary, was dedicated to the falcon-headed sun god Horus and to Hathor of Dendera, as well as to their son, the youthful Harsamtawe, 'Horus, the uniter of the two lands'.

The ground-plan (Fig. 40) shows the huge dimensions of the mighty pylon, the size of which can also be judged from the photograph taken from the west (Plate 255). Behind this pylon is the court (H on the plan), with colonnades on its eastern, southern and western sides. Here, as in the two hypostyles adjoining it, the columns have capitals showing numerous variants of leaf and bloom patterns. The tranquillity found in older pillared courts and halls is thereby lost, but the style of the time demanded variety and an abundance of forms. Low walls rising to about half the height of the columns, a characteristic of the temples of this late period, afford a view from the court into the first hypostyle, thus giving an effect of greater vivaciousness.

The vestibule (1 on the plan), with its two rows each of six columns, is separated by a comparatively thick wall from the so-called hall of pillars, with three rows of four pillars each. In both hypostyles a comparatively wide space has been left in the middle between the columns, to enable processions to pass on their way to the holy of holies, to which access is gained through two antechambers. From the second of these a passage runs right round the holy of holies, providing access to the chapels surrounding it on three sides. The existence of this passage makes the holy of holies (S on the plan) seem almost like a separate shrine-like building.

Round the complex of hypostyles and vestibules and the chapels surrounding the sanctuaries runs a disproportionately narrow ambulatory. The walls of this, like all other walls in the temple, are covered with a profusion of large reliefs and inscriptions, which, owing to their numbers and monotony, produce an almost depressing effect. They are, however, interesting for the students of religion and Egyptology. In contrast to New Kingdom temples, the above-mentioned wall does not encircle the temple at a considerable distance from the building, being incorporated with the pylon and fused with the back walls of the colonnades in the left and right sides of the court.

The temple at Edfu is the best-preserved that has come down to us from antiquity. No other temple gives us such a good idea of the general layout, the completely preserved roof and the spatial effect. We can see for ourselves how the light of the sub-tropical sky shines down on the court and from there floods into the vestibule, how it becomes more subdued as it penetrates into the hall of pillars, growing dimmer and dimmer in the antechambers, until in the holy of holies it is almost completely eliminated. Here one can still feel what light, space and shadow meant for worshippers in an ancient temple.

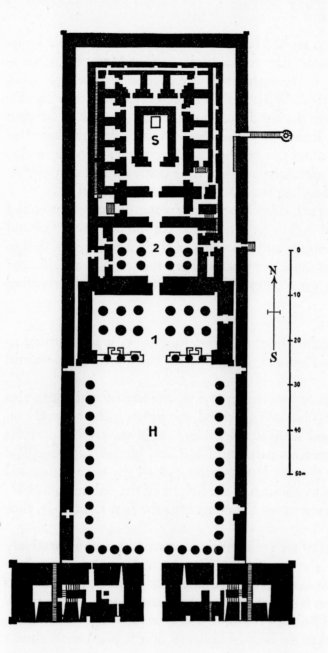

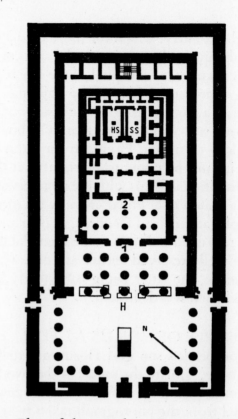

FIG. 41. Plan of the temple at Kom Ombo. On the south-west side, the pylon, which in the plan can with difficulty be distinguished from the thick perimeter wall.—H: The court. 1: Vestibule, with the two portals leading to it from the court and the two doorways to the hall of pillars (2). SS: Sanctuary of Suchos. HS: Sanctuary of Haroêris.

FIG. 40. Plan of the Horus temple at Edfu. At the southern end, the great pylon; behind it, the court (H). 1: Vestibule. 2: Hall of pillars. 3: Holy of holies.

Near the temple lies the 'House of Birth', likewise built in the form of a small temple, in which the ceremony of the 'confinement of the mother-goddess' was celebrated. As a result of the spread of the cult of Isis in the Egyptian late period and under the Roman Empire, such buildings became normal adjuncts to all larger temples.

THE TEMPLE OF SUCHOS AND HAROÊRIS AT KOM OMBO is, in its essential features, similar to the Horus temple at Edfu. It is not quite so long, and its pylon, as seen in the ground-plan, can hardly be recognized as such. Both these disparities can be seen by comparing Fig. 40 and Fig. 41, both drawn to the same scale. That the Kom Ombo temple was wider, was a necessary consequence of the fact that it was used for the separate cults of two divinities, for which reason a division into two parts was deliberately planned throughout the building.

In contrast to the temple at Edfu, at Kom Ombo there are three antechambers leading to the twofold holy of holies (HS and SS on the plan). Starting from the vestibule (1 on the plan), an ambulatory passes right round the complex of the hall of pillars, the three antechambers and the twofold holy of holies with its chapels. Behind these are seven unfinished rooms. Low walls between the pillars at the front of the vestibule, make it possible, as in Edfu, to see into the hypostyle from the court. Owing to the pylon's lack of depth and the thickness of the perimeter wall, as can be seen on the ground-plan, the transition from pylon to wall is almost imperceptible, though it may be assumed that the pylon, now no longer standing, was considerably higher than the wall. As at Edfu, a 'House of Birth' lay near the temple.

255–259. THE HORUS TEMPLE AT EDFU.
This great sanctuary, on a site that had long been sacred, was begun under Ptolemy III Euergetes I in 237 B.C. and the actual temple was finished in 212 under his successor Ptolemy IV Philopator. After a period of unrest and war, its decoration with pictures and inscriptions was resumed under Ptolemy VI Philometor and finally completed under Ptolemy VIII Euergetes II (146–116), ninety years after the laying of the foundation stone. Euergetes added the large vestibule, completed in 122, and adorned its walls with reliefs. Under Ptolemy X, Soter II and Ptolemy XI Alexander I (114–88) the court and its colonnades were built, and also the perimeter wall and the massive tower, though the reliefs on the latter were not executed until the reign of Ptolemy XIII Neos Dionysos (80–52). In 57 B.C. the building of the whole complex was finished.

255. GENERAL VIEW FROM THE SOUTH-WEST.
The photograph of the temple was taken from the mounds of rubble in the old town.

256. THE COURT OF THE TEMPLE.
Looking back from the north-east corner towards the inner façade of the pylon.

257. THE COURT OF THE TEMPLE.
Looking from the south towards the rear portion of the court and the front of the vestibule. Of the latter's twelve columns with richly adorned plant capitals, the six in the front row can be seen and, between them, six half-walls bearing sunk reliefs showing Ptolemy VIII Euergetes bringing offerings to the two chief divinities worshipped in the temple—the falcon-headed Horus and Hathor. To the left of the large portal in the centre, stands a colossal falcon with the double crown; to the right, near the entrance, lies the damaged body of a second falcon. The court is paved with stone flags and on three of its sides has colonnades, with a total of 32 pillars. In the middle of the court formerly stood the great altar, on which sacrifices were made to the gods of Edfu in the presence of the population.

258. THE HALL OF PILLARS IN THE TEMPLE.
Pillars with palm-frond and umbel-shaped flower capitals support the stone baulks of the roof. On the walls and shafts of the pillars, King Ptolemy VIII Euergetes II in the presence of the Edfu divinities.

259. THE HOLY OF HOLIES.
The granite chapel in the background belonged to the pre-Ptolemaic sanctuary, to which it was presented by King Nektanebos II of the Thirtieth Dynasty. In front of the holy of holies, which is a separate, shrine-like edifice, are two antechambers. In front of the simple granite shrine, beautifully built of noble material, there stands on a granite support, itself an offering, the modern replica of the divine bark which formed part of the ritual accessories of every Egyptian temple.

260. THE TEMPLE OF KOM OMBO.
The picturesque ruins of the temple building, seen from the south. This great temple was erected during the Ptolemaic period as a twin sanctuary. The chief gods worshipped in it were the crocodile-headed Suchos (Sobk) and the falcon-headed Haroêris; further, in connection with the former, the goddess Hathor and the youthful moon god Khôns-Hor; in connection with the latter, the 'good sister' (T-sent-nofret)—another manifestation of Hathor—and the 'Lord of the two lands' (P-neb-taui).
The reliefs in the actual building date from the reigns of Ptolemy VI Philometor (181–146), Ptolemy VIII Euergetes II (146–116) and Ptolemy XIII Neos Dionysos (80–52). Those in the court and on the outer walls are from the time of the Roman Emperors, in particular Tiberius.
The gateway has vanished except for a few fragments. Of the sixteen pillars of the colonnades which, as at Edfu, surrounded the court on three sides, only stumps are still standing. The vestibule has ten pillars with richly decorated 'flower-bunch' and palm-frond capitals. The ceiling of the hall of pillars was lower than that of the vestibule and was supported by ten papyrus pillars with open umbel-capitals.
The division of the temple into two parallel aisles, separated by the longitudinal axis of this building, which architecturally forms a single unit, is everywhere carefully observed: despite the fact that there is only one pylon, only one vestibule and only one hall of pillars, the provision of two doors in every wall as far as the two sanctuaries made it possible to celebrate separate rites in honour of each of the two chief gods and the goddesses connected with them.
The reliefs executed by order of the Emperors Macrinus and Diadumenianus are the latest that can be dated with certainty on the walls of the temples of ancient Egypt.

SHORT BIBLIOGRAPHY

I. GENERAL HISTORY AND HISTORY OF CIVILIZATION

Breasted, James Henry: *A History of Egypt*, Chicago, 1905.

Erman, Adolf, and Ranke, Hermann: *Ägypten und ägyptisches Leben im Altertum*, Tübingen, 1923.

Junker, Hermann: 'Die Ägypter,' in 'Die Völker des antiken Orients' (*Geschichte der führenden Völker*, vol. 3), Freiburg, 1933.

Kees, Hermann: 'Ägypten,' in 'Kulturgeschichte des Alten Orients' (*Handbuch der Altertumswissenschaft*, edited by Walter Otto), Munich, 1933.
Das alte Ägypten, Berlin, 1955.

Lange, Kurt: 'Pyramiden, Sphinxe, Pharaonen.' *Wunder und Geheimnisse einer grossen Kultur*, Munich, 1952.

Meyer, Eduard: *Geschichte des Altertums*, Vol. I; II, 1; III, Stuttgart-Berlin, 1913 and 1928.

Otto, Eberhard: *Ägypten. Der Weg des Pharaonenreiches*, Stuttgart, 1953.

Porter, Berta, and Moss, Rosalind L.B.: *Topographical Bibliography of Ancient Egyptian Hieroglyphic Texts Reliefs and Paintings*, Oxford, 1927–1951.—I. The Theban Necropolis, 1927.—II. The Theban Temples, 1929.—III, Memphis, 1931.—IV. Lower and Middle Egypt (Delta and Cairo to Asyût), 1934.—V. Upper Egypt: Sites (Deir Rifa to Aswân), 1937.—VI. Upper Egypt: Chief Temples (excluding Thebes), 1939.—VII. Nubia, the Deserts, outside Egypt, 1951.—Important for the topography and plans of buildings.

Scharff, Alexander: 'Ägypten,' in 'Handbuch der Archäologie' (*Handbuch der Altertumswissenschaft*, edited by Walter Otto), Munich, 1939.

Scharff, Alexander, and Moortgat, Anton: *Ägypten und Vorderasien im Altertum*, Munich, 1950.

Schneider, H.: *Kultur und Denken der alten Ägypter*, 3rd edition, Leipzig, 1924.

Spiegel, Joachim: *Das Werden der altägyptischen Hochkultur*, Heidelberg, 1953.

Steindorff, Georg: in K. Baedeker, *Ägypten und der Sudan*, 8th edition, Leipzig, 1928.

Wolf, Walther: *Die Welt der Ägypter*, Stuttgart, 1955.

Wreszinski, W.: *Atlas zur altägyptischen Kulturgeschichte*, I–III, Leipzig, 1923–1938.

II. WRITING, LANGUAGE AND LITERATURE

Budge, Sir E. A. Wallis: *Literature of the Ancient Egyptians*, London, 1914.

Erman, Adolf: *Die Hieroglyphen*, Berlin and Leipzig, 1917.
Ägyptische Grammatik, 4th edition, Berlin, 1928.
Die Literatur der Ägypter, Leipzig, 1923.

Gardiner, Sir Alan H.: *Egyptian Grammar*, London, 1950.

Lefebvre, Gustave: *Romans et Contes égyptiens de l'Epoque pharaonique*, Paris, 1949.

Maspero, G.: *Les contes populaires de l'Égypte ancienne*, Paris, 1911. (Also in English).

Scharff, Alexander: *Archäologische Beiträge zur Frage der Entstehung der Hieroglyphenschrift*. Proceedings of the Bavarian Academy of Sciences, 1942.

Schott, Siegfried: *Hieroglyphen*, Mainz-Wiesbaden, 1951.
Altägyptische Liebeslieder, Zürich, 1950.

Vandier, J.: *La religion égyptienne*, Paris, 1949.

III. RELIGION

Bonnet, Hans: 'Ägyptische Religion' (*Bilderatlas zur Religionsgeschichte*, 2nd–4th issues), Leipzig-Erlangen, 1924.
Reallexikon der ägyptischen Religionsgeschichte, Berlin, 1952.

Edwards, J. E. S.: *The Pyramids of Egypt*, Pelican Books, 1947.

Erman, Adolf: *Die Religion der Ägypter*, Berlin, 1934.

Junker, Hermann: *Pyramidenzeit. Das Wesen der altägyptischen Religion*, Einsiedeln-Zürich-Cologne, 1949.

Kees, Hermann: *Der Götterglaube im alten Ägypten*, Leipzig, 1941.

Otto, Eberhard: 'Gehalt und Bedeutung des ägyptischen Heroenglaubens.' *Zeitschrift für ägyptische Sprache und Altertumskunde*, No. 78, Leipzig, 1943.
'Die Lehre von den beiden Ländern in der ägyptischen Religionsgeschichte,' *Analecta orientalia*, Rome, 1938.

Roeder, Günther: *Volksglaube im Pharaonenreich*, Stuttgart, 1952.

Schott, Siegfried: 'Bemerkungen zum ägyptischen Pyramidenkult.'—*Beiträge zur ägyptischen Bauforschung und Altertumskunde* (edited by Hermann Ricke), No. 5, Cairo, 1950.

Sethe, Kurt: *Die altägyptischen Pyramidentexte*, 4 vols., Leipzig, 1908 ff. and:
Translations and Commentary (unfinished), 4 vols., Glückstadt, 1935–39.

Spiegel, Joachim: 'Die Idee vom Totengericht in der ägyptischen Religion,' *Leipziger Ägyptologische Studien* 2, Glückstadt, 1935.
Soziale und weltanschauliche Reformbewegungen im alten Ägypten, Heidelberg, 1950.

Wiedemann, Alfred: *Die Amulette der alten Ägypter*, Leipzig, 1910.
Der Tierkult der alten Ägypter, Leipzig, 1912.

IV. HISTORY, CIVILIZATION AND ART OF THE VARIOUS PERIODS

1. EARLY PERIOD AND OLD KINGDOM

Aldred, Cyril: *Old Kingdom Art*, London, 1949.
Breasted, James Henry: *Ancient Records of Egypt*, 4 vols., Chicago, 1906–7.
Goneim, Zakaria: *Die verschollene Pyramide*, Wiesbaden, 1955.
Lauer, Jean Philippe: *Sakkarah. Les monuments de Zoser*, Cairo, 1939.
Quibell, J. E.: *The Tomb of Hesy.—Excavations at Saqqara* (1911–12), Cairo, 1913.
Reisner, George Andrew: *History of the Giza Necropolis*, vol. I, Cambridge-London-Oxford, 1942.

2. FIRST INTERMEDIARY PERIOD

Stock, Hanns: 'Die erste Zwischenzeit Ägyptens.'—*Analecta orientalia*, No. 31, Rome, 1949.

3. MIDDLE KINGDOM

Aldred, Cyril: *Middle Kingdom Art*, London, 1950.
Evers, Hans Gerhard: *Staat aus dem Stein*, I, II, Munich, 1929.
Lange, Kirt: *Sesostris. Ein König in Mythos, Geschichte und Kunst*, Munich, 1954.
Winlock, Herbert E.: *The Rise and Fall of the Middle Kingdom in Thebes*, New York, 1947.

4. SECOND INTERMEDIARY PERIOD

Stock, Hanns: 'Studien zur Geschichte und Archäologie der 13. bis 17. Dynastie.' *Ägyptologische Forschungen* No. 12, Glückstadt, 1942.

5. NEW EMPIRE

Aldred, Cyril: *New Kingdom Art in Ancient Egypt*, London, 1951.
Blackmann, A. M.: *Das hunderttorige Theben*, Leipzig, 1926.
Capart, Jean, and Werbrouck, Marcelle: *Thèbes, la gloire d'un grand passé*, Brussels, 1925.
Carter, Howard, and Mace, A. C.: *The Tomb of Tutankh-Amen*, 3 vols., London, 1923–33.
Hölscher, Uvo: Medinet Habu, *Morgenland* No. 24, Leipzig, 1933.
Lange, Kurt: *König Echnaton und die Amarna-Zeit. Die Geschichte eines Gottkünders*, Munich, 1951.
Pendlebury, S. D. S.: *Tell-el-Amarna*, London, 1935.
Schäfer, Heinrich: *Amarna in Religion und Kunst.*—7th Circular of the Deutsche Orientgesellschaft, 1931.
Steindorff, Georg: *Die Blütezeit des Pharaonenreiches*, Bielefeld and Leipzig, 1926.
— and Wolf, Walther: *Die Thebanische Gräberwelt*, Glückstadt and Hamburg, 1936.
Wegener, Max: 'Stilentwicklung der thebanischen Beamtengräber,' in *Mitteilungen des Deutschen Instituts für ägyptische Altertumskunde in Kairo*, vol. IV, 1933.

V. ART HISTORY AND ARCHAEOLOGY

1. COMPREHENSIVE WORKS

Capart, Jean: *L'Art Egyptien*, 3 vols. (Architecture, la Statuaire, Les Arts Graphiques), Brussels, 1922–42.
Curtius, Ludwig: 'Die Antike Kunst, Ägypten,' in *Handbuch der Kunstwissenschaft*, Berlin-Neubabelsberg, 1923.
Hamann, Richard: *Ägyptische Kunst*, Berlin, 1944.
Komorzynski, Egon: *Altägypten. Drei Jahrtausende Kunstschaffen am Nil. Ein Blick auf Altägyptens hohe Kunst*, Phaidrosreihe, Vienna, 1952.
Lange, Kurt: *Ägyptische Kunst*, Zürich-Berlin, 1939.
Lepsius, Richard: *Denkmäler aus Ägypten und Äthiopien*, 12 vols, 1849–97.
Maspero, Gaston: *Geschichte der Kunst in Ägypten*, 2nd edition, Stuttgart, 1925.
Schäfer, Heinrich: 'Die Kunst Ägyptens,' in *Propyläen-Kunstgeschichte*, vol. 2, Berlin, 1925.
Von Ägyptischer Kunst, 3rd edition, Leipzig, 1930.
Steindorff, Georg: *Die Kunst der Ägypter*, Leipzig, 1928.

2. ARCHITECTURE

(a) Early Period and Old Kingdom

Badawy, Alexander: *A History of Egyptian Architecture*, vol. I, From the Earliest Times to the End of the Old Kingdom, Cairo, 1954.

Borchardt, Ludwig: *Das Grabdenkmal des Königs Ne-user-rê*, Leipzig, 1907.
Das Grabmal des Königs Sahurê, Leipzig, 1910.
Die Pyramiden, Berlin, 1911.
'Die Entstehung der Pyramide,' *Beiträge zur Ägyptischen Bauforschung und Altertumskunde*, Berlin, 1928.
Einiges zur Dritten Bauperiode der Grossen Pyramide bei Gise, Berlin, 1932.
Hölscher, Uvo: *Das Grabmal des Königs Chephren*, Leipzig, 1912.
Lauer, Jean-Philippe: 'La Pyramide à degrés,' *L'Architecture*. Impr. Institut Français d'Archéologie Orientale. Service des Antiquités de l'Egypte, Cairo, 1936.
Reisner, George Andrew: *Mykerinos*, Cambridge (Mass.), 1931.
Ricke, Herbert: 'Bemerkungen zur Baukunst des Alten Reiches,' I (No. 4 of the *Beiträge zur Ägyptischen Bauforschung und Altertumskunde*), Zürich, 1944 (contains, among other matters, the author's remarks on the tomb of King Djoser at Saqqâra).—II (No. 5 of the *Beiträge zur Ägyptischen Bauforschung und Altertumskunde*), Cairo, 1950 (contains: Grundformen der Königsgräber; Kultanlagen der Königsgräber; Grabkammern der Königsgräber).

(b) Middle Kingdom

Naville, Edouard: *The XIth Dynasty Temple at Deir El-Bahari*, Thirtieth Memoir of the Egypt Exploration Fund, London, 1910.

(c) New Empire

Chevrier, Henri: 'Plan d'ensemble de Karnak,' *Annales du Service des Antiquités de l'Egypte*, vol. 36, Cairo, 1936.

Davies, Norman de Garis: The Tomb of the Vizier Ramose (*Mond Excavations at Thebes*, I), London, 1941.

Gardiner, Alan H.: *The Temple of King Sethos I at Abydos*, vols. I–III, London and Chicago, 1933–38.

Hölscher, Uvo: *The Excavation of Medinet Habu*, vol. I (General Plans and Views), The University of Chicago Press, 1934.

3. SCULPTURE

Anthes, Rudolf: *Die Büste der Königin Nofretete*, Berlin, 1954.

Bissing, Fr. W. von: *Denkmäler Ägyptischer Skulptur*, Munich, 1914.

Borchardt, Ludwig: 'Statuen und Statuetten von Königen und Privatleuten im Museum von Kairo,' Part I (1911), Part 5 (1936), in *Catalogue Général des Antiquités Egyptiennes du Musée du Caire*.
'Denkmäler des Alten Reiches,' in *Catalogue Général du Musée du Caire*, vol. I, Berlin, 1937.

Drioton, Etienne: *Le Musée du Caire*, Paris, 1949.

Fechheimer, Hedwig: *Die Plastik der Ägypter*, Berlin, 1920.
Kleinplastik der Ägypter, Berlin, 1922.

Hermann, Alfred, and Schwan, Wolf: *Ägyptische Kleinkunst*, Berlin, 1940.

Catalogue: *The Egyptian Museum*, Cairo, 1951.

4. PAINTING

Davies, Nina M., and Gardiner, Alan H.: *Ancient Egyptian Paintings*, Chicago, 1936.

Lhote, André: *Les Chefs-d'oeuvre de la Peinture Egyptienne*, Paris, 1954.

Mekhitarian, Arpag: 'Ägyptische Malerei,' in Albert Skira, *Die Grossen Jahrhunderte der Malerei*, Geneva, 1954.
